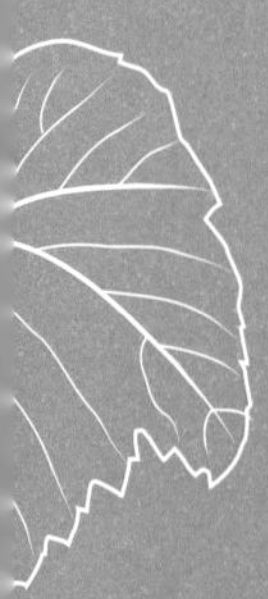

chenin blanc

gewürztraminer

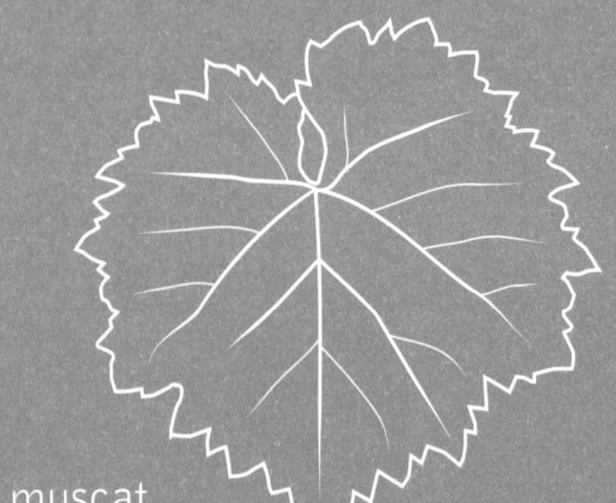

muscat

pinotage

pinot gris

riesling

syrah

WINE
in New Zealand

written by **Caroline Courtney**

photography by **Austin Langford**

art direction & design by **Stephen Woodman**

Acknowledgements

Montana Wines extends its sincere gratitude to the people who shaped this book.

Author Caroline Courtney;

Art director and designer Stephen Woodman;

Photographers Austin and Jane Langford;

Montana's wine education manager Mark Polglase, whose original training manuals formed the starting point for this book;

The many other members of Montana's staff who contributed their time, knowledge and abilities;

Winemakers and viticulturists in wineries around the country who helped with the chapter on wine regions;

Kevin Ireland and Jenny Bornholdt, who contributed verse on pages 1 and 146 respectively;

Terry Dunleavy, MBE, who compiled the historical timeline that outlines the development of New Zealand's wine industry;

Dr Hylton LeGrice, OBE, who read much of the book in its draft form and provided the team with valuable feedback;

Roger Smith, GeographX Ltd (www.geographx.co.nz) who created the computer-generated maps of each of the main winegrowing regions from topographical data sourced from Land Information New Zealand;

National Institute of Water and Atmospheric Research Ltd (NIWA) for supplying climate data for each of the country's main winegrowing regions;

Val Wadsworth of the Marlborough District Council.

National Library of New Zealand Cataloguing-in-Publication Data

Courtney, Caroline, 1956–
Wine in New Zealand / Caroline Courtney ; Austin Langford, photographer.
Includes bibliographical references and index.
ISBN 1-86962-093-3
1. Wines and wine making—New Zealand. 2. Grapes—Varieties—New Zealand. I. Langford, Austin. II. Title.
641.220993—dc 21

A GODWIT BOOK
published by
Random House New Zealand
18 Poland Road, Glenfield, Auckland, New Zealand
www.randomhouse.co.nz

First published 2003

ISBN 1 86962 093 3

Printed in China

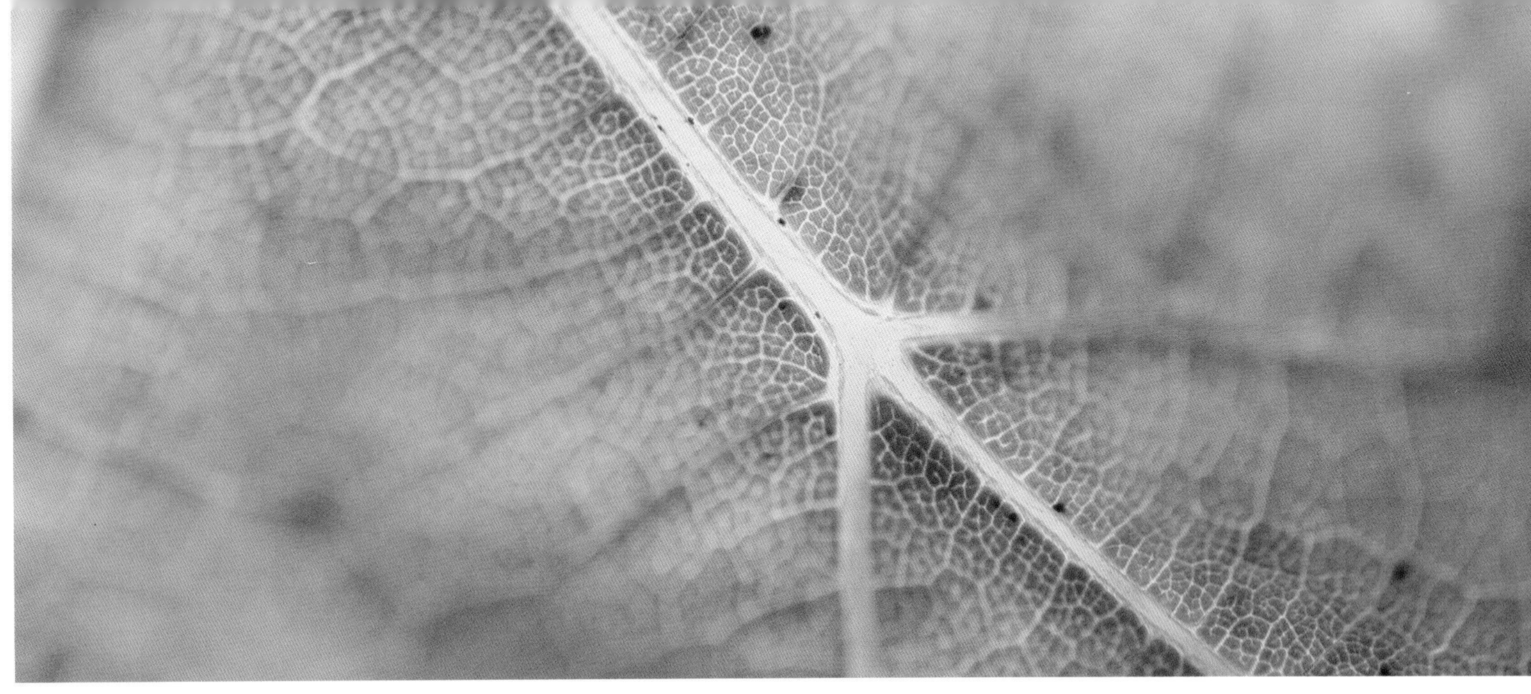

Contents

Foreword

The modern New Zealand wine industry has been built upon foundations laid down over 160 years by pioneers who were driven by passion, commitment and an ethos of hard work. Their efforts underpin the universal recognition which our nation's winemakers now receive for the unique qualities and excellence of our wines.

Montana, New Zealand's leading wine company, which is itself an amalgam of the heritage bequeathed us by a significant number of our wine industry forebears, has sponsored this book about our industry. The aim in producing it has been to help readers gain a basic understanding of the building blocks that combine to create the sensory experience we have come to expect from New Zealand wine.

The development of the New Zealand wine industry cannot be said to be complete. In future years we can expect its evolution to continue as we develop even greater understandings of the potential of our soils, how best to grow quality grapes on them, and so lift our wine quality to new heights of excellence.

In my long career as a winemaker I have found that the greater our understanding of wine, the more we can appreciate its infinite variety. I trust this book will unravel some of its mysteries – and help you find your next glass all the more rewarding.

Peter Hubscher
Managing Director
Montana Wines

'In vino felicitas et caritas'
'In wine there is happiness and friendship'

The riches of a clean, green land

Just one in every 500 bottles of wine produced in the world comes from New Zealand. That statistic probably surprises anyone who's had a good look recently at this country's ever-expanding winegrowing regions, now blanketed in vines where not so long ago sheep and cattle grazed or fruit trees grew.

Ours is a pint-sized industry, then, yet it is held in the highest esteem by wine aficionados everywhere. So sought after are our quality wines, in fact, we can't supply enough of them to international markets, even though the world at large is in the midst of a wine glut. So why exactly does the world clamour for New Zealand wines?

First understand our place, both figuratively and literally, within the international wine scene. New Zealand is part of what is known as the New World of winemaking, a disparate, loose collection of young winemaking countries that includes Australia, Argentina, Canada, Chile, South Africa and the United States. Many New World wine producers dug the age-old, classical grapes of Old World Europe into their countries' freshly tilled soils, then learned the crafts of winegrowing and winemaking as they went along – the hard way. Although they may have started out with a kind of bumbling enthusiasm, within a comparatively short space of time the best of them had developed confident and innovative approaches to winemaking. Now they produce, often with great expertise and flair, the fresh, flavour-packed, accessible wines that have become the hallmarks of the New World's style.

New Zealand has been part of all that, indeed, has been at the vanguard of New World winemaking modernism. Where we stand apart from most of the other members, however, is that ours is a cool-climate grapegrowing country – and herein lies our single biggest advantage. New Zealand's temperate climate is kind to grapes. It grants them the opportunity to ripen at a slow, leisurely pace, so they can build rich, intense fruit flavours and keep the trademark freshness and crispness they will one day flaunt in the glass.

It is a different story in a number of other parts of the world where, during summer, the onset of hot, continental air masses often gives rise to sweltering heatwaves that hurry the grapes into ripening, causing their acid levels to plummet. Longed-for aromas and flavours simply haven't enough time to develop to any great intensity.

New Zealand, then, is in the right place, poised at the right time, to compete with the world's oldest, most revered wine producers. Already the best of our Pinot Noirs rank among the world's finest, while some of our specialist Bordeaux-style red-wine producers are seeking to challenge the French originals. But no

From left to right, photographers Austin and Jane Langford, author Caroline Courtney, and art director and designer Stephen Woodman, pictured at Kerr Farm vineyard in Kumeu, Auckland, December 2002.

wine speaks more eloquently of how a New World country has redefined a classical European grape than our home-grown Sauvignon Blanc. A world apart from its French forebear in the Loire Valley, it has earned a global following with many connoisseurs now proclaiming it the touchstone for the variety.

Everything New Zealand has achieved to date has been made possible by embracing New World winegrowing and winemaking advancements with one arm and Old World philosophies with the other. By marrying the two we have the best of both worlds. Given a little more time, you can be assured we will make even better wines. Listen to the opinion of *The Washington Post* wine critic Michael Franz: 'Twenty years from now, what will be the country outside of Europe making the best wine?' The list of serious contenders includes only six countries, he says: Argentina, Australia, Chile, New Zealand, South Africa and the United States. 'All have their strengths. Any one of them could conceivably end up on top. However, my wager is riding on New Zealand.'

This book describes the styles of wine our country produces; shows you how to make the most of wine; clears up some persistent wine myths; tours our burgeoning winegrowing regions; and explains the art and science involved in winegrowing and winemaking. Within these chapters we have attempted to excite the interests of those who are not so familiar with New Zealand wine, as well as to satisfy the interests of those who already have a passion for it. Above all, though, we hope this book helps you appreciate our country's wonderful wines even more.

Old wine press at
Peregrine Wines,
Gibbston, Central Otago.

Laying the foundations

A brief historical timeline tracing the development of the New Zealand wine industry to the present day.

Compiled by Terry Dunleavy, MBE, inaugural CEO of Wine Institute of New Zealand Inc, 1976–1991.

Blessed are you Lord, God of all creation; through Your goodness we have this wine to offer, fruit of the vine and work of human hands; it will become for us our spiritual drink.

These words are used by Catholic priests in blessing the wine during the Mass, prior to its being consecrated into what Catholics believe to be, through a miracle of transubstantiation, the blood of Christ, as promised by Jesus at the Last Supper.

They are words which are especially relevant in a land which most New Zealanders believe to be 'Godzone'. A land which nature has endowed with an environment that grows wine grapes of uniquely high quality and distinctive flavours; a land in which a succession of human hands has crafted wines which have come to be a new marker of the spiritual significance of what it is to be a New Zealander. When, with a glass of wine in hand, I gaze across our clean, green land with its clear light and temperate climate, I am continually reminded that nothing says more about New Zealand than our wines.

Back in 1985, in a foreword I wrote for a book about wine, I made a prediction: 'Within my lifetime (and I am shortly 57) New Zealand will be better known throughout the world for the quality of our wines than for the quality of any of our other food and beverage products.' Eighteen years later in 2003 I can say that this prophecy has been achieved in the United Kingdom, Canada and Australia, and is well on the way in the United States and elsewhere.

Terry Dunleavy, photographed at his family-owned vineyard, Te Motu, on Waiheke Island.

The story of New Zealand's favoured wine styles, grape varieties and viticultural regions is told in detail in the following chapters. This short historical timeline serves to trace the work of those who gave birth to the New Zealand wine industry, as well as those who nurtured it into the world's pre-eminent boutique wine-producing country. It's a story that divides into three pivotal periods: the first beginning with the arrival of New Zealand's earliest settlers in the 19th century and ending at the turn of the 20th century; the second, tumultuous era beginning with the threat of prohibition and ending around 1960; and the third beginning with the modernisation of the industry through to the present day.

The beginning: 1819–1900

The earliest history of wine in New Zealand begins in Northland with the missionaries who come to this new land carrying vines.

1819 Missionary Samuel Marsden plants New Zealand's first vines, 100 different varieties in all, in Kerikeri, Northland. *'New Zealand promises to be very favourable to the vine as far as I can judge at present of the nature of the soil and climate,'* he writes.

1830s British Resident James Busby makes the first recorded example of New Zealand wine at Waitangi, Northland. Full of romantic idealism about the future of winegrowing in the new colony, he later muses, '*...the man who could sit under the shade of his own vine, with his wife and children about him and the ripe clusters hanging within their reach, in such a climate as this, and not feel the highest enjoyment, is incapable of happiness and does not know what the word means.*'

1838 Bishop Jean Baptiste Pompallier arrives in Hokianga, bringing French vine cuttings. When his priests establish mission stations around the country, they plant vines to supply sacramental wine and so pioneer winegrowing in Hawke's Bay and Gisborne.

1840 On 6 February Maori notables and representatives of the British Crown sign the Treaty of Waitangi which, 'from the official British perspective' writes historian James Belich, achieves full British sovereignty over the whole of New Zealand. The predominantly British working-class population who subsequently settle in New Zealand lack a tradition of drinking wine, a factor which slows the development of local winegrowing for more than a century.

1840 French, mainly peasant, settlers sponsored by the Nanto-Bordelaise Company arrive in Akaroa, intent on establishing vineyards on Banks Peninsula.

1843/1844 Two shiploads of hopeful winemakers from Germany arrive in Nelson, but soon become disillusioned and leave for South Australia. Their legacy is the name they give the district, Neudorf, today immortalised in the wines of Neudorf Vineyards.

1851 Father Lampila of Hawke's Bay plants the Mission Vineyards in Pakowhai and later transfers to Meeanee, then on to Greenmeadows in 1897, where today Mission Vineyards holds the distinction of being the oldest continuing winemaking enterprise in the country.

1863 Two English coppersmiths, Charles Levet and his 14-year-old son William, begin years of backbreaking work planting vines near the Kaipara Harbour, north of Auckland. They later become the first people in the country to earn their living solely from making wine.

1870s German immigrant Heinrich Breidecker produces wines in Hokianga, Northland. More than a century later, Breidecker's name is celebrated when the Wine Institute of New Zealand gives his name to a Geisenheim Riesling cross clone, CD49/84, which flourishes in southern latitudes.

1880 Spanish winemaker Joseph Soler wins six awards at the Melbourne International Exhibition. Since the late 1860s he has made wines from fruit grown on his two-and-a-half acre vineyard in Wanganui, supplemented with grapes purchased from Maori up the Whanganui River. Soler's wines later scoop prizes in London in 1886 and elsewhere.

1881 Wine sales are no longer confined to hotels. With the introduction of a new licensing scheme wineries are permitted to sell wine in quantities of no less than two gallons (9.1 litres) for drinking off premises.

1883 Wealthy farmer William Beetham of Wairarapa creates a tiny three-acre vineyard named Landsdowne which inspires landed gentry in Hawke's Bay to follow his example.

1891 Government grants winemakers the right to operate their own stills to make fortifying spirits.

1895 Prime Minister Richard John Seddon borrows the services of visionary viticulturist Romeo Bragato, then viticulturist to the government of Victoria, Australia, to report on New Zealand's winegrowing potential. After touring much of the country, Dalmatian-born Bragato reports prophetically, *'There are few of the places visited by me which are unsuitable to the vine. The land in your colony should yield a very large quantity of grapes per acre from which wine of the finest quality, both red and white and Champagne, could be produced.'* His infectious optimism triggers a rush to plant vines.

1896 Immigrants from the Dalmatian coast of Croatia working in the kauri gumfields of the Far North plant their first vines and thus begin the long tradition of Dalmatian winemaking in New Zealand.

The 1900s

Although it is acknowledged that New Zealand boasts the climate and soils to produce high-quality table wines, producers largely concentrate on making the fortified wines that appeal to the mainly British population's uneducated palate. Every winery has a still for distilling its own fortifying spirit. Auckland and Hawke's Bay now rank as the country's two most significant winegrowing regions. Industrious, predominantly Dalmatian immigrants, with designs on making their living from wine, settle in West Auckland and plant vineyards. By contrast, Hawke's Bay's pioneering winemakers comprise more established, gentlemen farmers.

1902 After having identified the vine-sapping aphid, phylloxera, on his first visit to New Zealand, Bragato returns to investigate its spread and accepts the post of government viticulturist at the viticulture research station at Te Kauwhata. Intent on steering New Zealand's fledgling wine industry on the path to quality winemaking, he imports phylloxera-resistant rootstocks and new varieties as well as training winegrowers in vine cultivation.

Romeo Bragato

1902 Lebanese immigrant Assid Abraham (A.A.) Corban plants a four-acre vineyard in Henderson and names it Mt Lebanon Vineyards. Corbans is to become one of New Zealand's winemaking giants.

1905 Anthony Vidal, Joseph Soler's nephew, plants vines in Hastings. Vidal Estate endures to the present day.

The Corban family at work in the vineyard.

1906 Joseph Soler steals the show at the New Zealand International Exhibition held in Christchurch when he enters five classes and wins three golds. Disgruntled Australian exhibitors kick up such a fuss that the New Zealand Cabinet, no less, order a re-judging by an expert the Australians accept. Second time around, Soler's wines collect all five golds!

1906 Romeo Bragato writes and publishes *Viticulture in New Zealand*, which sells 5000 copies, making it a bestseller by the standards of the day. In the book, he explains how to graft the scion of the classical *Vitis vinifera* varieties onto the rootstocks of phylloxera-resistant native American species of vines. But many growers ignore his advice and the phylloxera aphid continues to invade the nation's vineyards.

1908 The spectre of the temperance movement looms large. In the elections of the same year, the Masterton and Eden electorates vote to go 'no licence', thus banning the sale (but not the making) of all alcoholic drinks. A railway track marks the boundary between the 'dry' area which houses Corbans' winery and the 'wet' area. By erecting a little shop across the track in the 'wet' area, the family continues to sell wine legally.

1909 Romeo Bragato, disheartened by the growing influence of the temperance movement and the government's indifference to winegrowing, leaves New Zealand for Canada, where he dies the following year.

Pioneer winemaker Tom McDonald

1914 Prohibition mania extends into Parliament. In a debate on licensing laws Prime Minister William Ferguson Massey attacks Dalmatian-made wine, describing it as *'a degrading, demoralising and sometimes maddening drink'*.

1917 In the face of fierce anti-German sentiment during World War I, German immigrant Friedrich Wohnsiedler moves out of Gisborne to nearby Waihirere and establishes the region's first commercial vineyard and winery, Wohnsiedler.

1919 Prohibitionism comes perilously close to shackling the wine industry when the country votes in favour of national prohibition. Only when the votes of overseas servicemen are counted is the vote narrowly overturned. Thankfully, the vehemence behind prohibitionism gradually wanes from this point forward, enabling New Zealand's struggling wine industry to stand on a firmer footing and begin growing again.

1919 Josip Babich moves from Northland to Henderson, Auckland, where he establishes a vineyard. Today, family-owned Babich Wines exports fine wines around the world.

1920s

Vineyards planted in the European varieties are succumbing to phylloxera and various diseases. Disillusioned with these classical vines, growers increasingly replace them with disease-resistant European-American hybrid vines or Albany Surprise, varieties which sadly produce inferior-quality wines. Corbans emerges as the country's largest wine producer, a position it is set to hold until the early 1960s.

1927 19-year-old Tom McDonald purchases the Taradale vineyard of his employer, Bartholomew Steinmetz. Though Tom can only dream of what lies ahead, he is to become one of New Zealand's foremost pioneer winemakers and towering personalities.

1930s

New waves of Dalmatian immigrants settle in West Auckland. Fortified wines – Sherry, Port and liqueurs are still the mainstays of the industry – and remain so until the 1960s.

1933 Englishman Robert Bird establishes Glenvale at Esk Valley in Hawke's Bay, near the mouth of the Esk River. Under his son, Bob, the business in time becomes New Zealand's fifth largest winery.

1934 Croatian immigrant Ivan Yukich founds a tiny vineyard on the hills above Titirangi in Auckland and names it Montana. His sons, Frank and Maté, later shape Montana into New Zealand's leading wine company.

1935 The newly elected Labour Government proves a staunch ally of the wine industry. It is to expand and upgrade the Te Kauwhata viticulture research station, raise duties on imported wines and halve wine import licences. Thus, New Zealand wine can compete on a price basis with imported wine and demand for local product climbs.

'The history of winegrowing in New Zealand,' wrote Corban A. Corban in 1925, 'indicates how unsuitable an occupation it would be for a tired person.'

1940s

The tragedy of World War II ironically boosts the fortunes of local winegrowers. An influx of American servicemen sees demand for alcohol of any description exceed supply. Quality winemaking is well and truly relegated to the backburner as winemakers rush to cash in on the servicemen's thirst. But when the government relaxes import restrictions at the end of the decade, demand for local wine sinks in the wake of a sea of imported Australian wines.

1942 With large numbers of American servicemen flooding into the North Island, demand for wine, particularly cocktail-type drinks put together from fortified wines, sky-rockets. Not only is the servicemen's presence a boost for existing wineries, it also encourages others to make their foray into wine production.

1943 Nikola Nobilo, originally from the island of Korcula in Dalmatia, plants vines in Huapai in West Auckland and lays the groundwork for one of today's leading wine producers, Nobilo Wine Group.

1944 Tom McDonald sells out to Ballins Breweries of Christchurch, which renames the winery McDonalds Wines.

1945 New Zealand servicemen begin returning to New Zealand after the war, many of them having developed a taste for light table wines to quaff with food, especially those who served in Italy. The new-found demand for table wines, then mainly imported from Australia and South Africa, encourages New Zealand winemakers to seek their share of this growing market.

1947 Nikola and Vidosava Delegat establish a winery near Henderson and found Delegat's, today one of New Zealand's prominent producers.

1948 The government introduces the 'wine-reseller's' licence which allows growers and others to set up wine retail outlets.

Old winery truck at Opihi Vineyard, Pleasant Point, South Canterbury.

1950s

New Zealanders indulge in their passion for travel to Europe, whereupon they learn to enjoy wine with food. Meanwhile, new waves of immigrants from Europe's Old World winemaking countries, such as Italy and Yugoslavia, bring their enthusiasm for wine and food to New Zealand. Yet for most of this decade, drinking wine with a meal in a restaurant remains an illicit activity. Terry Dunleavy personally recalls bypassing the law in the customary fashion. He took a bottle of wine hidden in a brown paper bag to an unlicensed restaurant whereupon the proprietor surreptitiously opened it in the kitchen, poured the wine into a teapot and presented Terry and his friends with a set of teacups in which to drink it!

1951 The newly elected president of the Viticultural Association, George Mazuran, of Mazuran's in Henderson (still in operation today), begins his crusade to loosen the country's licensing laws. Armed with a soft voice and gentle charm that mask his keen intellect and steely determination, George cultivates the support of government ministers and MPs through frequent lobbying visits to Parliament as well as the introduction of annual field-day festivities for MPs and government officials. Another crusader of this era, Paul Groshek, goes so far as to petition Parliament with poetry: *'A drink of wine is like a garden of flowers ...it is not only a food, but an art in life...it is the spirit of companionship between man...'*

1951 Denis Kasza, a hugely talented and dedicated Hungarian oenologist, takes up the role as viticulturist at the Te Kauwhata research station and embarks on extensive experimental work. A decade later, he makes the country's first small commercial quantities of Chardonnay while working at McWilliams.

1952 Retiring Governor-General Lord Freyberg startles guests at the state luncheon held in his honour by declaring he believes that within 30 years New Zealand will produce wines that win international acclaim and asks that his prophecy is recorded.

1955 Parliament reduces the mininium quantities of table wine that winemakers and wine resellers can sell from two gallons (nine litres) to a quart (just over one litre) and to half-gallons for fortified wines. The number of wine reseller licences is increased and wine retail stores grow in number around the country.

1957 The government-appointed Winemaking Industry Committee reports on the state of the wine industry: *'The attributes of the craftsman and the ingredients of success in winemaking'* were *'honest, persistent endeavour, imagination, technical exactitude, with achievement as the most coveted award.'* It recommends a series of practical reforms, including the granting of more wine reseller licences. Reforms which, in the words of wine historian, Dick Scott, *'give this paragon a fighting chance in his more worldly surroundings'*.

1958 Import licences for wines and spirits are halved, while taxes are raised on beer and spirits, instantly creating buoyant demand for local wines.

1960s

Licensing laws continue to loosen and the wine industry enters a prosperous age. This is the decade that witnesses the rise of table wines known under Old World names, but mostly made from North American-European hybrid grapes: 'Hock' white wine, 'Moselle' semi-sweet wine, 'Sauternes' sweet wine, soft 'Burgundy' reds and firm 'Claret' reds, although the classical vines are making a comeback. Licensed restaurants spring up around the country. Serving wine with food, either in restaurants or at home on special occasions, becomes widely accepted practice. Corbans, McWilliams and Penfolds are to dominate the industry throughout the 1960s, but Montana's star is ascending.

1960 New legislation grants the first few licences to a sprinkling of restaurants and from this point forward the number of licensed restaurants grows.

1961 Frank and Maté Yukich form Montana Wines Ltd. Frank's missionary-like zeal for expansion and genius for marketing, combined with his brother Maté's practical hands-on support, transforms the face of the New Zealand wine industry over the next 10 years as the popularity of three of Montana's wines sweeps the country, first Montana Pearl in a distinctive bulb-shaped bottle with a screwcap closure; then the runaway success of Cold Duck; followed by Muscato Bianco in the mid-1970s.

1961 George Fistonich starts Villa Maria in Mangere, Auckland.

1962 McDonalds Wines amalgamates with Australian wine producer McWilliams Wines with Tom McDonald as production director. Aside from making fortified wines, the company introduces table wines that soon become household names: Cresta Doré white wine, Bakano red wine and Marque Vue sparkling wine. Tom McDonald is publicly acknowledged as the architect of exciting new ventures into Cabernet Sauvignon and Chardonnay.

1962 Alex Corban pioneers new wines, such as Premiere Cuvée sparkling wine using the Charmat process. Two years later, he crafts a wine that set new standards for table wine, Riverlea Riesling, made from Müller-Thurgau using the then new 'cold pressure' fermentation technique whereby the wine is fermented in sealed, stainless steel tanks under cool, temperature-controlled conditions.

1962 Between this year and 1963, production of New Zealand wine passes the million-gallon mark.

1963 Penfolds Wines (NZ) commences in Henderson.

1965 McWilliams Cabernet Sauvignon is New Zealand's most sought-after wine for the next 10 years.

1969 A group of Auckland businessmen form the Cooks New Zealand Wine Company. Cooks concentrates on varietal table wines and, with imaginative marketing, becomes one of New Zealand's leading wine producers as well as the first to pioneer wine exports to the United Kingdom. 'Cooks Chasseur' grows into one of the wines synonymous with this era.

Late 1960s The national vineyard grows as Corbans and later Montana pioneer large-scale contract grape-growing in Gisborne. Farmers plant surplus pockets of land in grapes and the wineries avoid the heavy capital costs involved in buying vineyards.

1970s

In the early 1970s many of New Zealand's wines are still made from the inferior hybrid varieties. The addition of sugar and water to wine during production is not uncommon. But as the decade progresses and demand for table wines continues to climb, producers increasingly focus on quality winemaking. Many of the hybrid varieties continue to be replaced with the classical varieties, particularly Müller-Thurgau. Auckland's large stake in the national vineyard falls, while regions further south such as Gisborne and Hawke's Bay expand. The most significant development of the decade is Montana's move into Marlborough, which quickly turns the district into the country's largest grapegrowing region.

Taking a break: Some of the workers who planted Marlborough's first large-scale vineyards in 1973.

1973 Montana Wines pioneers a new modern age of grapegrowing in Marlborough when it purchases vast tracts of land to convert to viticulture.

1973 Peter Hubscher becomes Montana's chief wine-maker. The introduction of new winemaking techniques results in such wines as the first Montana Gisborne Chardonnay, which quickly set a new benchmark for New Zealand-made Chardonnay.

1973 International drinks giant Seagram acquires a 40 per cent shareholding in Montana Wines. The local producer benefits immediately from access to technical expertise from Seagram operations around the world.

1974 Michael Morris and John Buck purchase what was originally pioneering 19th-century Hawke's Bay winemaker Bernard Chambers' winery and Te Mata Estate Winery is born.

1974 Winemaker Ross Spence and his brother Bill begin making wine in a tin shed in Swanson and later form Matua Valley Wines in Waimauku.

1976 The New Zealand Wine Institute opens for business, its aim to represent and promote the industry with a unified voice. A number of member producers have visions of New Zealand as a major wine-exporting country. Already Corbans is selling wine in Canada and the United States, while Cooks' export drive is focused on Britain.

1976 George Fistonich of Villa Maria buys A.J. Vidal & Sons in Hastings, now producing wines under the Vidal Estate label.

1980s

Tax incentives granted to land-based products encourage planting of many new vineyards. But as tax incentives are phased out and imports liberalised, the decade proves difficult, if not impossible, for winegrowers at times. Over-production creates a surplus of wine on the domestic market. Fierce price wars dominate the decade's middle years as the industry undergoes the painful process of rationalisation and adjustment to the new market environment. Meanwhile, on the export front it becomes clear that the industry needs a cooperative approach if it's to promote itself internationally. Indeed, the prospects overseas look tantilisingly bright, as New Zealand varietal Sauvignon Blancs and Chardonnays begin to build international reputations. Irrepressible winegrowers embark on a burst of new and, most importantly, quality plantings.

1981 Import licences are taken off wine to encourage competition within the industry.

1981 Montana Wines launches Lindauer méthode traditionnelle, which becomes another runaway success.

1982 Terry Dunleavy of the Wine Institute of New Zealand and the New Zealand trade commissioner in London, Don Walker, hold the first annual tasting of locally produced wines at New Zealand House in London. The wines have been airfreighted to London in RNZAF Hercules aircraft. At the time, New Zealand is exporting little more than 100,000 litres of wine to the United Kingdom.

1984 The lifting of sales taxes on Sherries and Ports by 54 per cent imposes more hardship on growers.

1985 The now combined Cooks/McWilliams wine company unleashes a fierce price war among producers when it slashes prices in a bid to sell off surplus stock. The other major producers follow suit and smaller producers struggle to stay in business.

1985 Cloudy Bay releases its debut Marlborough Sauvignon Blanc, a wine which wins plaudits in the United Kingdom and Australia.

1986 The government endeavours to rationalise the industry by funding a vine-pull scheme, whereby growers are paid $6175 per hectare to uproot vines. The aim is to cut the national vineyard area by a quarter. Canny winegrowers capitalise on the opportunity to replant with those varieties that are gaining favour among wine drinkers.

1986 Montana Wines takes over Penfolds and becomes the country's biggest producer with about 40 per cent of the market.

1986 Hunter's Fumé Blanc 1985 makes history at the annual *Sunday Times* Wine Fair in London by becoming the first wine ever to be voted top wine by the public on each of the fair's three days. Then it is selected as top wine by an eminent panel of wine judges. It wins the top wine award again in 1987 and makes it a hat-trick in 1988.

1987 New Zealand has its first stand at the London Wine Trade Fair.

1987 Seagram decides to exit Montana and gives Montana board chairman, Peter Masfen, a 24-hour option to buy its stake in the company. Peter buys the shares and brings Montana under the control of Corporate Investments Ltd.

1987 Montana Wines buys Tom McDonald's former winery in Church Road and refurbishes it. The Tom McDonald Cellar is named in Tom's honour and the winery later becomes Church Road.

1989 The Sale of Liquor Amendment Act creates more licences for wine and other beverages. But an amendment that would have permitted the sale of table wine in supermarkets and grocery stores has been lost during the committee stages of the Bill. Only when a poll of three Auckland supermarkets' customers demonstrates the overwhelming public demand for the right to buy wine with groceries does MP Fred Gerbic succeed in having the clause re-committed and lobbying by Terry Dunleavy subsequently sees it passed.

1990s

New Zealand wine achieves export success in Europe, the United States and Asia, including Japan. Indeed, the export market drives the industry's growth. New Zealanders increasingly appreciate the qualities of local wines now that they are attracting so much attention overseas. Overseas investors start eyeing the country's wine industry, while new wineries mushroom up and down the country.

1990 On 1 April the first licences for supermarkets and grocery stores take effect. The sale of wine in supermarkets is to transform the image of wine in New Zealand society.

1990 Montana Sauvignon Blanc 1989 wins the Marquis de Goulaine trophy at the London International Wine Challenge.

1991 The New Zealand Wine Guild forms and sets up a promotional office in London. Rosemari Delegat of Delegat's chairs the industry group on export strategies.

1995 One hundred years after Romeo Bragato made his report to the government, the New Zealand Grape Growers Council holds the first conference named in his honour, now an annual symposium on viticulture and oenology.

Peter Scutts wielding a sabre to crack the neck off the bottle in the time-honoured French fashion at the launch of Deutz Marlborough Cuvée in 1990.

Prime Minister Helen Clark opens the Montana Brancott Winery visitor centre in September 2000, pictured here with managing director Peter Hubscher (centre) and then board chairman Peter Masfen (right).

2000 onwards

Big overseas companies purchase a string of New Zealand's larger wineries, thus creating new export avenues for their wines.

2000 Montana purchases Corbans Wines.

2000 BRL Hardy buys Nobilos (the former later merging with Constellation Wine Group).

2001 Quality-driven member wineries launch the New Zealand Screwcap Wine Seal Initiative to promote and educate producers and consumers about screwcaps (with Michael Brajkovich of Kumeu River Wines as chair of the initiative).

2001 Montana Wines becomes a wholly owned subsidiary of international drinks giant Allied Domecq.

2002 The Wine Institute of New Zealand combines with the New Zealand Grape Growers Council to form a single body.

2002 New Zealand is exporting almost 23 million litres of wine, mostly to the United Kingdom, United States and Australia.

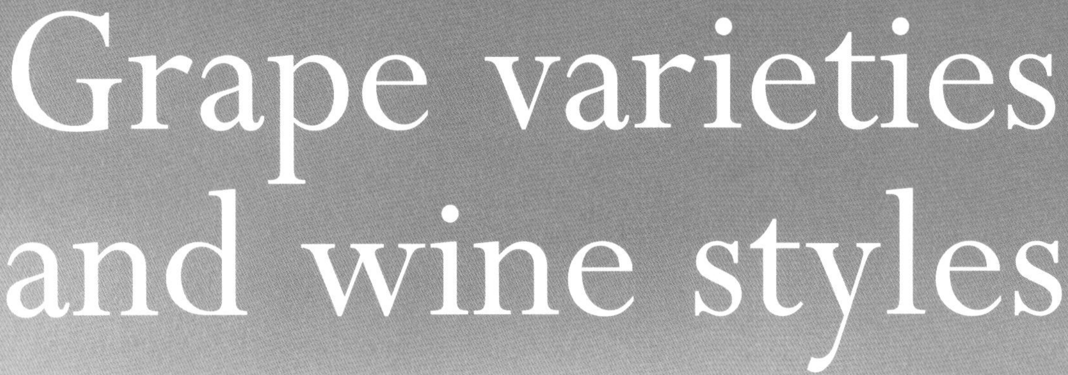

Grape varieties and wine styles

In New Zealand, wine producers name most of their wines after the grape varieties from which they are made, unlike Old World winemaking countries which mainly label their wines after regions.

In the wild, vines are forest-dwelling climbers which compete with other plants for light, space, nutrients and soil moisture. They're used to struggling to stay alive. Several survival mechanisms, such as a measure of tolerance to drought (due to their ability to spread deep roots) and their deciduousness, which means they can withstand the cold, for example, allowing them to grow where less-hardy plants would perish. Such adaptability has made vines perfect for cultivation since the Stone Age, when the first wines were probably made.

Vitis vinifera vines were first introduced to New Zealand in the early 19th century by European settlers. But by the 1940s most of these classical varieties had been replaced with hardier North American-European hybrids, which made inferior-quality wines. Only in the 1960s did the classical *Vitis vinifera* varieties start making a strong comeback, at a time when, not coincidentally, New Zealand's wine industry was beginning to reinvent itself as a quality producer.

A wine's varietal composition tells us more about the flavour characteristics we can expect from it than anything else. That said, its region of origin supplies us with a number of clues about the wine's style, too. Wines grown in the warmer North Island tend to be softer and more full-bodied than the same varietals raised in the cooler climes of the South Island, which typically crafts leaner, more-elegant wine styles. South Island white wines usually display greater concentrations of citrus fruit characters than their North Island cousins, whereas with wines from the North the accent tends to be on tropical fruit flavours.

Which styles of wine do you enjoy the most? More than likely your answer includes wine styles known by their grape variety – Sauvignon Blanc or Pinot Noir perhaps – because that's how we label the vast majority of our wines in New Zealand.

Labelling by variety is a New World convention, known as 'varietalism', practised in other comparatively young wine-producing countries besides ours. By contrast, Old World producers, such as France and Italy, for the large part follow the time-honoured tradition of naming their wines after the centuries-old winegrowing regions in which they are made.

'Varietalism' does have advantages for the wine consumer. It's a very simple way to identify wines. Buy a bottle of wine labelled, for example, Sauvignon Blanc and even if you know nothing about its origins or its producer, you at least have a general idea of what to expect when you open it. Every wine variety has its own unique, immutable flavour characteristics, a defining, recognisable essence that sets it apart from the others.

But where 'varietalism' isn't helpful is in expressing the infinite range of wine styles each grape variety can produce. Chardonnay is a classic example. So malleable

is this variety that the name 'Chardonnay' on the label tells us next to nothing about the style of wine inside the bottle. Depending on where and how the wine was made, it may be light bodied and unoaked or, quite the opposite, big, rich and oaky. Wines, like people, are products not only of their genes, but also of their environments. Take two genetically identical vines, plant them in dissimilar climates and soils and invariably they yield grapes with distinctly different flavour profiles. It is by capitalising on such differences that producers put their own unique stamp on each wine they make. This relationship between nature and nurture in winemaking also explains why no two producers' wines are the same – and why wine itself is such a fascinating and absorbing subject.

Virtually all the world's wines are made from the classical European species of vine, *Vitis vinifera*. They number several thousand separate varieties and while around a thousand or so are used for winemaking, only about 40 are cultivated on a large scale. In New Zealand, we grow fewer than 20 *Vitis vinifera* varieties in significant quantities, although our winegrowers are experimenting with many more, such as promising, perfumed Viognier and the Italian mainstay, Sangiovese.

Today, white-wine grapes dominate the national landscape with the country's biggest export varietal, Sauvignon Blanc, being the most extensively planted grape, followed in second place by Chardonnay. Yet among New Zealand wine drinkers, Chardonnay wears the crown for most popular wine, accounting for about one quarter* of all still bottled wine sold in New Zealand. In fact, we drink about one-and-three-quarter glasses of Chardonnay to every one glass of Sauvignon Blanc. As for red wine, its popularity surges during the colder months along with the nation's electricity consumption. Winter is the one time of year when we buy more red than white wine. While Cabernet Sauvignon/Merlot blends are our preferred winter warmers, Shiraz and Pinot Noir (the last is the country's third most planted grape variety) are increasingly in demand. This chapter explores the key grape varieties and wine styles produced and enjoyed in New Zealand today. It begins with white wines, followed by red varieties, each set out in order of their individual share of the national vineyard. Sparkling wines, dessert styles and fortified wines follow separately.

*ACNielsen, Grocery, MAT to 18 May 2003.

This gnarly, 20-year-old Riesling vine at Corbans' Omihi vineyard in Amberley, Canterbury, is in its prime of life.

Myth: old vines produce better wines. True or false?

True. Mature vines, aged eight years or more, produce better wines than their younger relatives. Unlike young vines they are likely to have reached happy equilibrium between canopy size, root volume and crop levels. And their deeper roots are no longer at the mercy of sudden changes to nutrient and moisture levels that occur closer to the soil's surface. It is also believed that mature vines store more carbohydrates in their bulkier trunks and roots, furnishing them with substantial reserves with which to trigger vine and fruit development.

Sauvignon Blanc

Sauvignon Blanc

Sauvignon Blanc and New Zealand: wine drinkers the world over can't help but speak of them in the same adoring breath. They're as inseparable from one another in everyone's minds as Peter Jackson's *The Lord of the Rings'* Middle Earth is from this country's awe-inspiring landscape.

The romance between Sauvignon Blanc and New Zealand began in earnest during 1976 when Montana Wines took a calculated gamble and planted vast tracts of Marlborough farmland in the classic French variety. Back then, no one in this country knew too much about Sauvignon Blanc and knew even less about Marlborough's ability to grow it.

It was a leap into the unknown that paid off. In 1979, Montana produced the first-ever Marlborough Sauvignon Blanc, a delightfully pungent, herbaceous and crisp creature, quite distinct from Sauvignon Blancs produced elsewhere in the world. It quickly became obvious to local winemakers that Sauvignon Blanc and Marlborough had given us New Zealand's wine marriage of the century, a delicious pairing of a light, little-understood variety with a cool, austere and equally little-understood grapegrowing region.

Within the space of 10 years, the rest of the wine world was as enamoured with our Sauvignon Blancs as we were. At the 1990 International Wine & Spirit Competition in London, the 1989 vintage of Montana Marlborough Sauvignon Blanc collected the Marquis De Goulaine trophy for best Sauvignon Blanc in the show. Other producers' successes followed and soon Marlborough Sauvignon Blanc, crafted by the likes of Montana, Cloudy Bay and Hunter's, focused the wine world's attention on tiny New Zealand and, more specifically, its exciting winegrowing newcomer, Marlborough. Marlborough-style Sauvignon Blancs set a new world standard and paved the way for New Zealand's other wine styles and regions to win international recognition. We have a lot to thank them for.

Today, Sauvignon Blanc is New Zealand's most planted variety and is grown with success in each of our main winegrowing regions. Those produced in the North Island tend to be softer as well as less herbaceous than their southern cousins and may show more gooseberry and tropical fruit characteristics. Still, more than 80 per cent of local Sauvignon Blancs are grown in Marlborough, many of them displaying the overtly pungent, grassy-green, herbaceous personality that overseas markets chiefly associate with the New Zealand style.

Most come unoaked, although oaky, toasty-flavoured (and longer-living) Sauvignon Blancs reminiscent of Pouilly-Fumé from the Loire, France, are becoming more commonplace here.

Say it right
So-veen-yon Blonc

Styles

In New Zealand, Sauvignon Blanc is generally a dry wine, light to medium bodied, and usually unoaked. As a general rule, unoaked Sauvignon Blanc is at its best within two years of vintage. After that, it may lose its varietal freshness and take on tinned peas or tinned asparagus flavours. Oaked versions are either labelled 'oak-aged' or Fumé Blanc. The chalky regions of Sancerre and Pouilly in the upper Loire Valley, France, are renowned for unblended Sauvignon Blancs, flinty and assertive in style. In Bordeaux, they blend Sauvignon Blanc with Sémillon to create the world's most famous sweet wines, Sauternes, and dry styles such as Graves.

Flavours and aromas

At the less-ripe end of the spectrum Sauvignon Blanc exhibits fresh cut-grass and green capsicum aromas. Riper styles may show red capsicum, gooseberry and occasionally tomato stalk, whereas the very ripe styles display melon, nectarine and passionfruit aromas and flavours. Fermented and/or aged in oak they take on toasty, nutty characters. When malolactic fermented you'll also notice buttery characters.

Food matches

Good with tangy-flavoured foods. Also avocado, antipasto, quiche, oysters, smoked salmon or trout, seafood (such as smoked mussels and crayfish), asparagus and chicken as well as vegetable dishes and salads without too much vinegar. Also herb, onion and garlic-flavoured sauces. Team with green herb-flavoured foods.

'The great thing about Marlborough,' said British wine expert, Oz Clarke, a few years back, 'is that it produced for the first time since the war, maybe this century, a flavour which no one's ever found before. Marlborough flavour is unbelievably strong, unbelievably memorable ...'

Sauvignon Blanc blends In New Zealand, usually produced as 100 per cent Sauvignon Blanc, although occasionally a little Sémillon may be added to lend structure and length. Bordeaux Sauvignon (Blanc) is traditionally blended with Sémillon to produce both dry (for example, Graves) and sweet (for example, Sauternes) wines.

Viticulture A vigorous-growing variety which ripens mid to late season. In cool climates, it retains high levels of aromatic and flavouring substances called methoxypyrazines, which give these wines their characteristic herbaceous edge. (New Zealand Sauvignon Blanc retains about three times as much methoxypyrazine as its Australian counterpart.) Thin-skinned, Sauvignon Blanc is prone to splitting and rotting after warm, heavy rains. Grapes growing on young plants (whose roots reside in shallower soils) are especially at risk of bunch splitting. Using low-vigour rootstocks and planting Sauvignon Blanc on low-fertility soils helps constrain the vine's tendency to produce vigorous, prolific plant growth.

Yields Usually 10–15 tonnes per hectare. Low to moderate yields produce more intensely flavoured fruit.

New Zealand plantings New Zealand's most prevalent grape variety, grown in every region (having overtaken Chardonnay's supremacy in 2002).

Winemaking Styling fresh, crisp, fruit-forward Sauvignon Blanc requires minimal winemaking intervention. A long, slow, cool fermentation in temperature-controlled stainless steel tanks is the norm. Partial malolactic fermentation and lees-ageing adds complexity and texture to the finished wine.

New Zealand history Probably first arrived in New Zealand in the 1960s, but was not seriously planted until the 1970s. West Auckland's Matua Valley produced the first trial Sauvignon Blanc in 1974. In 1976, Montana put Marlborough's and the country's first large-scale commercial plantings of Sauvignon Blanc in the ground.

Origins Sancerre and Pouilly in the Loire Valley and Bordeaux, France.

Worldwide plantings France, United States, Chile and South Africa.

Popular clones The mainstay of New Zealand's Sauvignon Blanc wine production is the overtly fruity UCD1 from California, first planted in the 1970s and, as luck would have it, a clone which reaches full expression in New Zealand. Other clones do come into the local picture, but to a lesser extent. Two new Bordeaux imports are used for style variation: 316 and 317 appear to give slightly riper, more tropical fruit flavours and lower yields.

Chardonnay

Chardonnay

Big, biddable and versatile: character traits that sum up one of New Zealand's – and the world's – favourite wine grapes: Chardonnay.

Chardonnay is eminently versatile and adaptable. Winemakers can shape this variety into simple, fruit-driven wines, with or without oak or, at the opposite end of the style spectrum, craft it into rich, powerful, multi-faceted, long-living wines using myriad Burgundian-style winemaking methods. The choice is theirs. With Chardonnay, the winemaker is always the final arbiter. Not that Chardonnay surrenders entirely to the winemaking process. No matter where or how they're made, the better-quality styles always share a few things in common – they're invariably medium- to full-bodied wines with a lovely balance of fruity intensity and structure.

Chardonnay's spiritual home is in Burgundy, France, on the Côte d'Or, south of Champagne, but it grows just about everywhere *Vitis vinifera* vines put down roots, thriving in cool, as well as warm, climates. Marlborough's cool climate produces crisp (higher acid), steely, more citrusy flavoured Chardonnays, even when made from very ripe fruit. In the North Island the flavour profile leans towards riper, rounder fruit flavours. Gisborne Chardonnay shows tropical- and stone-fruit characters. Hawke's Bay's Chardonnays are typically a mix of tropical and citrus fruits.

Never underestimate Chardonnay because it's on shop shelves everywhere. Such is its backbone that leading-edge versions can only keep getting better as New Zealand winegrowers and winemakers build on their understanding of Chardonnay clones, sites and suitable rootstocks. In fact, right now some of New Zealand's foremost white winemakers have their sights set on crafting super-premium Chardonnays.

Say it right
Shar-don-nay

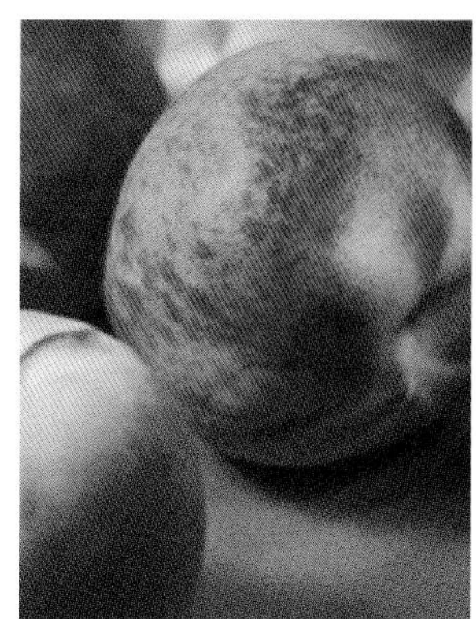

Styles
Chardonnay comes in a multitude of styles: everything from simple, unoaked versions to big, powerful, complex Burgundian-style wines. Most are medium- to full-bodied wines, their breadth and weight often having more in common with reds than many whites. Chardonnay is also one of the main varieties in Champagnes and sparkling wines and comprises 100 per cent of the Blanc de Blancs styles (see page 74).

Flavours and aromas
Cooler regions tend to produce crisp, citrus and apple, sometimes flinty-flavoured Chardonnays. Warmer regions in general make melon, tropical pineapple and occasionally peach- or nectarine-flavoured wines. Depending on the winemaking treatment Chardonnay receives you may note vanillin (from oak), butter, butterscotch, nuttiness, yeast flavours, toast (also from oak), oatmeal, honey and butter or cream (from a malolactic fermentation).

Food matches
Most seafood, rabbit, light cheeses, avocado, steamed mussels, oysters, poached salmon, whitebait, roast chicken and veal. Team the more intensely flavoured (and usually more expensive) styles with stronger-flavoured dishes. Also a favourite with cream, cheese, garlic or lemon-flavoured sauces.

Chardonnay blends In its still wine form, usually bottled as 100 per cent Chardonnay. In méthode traditionnelle and Champagnes it typically comprises anywhere between 30 and 70 per cent of the blend.

Viticulture An early-ripening variety which happily puts down roots in a variety of soils and climates, but generally grows the best-quality fruit on soils of low to moderate fertility. Chardonnay buds early so is at risk from spring frosts in frost-prone districts. It is susceptible to powdery mildew. Winegrowers usually harvest Chardonnay at a ripe 21–24°Brix for still wine and around 18–21°Brix for sparkling wine.

Yields Grown in New Zealand, Mendoza clone Chardonnay crops 7–12 tonnes per hectare. Many of the newer clones may crop more heavily.

New Zealand plantings New Zealand's second most planted variety, after Sauvignon Blanc, and grown in all the major winegrowing regions (predominantly Marlborough and Gisborne, followed by Hawke's Bay).

Winemaking To build on Chardonnay's base aromas and flavours winemakers can draw upon a raft of tools. Among them, gentle whole-bunch pressing; a shorter, warmer barrel fermentation which adds structure and complexity to the wine; ageing on lees (yeast sediment) for up to 12 months to impart yeasty, bready flavours; lees-stirring; malolactic fermentation to soften the wine and impart buttery crème brûlée characters; and oak (either French or American) barrel maturation – used more often than not when making New Zealand Chardonnay, although simple unoaked Chardonnays are becoming more common.

New Zealand history Produced experimentally at the government viticulture research station in Te Kauwhata in the late 1950s by Denis Kasza, a Hungarian oenologist.

Origins A native of Bourgogne (Burgundy), France. The grape of great white Burgundy whose famous names include Meursault, Montrachet and Chablis.

Worldwide plantings Now grown and produced around the world in countries such as Italy, eastern Europe, Chile, South Africa, Australia and United States.

Popular clones Mendoza clone is one of the most popular. It tends to grow 'hen and chicken bunches' (large and small grapes), hence is relatively low yielding and produces intensely flavoured wines. Another very important mainstay is clone UCD6. Quite citric and lemony, it crops more reliably than Mendoza and produces larger-sized berries. Clone UCD15 is popular too: when ripe, it yields grapes with more tropical fruit flavours than Mendoza.

Riesling

Riesling

Riesling is to wine what the diamond is to the world of precious gems – the most brilliant, transparent and aristocratic of all the aromatic whites. Many wine connoisseurs go so far as to argue it deserves the world crown for best white wine.

Not that it enjoys the fashion-icon status of that other great white, Chardonnay. Riesling has, until recently, been under-appreciated by the current generation of wine drinkers, although it is now fast winning over a new wave of fans. Diamonds, after all, are forever.

Enjoy this intensely aromatic variety young or old. Tight, steely, limey New Zealand Rieslings make good drinking in their youth, but they wax even more lyrical with age. Most good local versions don't even hit their straps until they reach five, or maybe six, years old.

More than 80 per cent of this country's Riesling grows in the South Island where the cooler climate produces wines with the fresh, crisp acidity that helps them age gracefully. Winemakers tend to style our Rieslings as off-dry wines with a touch of residual sugar to help balance their fresh acid backbone. But bone-dry versions, styled after Alsatian wines, are gaining ground here.

How does a late-ripening variety like Riesling do so well in the cool climates of New Zealand and countries such as Germany? The answer lies in Riesling's peculiar ability to achieve full, ripe aromas and flavours at very low Brix or sugar levels.

Say it right
Reece-ling

Styles
Local Rieslings range in style from bone-dry to sweet late-harvest styles and everything in between. In terms of body, they span between light- to medium-bodied wines. Longer skin contact during winemaking produces fuller-flavoured Rieslings; those made without skin contact are more elegant wines. Good New Zealand Rieslings can easily age for 10–15 years. Riesling tends to have slightly lower levels of alcohol than other wines.

Flavours and aromas
Powerful aromas of flowers and sometimes honey. When young, apple, citrus, lemon, lime and tropical fruit flavours – characters which concentrate over time. As they age, Rieslings develop toasted and honey flavours.

Food matches
Very versatile: team with roast pork, scallops, seafood, chicken, fish and lightly spiced foods, particularly Asian dishes.

Riesling blends Most often produced as 100 per cent Riesling. Occasionally, lower-priced versions are blended with Müller-Thurgau.

Viticulture Prone to botrytis, Riesling grows best in cool, dry climates. It has a capacity to produce heavy yields of inferior grapes unless managed appropriately. A late-ripening variety, Riesling likes a long, hot summer and settled autumn to develop ripe, intensely flavoured fruit. Left even longer on the vines to raisin a little, Riesling's sugars and acids concentrate to produce the luscious fruit for its famous sweet late-harvest wines and botrytised styles.

Yields Low to moderate cropper: generally about 8–13 tonnes per hectare. Lower yields are essential to achieving flavour intensity in the crops.

New Zealand plantings More than 80 per cent of New Zealand Riesling grows in the South Island, namely Marlborough, Canterbury, Waipara, Nelson and Central Otago.

Winemaking Very similar to crafting Sauvignon Blanc in that sophisticated winemaking techniques are kept to a minimum. Since it is particularly prone to oxidation, Riesling needs better protection from oxygen than any other variety. Most winemakers apply higher amounts of either sulphur dioxide or ascorbic acid (vitamin C) and cover the juice/wine with a blanket of carbon dioxide gas before, during and after fermentation. (However, a few New Zealand winemakers do expose their Riesling to oxygen and still produce good, crisp wines.) Winemakers may either stop fermentation when there's a little residual sugar left or, very occasionally, add some unfermented grape juice to the wine (known as back-blending, a procedure used in Germany).

New Zealand history One of the earliest varieties planted in New Zealand, as styles of Riesling were popular among some British immigrant wine drinkers. But Riesling didn't really take off until the 1970s, when it was tagged Rhine Riesling to distinguish it from Riesling Sylvaner, the then popular name for Müller-Thurgau. In the past used to be called Rhine Riesling or Johannisberg Riesling. Wines called Cape Riesling, Laski Riesling and Welschriesling are not, in fact, true Rieslings.

Origins The great grape of Germany. One hundred years ago its wines were as highly valued as the best of French wines.

Worldwide plantings The Rheingau and Moselle regions of Germany produce the world's most famous. Also Alsace in France, Italy, Austria, Hungary and South Australia.

Popular clones Two clones, both German developed, make up most of New Zealand's plantings: GM110 and another German clone imported by the Te Kauwhata viticulture research station.

Sémillon

Life isn't fair. Why should Sémillon be relegated to the back-room jobs when it can create wonderful stand-alone varietal wines? There's no easy answer to that. But if the winemakers now pioneering New Zealand's 100 per cent Sémillon wines have things their way, many more of us will soon wake up to its virtues.

One of the world's most planted varieties, Sémillon nonetheless leads a strangely anonymous life in this country. In France, it is blended with Sauvignon Blanc to create the great, dry white wines of Graves and the very famous, very exclusive sweet wines of Sauternes, but in New Zealand most of it disappears into blends without receiving so much as a mention on the label. Only on rare occasions does it get to show off its singular talents as a straight varietal wine or as a botrytised Noble Sémillon dessert wine (see sweet dessert wines, page 76).

Yet New Zealand varietal Sémillon has much to offer. Our cool climate accentuates the variety's bright, grassy-green characters and keeps its acids firm, resulting in fresh, zingy wines with Sauvignon Blanc-like qualities. Those grown in warmer climates – such as Gisborne – also take on ripe, rich, tropical fruit characters. New Zealand Master of Wine Bob Campbell has gone so far as to declare Sémillon an inherently superior variety to Sauvignon Blanc. Even so, until wine drinkers become more adventurous with it, Sémillon is a long way from becoming a mainstream varietal. And that's a pity.

Say it right
Semi-yon

Styles

Sémillon produces excellent, dry varietal wines either akin to Sauvignon Blanc's fresh, zingy herbaceousness when cast in the typical New Zealand style or more Chardonnay-like when made in the fuller-bodied, oak-aged, typically Australian style. Sémillon is most famous for ultra-sweet botrytised Sauternes-style dessert wines, or Noble Sémillon, crafted in the traditional Sauternes manner. Varietal Sémillons can be drunk young, but also age well. Sweet dessert Sémillons age even better.

Flavours and aromas

In its varietal form, wines from warmer New Zealand climates show delicious lime, lemon, melon and tropical pineapple characters. Poorer examples exhibit broad-bean flavours. (Australian Sémillons may show limey, biscuity, yeasty, and Riesling-like kerosene characters.) In its dessert wine form, expect concentrated honeyed, marmalade and peachy flavours.

Food matches

Very food friendly. As a dry, varietal wine serve with seafood, light pastas, chicken and fish in cream sauces. It also has a special affinity with garlic. As a sweet Sauternes or Sauternes-style wine team with crème brûlée, baked peach and nectarine desserts and blue cheeses.

Sémillon blends Often used as a blending partner in Sauvignon Blanc to accentuate herbaceous characters and add fresh, cut-grass characters. When blended with Chardonnay, Sémillon adds a fresh-flavoured herbaceousness, lifts the wine's acidity and imparts it with a certain delicacy, creating a style of Chardonnay that suits apéritif drinking.

Viticulture Relatively easy to grow, Sémillon produces rather large, slightly egg-shaped, disease-resistant grapes. Early efforts to grow the variety in New Zealand tended to result in overly herbaceous fruit. But, today, better canopy management techniques, crop yield control measures and improved fruit exposure allow New Zealand viticulturists to grow excellent, well-ripened fruit.

Yields In Gisborne, yields of 12–17 tonnes per hectare. For botrytised wines, yields of 2–3 tonnes are more typical.

New Zealand plantings Represents about 3 per cent of the national vineyard. Most is planted in Gisborne, followed by Marlborough and Hawke's Bay.

Winemaking Dry varietal Sémillons tend to receive partial barrel fermentation and storage on yeast lees, thus resulting in deeper-coloured, more complex wines.

Origins A likely native of Bordeaux, France.

Worldwide plantings Notably Graves and Sauternes in France, Australia (including the Hunter Valley, where it makes a very long-living wine) and Chile.

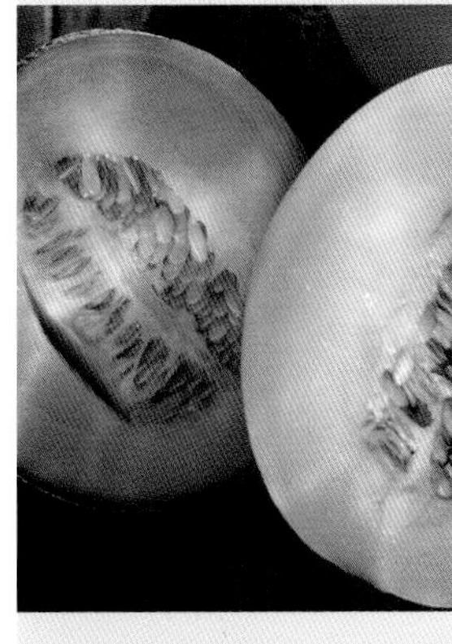

Pinot Gris

Pinot Gris

Pinot Gris is something of a chameleon. Versatile enough to make light-bodied, fresh and fruity wines and equally adept at making rich, robust, mouth-filling wines – the latter offering an excellent alternative to Chardonnay.

Pinot Gris may be styled as a dry or off-dry (slightly sweeter) wine, may come either oaked or unoaked and, in true chameleon-like fashion, may vary in colour from vintage to vintage. Some Pinot Gris are almost white, others pinkish or yellowy-bronze. So here's a tip: always read a Pinot Gris' label closely so you know exactly what you're buying.

As you'll see in the wine regions chapter, several of New Zealand's winegrowing regions have high hopes for Pinot Gris, a variety which is becoming increasingly fashionable among the wine-drinking public at large. In response to its burgeoning popularity, plantings of Pinot Gris doubled between 2001 and 2003 and are predicted to continue to climb over the next few years. Nothwithstanding its recent growth spurt, however, Pinot Gris still only accounts for three per cent of the country's white variety plantings.

Hence, the majority of New Zealand Pinot Gris winemakers have had little more than four or five years' experience with it. There's still a lot more work to be done, evaluating new plantings and defining wine styles. One thing's for sure, though – the standard of Pinot Gris produced here thus far demonstrates its enormous potential for New Zealand.

Well-loved in Europe, where several countries have laid claim to it as their own, Pinot Gris has a number of aliases. In Italy, it goes by the name Pinot Grigio and is exported in large volumes around the world. In Burgundy, France, Pinot Gris assumes the name Pinot Beurot; and in Germany, it is labelled Ruländer when on the sweeter side, Grauburgunder when dry.

Say it right
Pee-no-gree

Styles
Two main New Zealand styles of Pinot Gris are emerging: a fruit-driven style which often has a touch of residual sugar; and a dry style with a hint of oak as well as buttery and yeasty flavours to complement its fruit flavours. Tends to produce rich, mouth-filling wines with a slightly higher alcohol content than some other white wines and lowish acidity. The richest wines have an oily, unctuous quality to them. Pinot Gris grown in New Zealand's cooler regions shows higher levels of acidity and may benefit from cellaring.

Flavours and aromas
Delicate bouquet. Flavours of apples, pears, honeysuckle through to riper stone-fruit, especially apricot when grown in the north. Spice and smoke flavours if oaked.

Food matches
Serve with creamy pastas, calamari, scallops, whitebait, poached fish, shrimps, prawns, crab and shellfish.

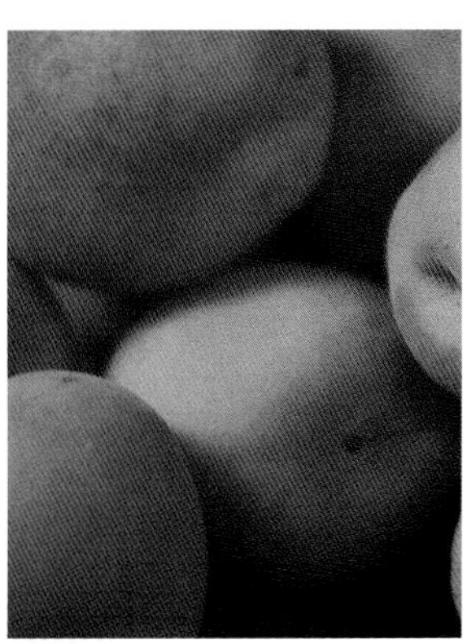

Pinot Gris blends Usually produced as a 100 per cent varietal wine in New Zealand.

Viticulture Pinot Gris vines grow grapes which vary in colour from greyish-blue ('gris' means 'grey') to pinkish-brown. With its tendency to overcrop, Pinot Gris must be managed for low yields in order to produce quality fruit, with ripe, concentrated flavours. In stages of early maturity, it can look very similar to Pinot Noir. It ripens mid season when it produces fruit with comparatively low acidity and high sugar levels, which in turn are responsible for the slightly higher alcohol levels present in Pinot Gris wines.

Yields Approximately 10–15 tonnes per hectare.

New Zealand plantings Mainly Marlborough, Central Otago and Hawke's Bay.

Winemaking
By and large subjected to gentle pressing and fermented at around 10–11°C. Some winemakers may ferment a portion of the wine in oak barrels and/or mature the wine in oak on yeast lees.

New Zealand history Recommended by government viticulturist Romeo Bragato in 1906.

Origins Burgundy, France. A close cousin of Pinot Noir.

Worldwide plantings Italy, Burgundy and Alsace in France, Austria, Romania, Hungary and Russia.

Popular clones Like Pinot Noir, Pinot Gris is, genetically speaking, very unstable and thus prone to mutation. In fact, it's not unusual to see different coloured grapes on the same bunch. New Zealand has imported a number of Pinot Gris clones, but while individual growers may have considerable experience with individual clones, collectively New Zealand's wine industry still has more to learn about them.

Gewürztraminer

Gewürztraminer

If Gewürztraminer were a woman, she would be a demure, sensitive, pretty-in-pink, floral-prints and rose-petal scent kind of girl one moment, the next a racy, exotic beauty you wouldn't forget in a hurry.

Gewürztraminer's delicate aromas of rose petals, lychees and allspice on the nose don't prepare you for the big, bold and powerful palate rush that follows. In fact, palate-wise Gewürztraminer is closer in breadth and weight to Chardonnay than it is to that other great aromatic variety, Riesling.

It thrives in cool climates – one reason why New Zealand produces impressive Gewürztraminer worthy of keeping company with the world's best, notably those produced in Alsace in France. Our local winemakers focus on capturing the wine's varietal characters – the floral, lychee and spice aromas of cinnamon, cloves and ginger which gather in intensity on the palate.

Alsatian Gewürztraminer has more yeasty characters (the effect of staying on its yeast lees longer) and creaminess (the result of malolactic fermentation), neither of which are part of standard Gewürztraminer winemaking practice in New Zealand. The heavier, more musky-scented styles of Gewürztraminer usually hail from warmer climes than ours.

New Zealand grows Gewürztraminer in small quantities around the country, most notably in Gisborne, Marlborough and Hawke's Bay. But the majority flow from Gisborne and boast the body to balance their tropical fruit flavours, along with smooth, approachable textures. Generally, the further south you travel, the more minerally the Gewürztraminer becomes.

Say it right
Ge-vurts-tra-meen-er

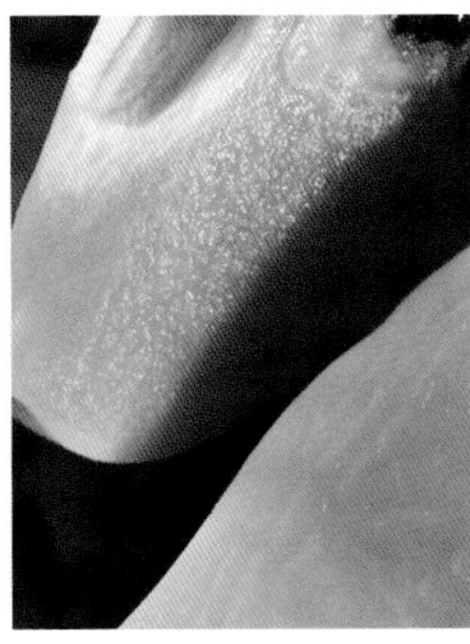

Styles

An aromatic, low-acid variety, usually made without oak. Styles range from the fat, full-bodied and almost oily models to the steely and minerally. Most are dry to off-dry, but can vary between bone-dry style to ultra-sweet late-harvest or botrytised styles. Since Gewürztraminer's acidity is often lower than other varieties, many are best enjoyed within two years of vintage, although well-made and late-harvest versions (known as Vendange Tardive in the Alsace region of France) benefit from cellaring.

Flavours and aromas

Perfumed scents of rose petals, lychee and allspice, which carry through onto the palate where they gain in intensity. May have only hints of spiciness (cinnamon, cloves and ginger), with more emphasis on the floral notes, however. Sometimes displays apricots, tropical mango, passionfruit and grapefruit, too. Malolactic-fermented versions show an ice-cream flavour.

Food matches

Living up to its name 'gewürz', which means spicy in German, it makes a perfect partner for spicy foods, so long as they aren't too hot. Try with mild curry and chilli dishes, especially if there's some sweetness in the dish. Works well with Thai cuisine, Japanese dishes with wasabi or horseradish, roast pork and hot ham. And good with cinnamon-flavoured apple desserts with raisins and cream.

Gisborne's award-winning Montana Patutahi Estate 'P' Gewürztraminer has a cult following among Gewürztraminer fans.

Gewürztraminer blends Usually produced as a 100 per cent varietal style, although very small amounts blended with Pinot Gris and Riesling wines add an attractive aromatic lift.

Viticulture When vine vigour is well controlled, it grows good fruit on fertile sites as well as sites of low to medium fertility. Gewürztraminer is very prone to poor fruit set under unfavourable flowering conditions. And as Gewürztraminer buds early, it's susceptible to frost damage. Its relatively small leaves and tendency to double-bud can make for congested, shady vine canopies, hence growing quality Gewürztraminer requires labour-intensive leaf plucking and shoot thinning to keep the canopies open as well as fruit thinning to produce intensely flavoured fruit. Knowing the exact moment to pick is the key to good-quality Gewürztraminer – it needs harvesting as soon as its aromatic spiciness peaks, but before the acid levels plummet.

Yields Normally 7–11 tonnes per hectare.

New Zealand plantings Mainly Gisborne, with lesser plantings in Marlborough and Hawke's Bay.

Winemaking May pass through crusher and then receive cold soaking (thus giving the juice a little time in contact with its skins) before being gentle pressed. Alternatively it may by-pass the crusher and go directly to the press. Removing Gewürztraminer's unusually high levels of protein (which may render it unstable in the bottle) prior to fermentation, without sapping the wine of flavour, colour and body is the winemaker's greatest challenge. Fining with bentonite clay is usually the best solution. As it is a low-acid variety, malolactic fermentation is rarely used.

New Zealand history First imported in the 1950s. The Te Kauwhata viticulture research station reintroduced it in the early 1970s and it was one of the varieties Bill Irwin of Matawhero Wines in Gisborne pioneered. It's now enjoying a reputation as a premium varietal wine.

Origins Born in the small town of Tramin or Termeno in northern Italy about 1000 years ago. Gewürztraminer's name means 'spicy Traminer'.

Gewürztraminer produces small, pretty, pinkish grapes. The bunch pictured here is only just beginning to ripen, hence some of the grapes are still green.

Worldwide plantings Built its reputation in Alsace in France, on the north-eastern border with Germany. Alsace's Hugel, Schlumberger and Trimbach styles are legendary. Also grows well in Germany and in Italy's Alto Adige.

Müller-Thurgau

Müller-Thurgau holds a special place in our winemaking family tree. The humble grandmother of modern New Zealand white wines, two generations ago it introduced thousands of New Zealanders to the pleasures of wine.

A light, attractive, fruity variety, Müller-Thurgau's golden era in New Zealand began during the 1960s when two then new Müller-Thurgaus – McWilliams' Cresta Doré and Corbans' Riverlea Riesling – convinced Kiwis we could make perfectly good aromatic white wines of our own.

A flurry of plantings in the 1970s established early-ripening, high-yielding Müller-Thurgau as New Zealand's most planted variety (a matriarchal position it was to hold onto until 1992 when Chardonnay finally knocked it off its pedestal). As New Zealand's wine industry gathered momentum over the 1970s, Müller-Thurgau became the guinea pig for a raft of newly introduced winemaking techniques – such as batch pressing and the now standard long, slow, cool fermentation – which so improved the wine's taste that it became a national favourite. Ask anyone to remember which wines they drank regularly in the 1970s and, chances are, they'll name that classic Müller-Thurgau, Wohnsiedler, from Gisborne.

Now Müller-Thurgau's glory days are long since over, despite the fact that it's capable of producing very good, well-rounded, flavoursome wines with the ability to age well. While it is still used in some casks, plantings of this German variety continue to decline as winegrowers pull out old vines and replace them with the classical French varieties today's generation of sophisticated wine drinkers prefers. Müller-Thurgau's last New Zealand stronghold is Gisborne, but even in its native Germany, where it produces a sweeter, less-alcoholic style than our own, it has become less popular.

Say it right
Moo-ler-tour-gow

Styles
A light-bodied, typically slightly sweet wine, styled as an easy-drinking, low-priced wine and mostly packaged in casks. Drier styles do exist, but are less common.

Flavours and aromas
A fruity wine, which combines floral characters with citrus characters and lacks the firm acid backbone of its Riesling parentage.

Food matches
Sweeter styles team well with sweet and sour chicken and pork, pork with apple sauce and lightly spiced Asian food. Enjoy drier styles with fish.

Müller-Thurgau blends Often blended with Muscat.

Viticulture Ripens early but, contrary to the myth, is not that easy to grow in New Zealand because it is susceptible to all sorts of diseases.

Yields High-cropping variety: normally yields about 17–20 tonnes per hectare.

New Zealand plantings Represents only three per cent of the national vineyard and still declining. Mostly planted in Gisborne, followed by Hawke's Bay.

Winemaking Most Müller-Thurgau is stop-fermented to leave a little residual sugar in the wine.

New Zealand history Was first imported into New Zealand in the 1930s, but was not widely planted until the 1960s when it was grown extensively to satisfy the domestic market for off-dry, fruity Germanic-styled white wine. Became less popular in the 1980s as local wine drinkers discovered Chardonnay and Sauvignon Blanc, but only in 1992 did Chardonnay overtake Müller-Thurgau as New Zealand's most planted variety.

Origins A German hybrid, the crossing of Riesling and the German Sylvaner variety by a Dr Herman Müller who wanted to combine the fine characters of Riesling with the reliability of the Sylvaner variety. Often called Sylvaner Riesling.

Worldwide plantings Germany, Italy (Alto Adige), Switzerland, Austria and eastern Europe.

Chenin Blanc

Chenin Blanc

Call Chenin Blanc a great all-rounder, but never a jack-of-all-trades. Most New World Chenin Blanc may be rather ordinary, but in its native home of France, it produces some of the world's finest wines. Now it's making some very impressive varietal wines in this country.

In New Zealand, versatile Chenin Blanc usually disappears into sparkling wines and rank-and-file cask blends, where the variety's characteristic firm acid backbone plays a small but valuable support role. Dry varietal Chenin Blancs are few and far between – although a handful of Gisborne and Hawke's Bay producers do make strikingly crisp yet ripe, tropical fruit-flavoured wines from vines managed for lower yields. Chenin Blanc has never been, and probably never will be, big in New Zealand. Nevertheless, winemaker interest in it is slowly reawakening.

Elsewhere in the New World, Chenin Blanc has long been appreciated, if only for expediency. The fruit's ability to retain acidity – even in hot grape-growing climates – proves extremely useful. In South Africa, high-yielding Chenin Blanc (called Steen) ranks as the country's most planted variety and finds its way into everything from basic table wine to fortified wines and spirits. In California's hot Central Valley, Chenin Blanc produces crisp base wines for inexpensive commercial blends and in Australia it assists with acidity in Chardonnay and/or Sémillon wines.

But only in the cooler climate of the Loire, France, does classical Chenin Blanc express its true potential. There Chenin Blanc-dominant wines prove outstanding, whether they're styled as rich, concentrated, acidic dry wines, sweet but acidic botrytised dessert wines or sparkling wine called Crémant de Loire. Could cool-climate New Zealand produce varietal Chenin Blanc to rival the Loire, then? Time will tell. As wine writer Michael Cooper says in his *Wine Atlas of New Zealand*, '...New Zealand's finest Chenin Blancs are yet to come.'

Say it right
Shennin-blonc (often called Pineau in France)

Styles
Our varietal Chenin Blancs are usually medium- to full-bodied dry white wines with firm to high acidity. Although today's versions are riper and less acidic than earlier examples they may benefit from cellaring to further soften their acidity.

Flavours and aromas
Fruity apples, pears, peaches, and tropical fruit flavours of pineapples. The best have delicious honeyed characters.

Food matches
Can be served as an apéritif. Team it with dishes that have no sweetness and are soft and delicate in flavour: such as poached or steamed fish, seafood, shellfish, savoury-flavoured consommés and lightly flavoured pasta.

Chenin Blanc blends In New Zealand, often blended into sparkling wines where Chenin Blanc's acid backbone lends support to Chardonnay and Pinot Noir. Frequently blended with Müller-Thurgau to make bulk cask wines.

Viticulture A naturally vigorous variety whose tendency to crop heavily needs to be kept in check if it's to produce quality fruit. Grown on carefully chosen, sunny sites and managed using modern viticulture practices, this late-ripening variety produces lighter crops of riper, richer-flavoured fruit with lower levels of acidity. Its tight bunches are prone to botrytis fungal disease.

Yields Can be high yielding: 12–18 tonnes per hectare in some situations.

New Zealand plantings Mainly Gisborne and Hawke's Bay. Plantings declined throughout the 1990s but have recently stabilised. Still only represents a tiny one per cent of the national vineyard.

Winemaking Maturation in oak suits this variety well.

Origins Centuries old, it probably originated in the Loire Valley, France.

Worldwide plantings The Loire Valley, particularly the Anjou-Touraine, in France, Australia, United States (notably California), South Africa and South America.

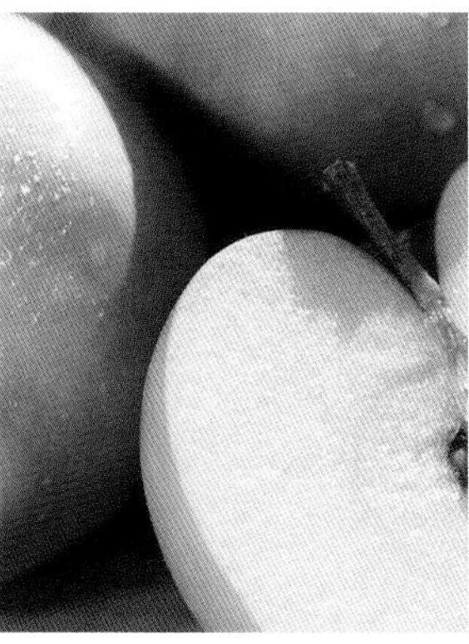

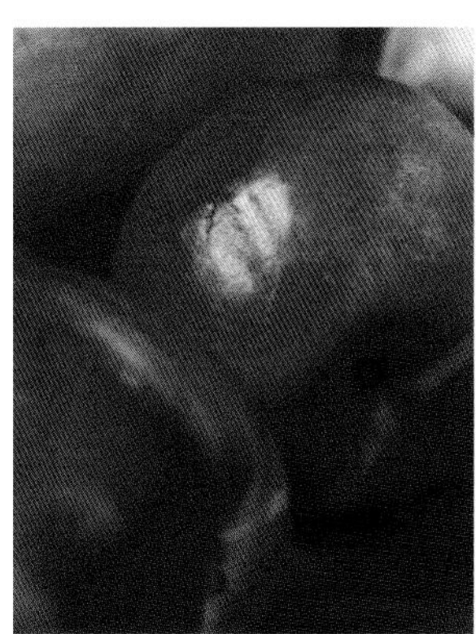

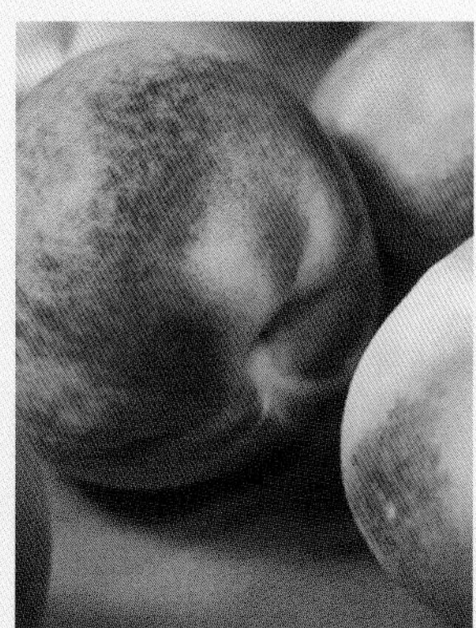

Muscat

Think Muscat and you may automatically put it in the same league as Müller-Thurgau. Many people do, since the two often wind up in casks together. Yet Muscat has enormous potential in New Zealand, say our winegrowers and winemakers.

It's already producing a sprinkling of exciting varietal wines, but wait 10 years or so, as winegrowers experiment with lower-yielding, smaller-berried, highly scented and spicy clones, then witness musky Muscat enjoy a renaissance, just as aromatic Gewürztraminer is doing today.

Muscats comprise a large family of red and white grapes who collectively bear intense musky, scenty aromas and possess sweet, table-grape flavours. Drink their wines and you can actually taste the grapes. There's something else that's out of the ordinary about them, too: their fruit flavours have a remarkable ability to remain intact after fermentation, something very few other grape varieties can claim to do with quite the same degree of harvest-fresh intensity.

The world knows and loves Muscat principally through Asti (Spumante), the low-alcohol, sparkling wine from the Asti region of northern Italy, although the variety makes some wonderful dessert wines and liqueurs as well. Here in New Zealand, we know it best as the grape that brings us a locally produced old favourite, Bernadino Spumante, an Italian-style sparkling wine.

We also enjoy eating Muscat grapes. The large, fleshy fruit can be served fresh or dried as raisins. The most common Muscat grape grown in New Zealand – Dr Hogg – is in fact an old English table grape.

Say it right
Muss-cat

Styles
Best known for Asti (Spumante) and, in New Zealand, Spumante-style sparkling wines. Also makes sweet dessert wines, occasionally white Port-style wines and liqueurs – the last notably the Muscats of Rutherglen in north-east Victoria.

Flavours and aromas
Powerful musky scents and sweet flavours that taste of table grapes.

When to serve
As an Asti, serve as apéritif party wine. Serve liqueur Muscat at end of meal with cheese or instead of Port to people who enjoy a sweeter-style after-dinner wine.

Muscat blends May partner Müller-Thurgau in inexpensive still white-wine blends and sparklings.

Viticulture Dr Hogg Muscat yields well, but ripens late in the season when it can fall foul of the colder temperatures. Early White Muscat ripens sooner, but is prone to attack from birds, which triggers fungal disease.

Yields High: 18–20 tonnes per hectare, or about 4–8 tonnes per hectare for dessert wines.

New Zealand plantings Currently represents only one per cent of New Zealand's plantings, with more than 80 per cent of the vines in Gisborne. Plantings have declined in the last decade, but have now stabilised.

Winemaking Its slippery skins make it hard to press. Generally cool fermented to produce a low-alcohol (9–10 per cent) wine. Carbonated and sweetened to make Asti-style sparkling wine.

New Zealand history In the 1960s and 1970s New Zealand produced what was called Royal Muscat – a fortified oak-aged sweet Muscat in a cream Sherry style. New Zealand Asti-style sparkling wines won many gold medals at local wine competitions in the 1970s.

Origins Grown around the Mediterranean for centuries. First planted in the New World in South Africa in the 17th century, where it was made into a rich dessert wine, called Constantia, favoured by London's and Amsterdam's wealthy.

Worldwide plantings Greece, Italy and elsewhere around the Mediterranean.

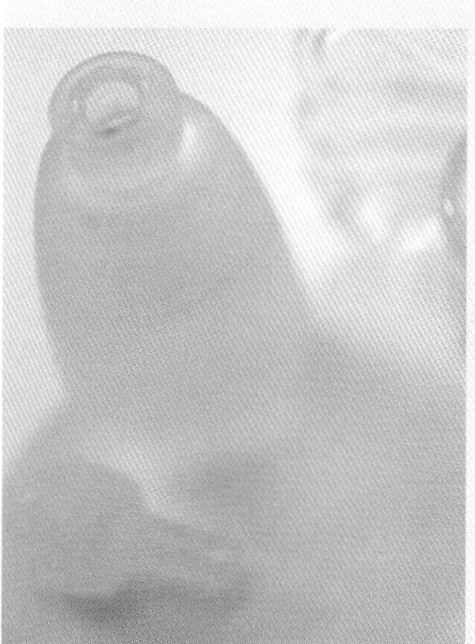

Pinot Noir

Pinot Noir

Young, elegant and upper-class, Pinot Noir is the debutante of New Zealand wine society. Many local producers are pinning hopes on it blossoming into our signature red varietal wine.

Already New Zealand's reputation for quality Pinot Noir is such that the country belongs to a tiny, elite group of producers whose wines the world puts on a pedestal. The best of our Pinot Noirs embody both power and elegance. Rich, soft, silky-smooth, mouth-filling fruity wines, they're highly sought-after in a world that simply doesn't have enough good varietal Pinot Noir to go around. No wonder local producers in the south of the North Island and in the South Island are rushing to plant this cool-climate-loving variety. Pundits predict Pinot Noir is set to become the country's next big wine style: a premium red to stand alongside our Sauvignon Blanc on the international stage. Pinot Noir already occupies more of the national vineyard area than any other red variety and, indeed, is the country's third most planted variety, red or white. Since the late 1990s, its rate of growth has been phenomenal: by 2005, the number of hectares in Pinot Noir will have increased around 700 per cent on 1995 plantings.

Pinot Noir leads a double life. In its native home of France it is the variety entirely responsible for classic red Burgundy and it plays a vital role in Champagne as well. Likewise, in New Zealand Pinot Noir not only makes lush, highly desirable red varietal wines, but also adds fullness and length to our méthode traditionnelles.

Most of New Zealand's newer plantings of Pinot Noir, however, are destined to satisfy demand for stand-alone varietal wines, not sparkling wine. Few places outside Burgundy boast the ideal growing conditions to produce premium varietal Pinot Noir. In warm climates it produces insipid, ill-balanced wines, but our cooler, drier regions suit the grape's notoriously touchy temperament well.

Certainly, Pinot Noir is no easy variety to work with. Winegrowers call it a very 'transparent grape', meaning it is deeply affected by every tiny aspect of its growing environment as well as the people who nurture it into wine. Pinot Noir's thin-skinnned grapes are delicate and hyper-sensitive, predisposed both to fungal diseases in the vineyard and oxidation in the winery.

To many winegrowers and winemakers, then, producing varietal Pinot Noir represents the ultimate challenge. No other variety seems to awaken quite the same passions as Pinot. Take how every year local producers rally together for the Southern Pinot Noir Workshop to share their experiences with the variety and taste the wines. 'It's a hugely cooperative, and collaborative event,' says Ata Rangi's Phyll Pattie. 'That really surprises the overseas guest speakers and winemakers who attend. They cannot believe the

level of openness, mutual support and education on technical issues and so forth that goes on.' New Zealand producers also host a Pinot Noir conference. The first such event, held in 2001, enticed hundreds of Pinot Noir fans from around New Zealand and the globe to Wellington to celebrate the variety. For many of them, it was a chance to catch up with old friends: everyone knows everyone in the New World of Pinot Noir, whether they live in Oregon, USA, or Martinborough, New Zealand.

With all the difficulties inherent in producing Pinot Noir, it is generally on the pricey side. That said, finding a good Pinot Noir under $20 in New Zealand today isn't quite as challenging as making one.

Say it right
Pee-no-nwah

Styles
Soft, lush, silky smooth fruity red wines, light- to medium-bodied, with less tannins than other reds and a velvety finish. Good Pinot Noir has a mouth-feel that rivals that of heavier reds crafted from Cabernet Sauvignon or Syrah. Very approachable wines which, in most cases, don't require long cellaring.

Flavours and aromas
Reminiscent of sweet fruit: strawberries, raspberries, cherries and plums. With age, develops complex mushroom and earthy characters.

Food matches
Serve lighter styles with fresh salmon, quail, turkey and veal, fuller-flavoured versions or oak-aged versions with lamb, duck, venison and roast chicken. An excellent alternative to fuller-bodied reds in summer or over lunch.

Pinot Noir blends In its still-wine form, Pinot Noir is always crafted as a stand-alone wine. But when used to make méthode traditionnelle, it is blended with Chardonnay and, to a lesser extent, Pinot Meunier. (See sparkling wines, page 73.)

Viticulture Pinot Noir is one of the most difficult grapes to grow. It likes dry conditions with a long ripening period, like those typically found in the cooler regions of New Zealand. An early budder, it is vulnerable to late spring frosts. Its thin-skinned, tight bunches of small grapes are prone to fungal disease later in the season. Over-crop Pinot Noir and the colours and flavours in the grapes dilute, since the variety has fewer pigments (anthocyanins), flavouring substances and tannins than other reds. It prefers devigorating soils, although these can be quite variable in composition: free-draining gravels can grow good Pinot Noir as can loess soils on slopes. There are also some interesting Pinot Noir developments on soils with limestone influences.

Yields A low cropper: 6–8 tonnes per hectare is the maximum for a good-quality wine.

New Zealand plantings New Zealand's most planted red-grape variety. Today, more than 80 per cent of Pinot Noir vines are dedicated to producing varietal wines. Marlborough is New Zealand's biggest Pinot region, followed by Central Otago, Wairarapa and Canterbury/Waipara.

Winemaking See making Pinot Noir, page 256.

New Zealand history One of the great grapes viticulturist Romeo Bragato recommended for New Zealand back in 1895. Planted in tiny quantities in the 19th century in areas such as Hawke's Bay and Masterton.

Origins An especially old vine whose origins probably date back two millennia. By the 18th century, strong, full and relatively tannic Pinot Noirs from the Nuits-St-Georges region had become the benchmarks.

Worldwide plantings Grows best in cool climates, namely France's Burgundy, and Oregon, United States. Also grown in Alsace and cooler parts of California, Australia, Italy and Spain.

Don and Carole McCrone, owners of McCrone Vineyard in Oregon, USA, first met fellow New World Pinot Noir producers Clive Paton and Phyll Pattie of Martinborough's Ata Rangi Vineyard at a Pinot Noir conference in Oregon, back in 1988. Today, the McCrones spend half the year in Martinborough, where they are not only Clive and Phyll's next-door neighbours, but also work with them. Ata Rangi Vineyard is set to make premium, single-vineyard Pinot Noir from the couple's recently established Martinborough vineyard, mirroring the relationship the Oregonians have with top American Pinot producer Ken Wright Cellars, who crafts their Oregon-grown grapes into Ken Wright Cellars McCrone Vineyard Pinot Noir. Their relationship with Ata Rangi sets an exciting precedent in New Zealand, one that takes the New World's collaborative approach to producing and marketing Pinot Noir a step further.

Popular clones Pinot Noir is very prone to mutation, so there are hundreds of clones available. The better-performing clones grown in New Zealand include clones UCD 5 and 6 and the Dijon clones from Burgundy (the latter have been widely planted recently and appear to have a tendency to produce relatively open bunches and smaller berries). The Swiss clone AM 10/5 has been around for a long time and is still widely used today.

Merlot

Merlot

Mention Merlot and the conversation soon turns to Cabernet. Like two brothers, they are fated to be compared with one another always.

Certainly, Merlot has spent a long time in Cabernet Sauvignon's shadow. In terms of red wine, up until the mid-1990s New Zealand was Cabernet-obsessed, even though early-ripening Merlot performed more reliably than slow-to-ripen Cabernet in our relatively cool climate. Merlot usually ended up playing the support role in Cabernet-dominant Bordeaux-style blends. It was better known for its ability to iron out Cabernet's harsh tannins and offset any under-ripe, herbaceous flavours than as a variety with the ability to carry a blend or make premium, stand-alone varietal wine.

Now, at last, Merlot is enjoying time in the sun. Straight varietal Merlots and Merlot-dominant blends have become increasingly commonplace in the last few years as new clones and rootstocks have allowed winegrowers to consistently produce well-structured fruit. Winemakers, in turn, can now afford to rely less and less on Cabernet Sauvignon to supply Bordeaux-style blends with their structures.

Merlot-dominant wines aren't new in Bordeaux, France, however. Château Pétrus, one of the world's most expensive wines, costing hundreds of dollars per bottle, comprises almost all Merlot. In Pomerol and St-Émilion (around Libourne in the so-called Right Bank area of Bordeaux) Merlot dominates plantings. Back in the early 1950s, Libourne grew mainly Cabernet Sauvignon and Malbec, although neither was ideally suited to the area, until a severe frost in 1956 killed many of the vines, and afforded winegrowers an opportunity to replant with more fitting varieties – mostly Merlot and a little Cabernet Franc. You could say New Zealand has had to learn much the same lessons about Merlot and Cabernet Sauvignon. In this country, Merlot is a more forgiving variety than Cabernet, performing well in regions not necessarily recognised for their Bordeaux reds, such as Marlborough and Gisborne.

Say it right
Mer-low

Styles
Round, plump-bodied wines with soft, fruit flavours and velvety mouth-feel. Traditionally blended with other Bordeaux reds. As a stand-alone wine is less tannic than Cabernet and matures sooner in the bottle.

Flavours and aromas
Rich, plummy fruit, sweet dark berries, chocolate aromas, perhaps beetroot and a hint of spice. Less prone to herbaceous/minty characters in cooler vintages than Cabernet Sauvignon.

Food matches
Delicious with full-flavoured New Zealand lamb, venison, wild pork, pan-fried liver, veal cutlets with tomato, black olives and herbs, pheasant and duck. Good with Mediterranean dishes and berry or plum sauces. Some like it with chocolate or ice cream!

Merlot blends Along with Cabernet Sauvignon, Cabernet Franc and Malbec, one of the cornerstones of the Bordeaux blend (known as Claret in France). Merlot-dominant blends are becoming increasingly common in New Zealand.

Viticulture Merlot ripens approximately one week ahead of Cabernet Sauvignon in New Zealand conditions. But, on the downside, as Merlot buds earlier as well, it's prone to damage from spring frosts and, if weather conditions are unfavourable over flowering, poor fruit set. Being quite thin-skinned, it's susceptible to fungal diseases. Happy in clay soils, indeed, it may over-crop on fertile land without good viticulture management. New and improved rootstocks and clones are helping produce better-structured wines.

Yields Yields 5–12 tonnes per hectare, about the same as Cabernet Sauvignon, depending on the site.

New Zealand plantings About 70 per cent of New Zealand's Merlot is in Hawke's Bay, with the majority of the balance split between Marlborough and Gisborne. A rush of plantings, starting in the mid-1980s, has seen it become the second most planted red grape variety in New Zealand.

Winemaking See red winemaking, page 250.

New Zealand history The Vidal winemaking family (descendants of Spanish immigrant winemakers Joseph Soler and Anthony Vidal) grew some of New Zealand's earliest Merlot in Hawke's Bay.

Origins Born in Bordeaux, where it is now the most planted red variety. (Merlot is the main red grown in the clay soils of Pomerol and St-Émilion. Only in the warmer shingly soils of Médoc and Graves is Cabernet Sauvignon more common.)

Worldwide plantings Widespread in countries such as France, Italy, Hungary, Australia, Chile and United States.

Popular clones While a range of clones and selections of Merlot exist and have been planted for some years, in the late 1970s two clones were imported from California. These clones, UCD 3 and UCD 6, are currently the most widely planted. More recently, however, new French clones, most notably clone 481 (or more correctly known as clone 181) are producing bigger-structured wines. They grow smaller grapes (with therefore a higher skin-to-juice ratio and more colour, tannin and flavour concentration) and they don't over-crop to the same extent as the older, mass-selected clones (meaning those clones with vague, indeterminate origins).

Cabernet Sauvignon

Cabernet Sauvignon

Think of the varieties in a typical Bordeaux-style red wine, Cabernet Sauvignon, Merlot and Cabernet Franc, as the three tenors and Cabernet Sauvignon as Pavarotti. It's the fuller bodied of the trio, rich, masculine and with great tannic staying power.

Still the world's most famous red, Cabernet Sauvignon (unlike Pavarotti) doesn't often perform solo, however. Instead, it makes a much more harmonious, better balanced wine when in the company of Merlot and Cabernet Franc, two grapes with the ability to soften its otherwise very vocal tannins. Certainly, Cabernet Sauvignon is endowed with excellent structure (taste and mouth-feel on the palate), but as a stand-alone wine it can at times be a little astringent, especially when young. Cabernet Sauvignon is a variety that needs oak like a tenor needs the stage, too. All those big, loud tannins soften when the wine matures in oak barrels (see page 264).

One of the first grape varieties planted in New Zealand back in the 19th century, Cabernet Sauvignon doesn't perform well everywhere in the country. The biggest viticultural challenge is to get it to ripen fully. It craves warmth, which is why hotter and sunnier sites regularly produce excellent lush, characteristically blackcurrant- and blackberry-flavoured Cabernets and why cooler vineyards generally turn out rather unripe, herbaceous-flavoured examples. Grown in cooler climates, Cabernet Sauvignon contains high levels of naturally occurring methoxypyrazines, the same substances that bestow our world-beating Sauvignon Blancs with their sought-after grassy-green characters. In Cabernet Sauvignon methoxypyrazines usually perform a less constructive role, although in small quantities they do supply the wine with peppery and minty characters. Cabernet's tendency to produce wines with unripe flavours when grown on cooler sites is one reason why Merlot-dominant red wines are becoming far more common.

Say it right
Cab-air-nay Saw-vee-nyaw

Styles
Full-bodied, dry, well-structured, rich-flavoured tannic red wines which should age well. The very best New Zealand examples will cellar for more than 10 years. Cabernet Sauvignon wines produced from young vines can be astringent and aggressive on the finish (or aftertaste).

Flavours and aromas
Blackcurrants, blackberries, black cherry, cedarwood, oak. When grown in cooler climates the wines may show mint and chocolate characters. Some have savoury, earthy, smoky cigar-box flavours.

Food matches
A fine accompaniment to red meats, winter casseroles and stews, goat, venison, wild fowl, strong-flavoured cheeses, pizza and eggplant.

Cabernet Sauvignon blends When made in the Bordeaux style, is blended with Merlot, Cabernet Franc and maybe a little Malbec. Australian blends may contain Shiraz as well. Until recently, Cabernet Sauvignon typically comprised the principal wine in New Zealand Bordeaux-style reds, but as Merlot increasingly takes over that lead role, it's playing second fiddle.

Viticulture A late-ripening variety, usually the last to be harvested (with the exception of late-harvest styles for dessert wine). Performs best in warm summer climates on devigorating soils, including stony gravels. Cabernet struggles to ripen optimally in cool growing seasons. On the plus side, its loose bunches of thick-skinned grapes prove moderately resistant to rot and autumnal rains. The use of better (low-vigour) sites as well as improved clones, rootstocks and canopy management techniques have seen New Zealand's Cabernet Sauvignon improve markedly in the last decade.

Yields A moderate cropper: yields 5–12 tonnes per hectare. To produce premium wines, yields of less than seven tonnes per hectare are necessary.

New Zealand plantings New Zealand's third most planted red variety. More than 80 per cent of the country's Cabernet Sauvignon hails from the warmer North Island winegrowing regions, namely Hawke's Bay and Auckland/Northland and Waiheke Island. Very little grows anywhere further south than Marlborough.

Winemaking See red winemaking, page 250.

New Zealand history Probably one of the first grapes planted in New Zealand, arriving here either with James Busby or French settlers in Akaroa. An early Te Kauwhata version won a gold medal at the 1908 Franco-British Exhibition. By the start of World War I, in 1914, most plantings were already concentrated in Hawke's Bay. Cabernet was the 'big' red grape from the 1960s through to the mid-1990s.

Origins The backbone of French Claret, its reputation has been built in the Médoc and Graves regions of Bordeaux, France. DNA fingerprinting shows it is a relatively recent crossing of Cabernet Franc and Sauvignon Blanc.

Worldwide plantings France, Italy, Spain, Russia, Chile, Argentina, United States (California), Australia and South Africa.

Popular clones The key clones are UCD 7 and 8, as well as the mass-selected clone (of indeterminate origin) and a range of selected vineyard clones. More recently a number of improved clones which may favour our cool-climate conditions have been imported from several sources.

Cabernet Franc

A gentle, genial character – known as Cabernet Frank in some parts of Italy – you could go so far as to call it the Uncle Frank of red Bordeaux varieties.

It's softer and fruitier than Cabernet Sauvignon, being lower in acids, extract and tannins. In New Zealand, winemakers use Cabernet Franc almost exclusively to impart those soft, fruity qualities to their Bordeaux-style wines, often blending it in such small proportions that it doesn't rate a mention on the label. Stand-alone varietal styles are a rarity.

Cabernet Franc is a minor player, in other words, and probably destined to stay that way. It has neither the structure and bullishness of robust Cabernet Sauvignon, nor the seductive fruitiness or fleshiness of Merlot. Some winegrowers see it as a compromise grape, a variety to plant in areas where the climates aren't able to reliably ripen Cabernet Sauvignon or a good stand-in variety to blend with Cabernet grown in cooler vintages.

Yet Cabernet Franc is the chief grape in the highly esteemed Château Cheval Blanc of St-Émilion in France. And in the middle of the Loire Valley they produce attractive, moreish medium-weight varietal reds out of Cabernet Franc, known locally as Frenchman's Reds.

Say it right
Cab-air-nay Fronc (certain styles are known as Bouchet in France)

Styles
Typically makes light- to medium-bodied, fruity wines, although it's capable of producing full-bodied Bordeaux styles. Frequently has a very linear palate – that is, a gentle approach (or 'attack') which follows through to the mid-palate and a long finish with good fruit sweetness.

Flavours and aromas
Elegant perfumed wines with violets, raspberries and confectionery characters. Also some blackberry, black-currant and mint (lighter in character than those found in Cabernet Sauvignon).

More often used in New Zealand nowadays as a blending component, Cabernet Franc wine is both lighter in colour and tannins than Cabernet Sauvignon.

Cabernet Franc blends A staple, but relatively minor blending partner in Bordeaux-style reds. May typically comprise five to 30 per cent of a blend, sometimes more. Its sweet finish is useful in Cabernet Sauvignon and Merlot blends as they both often have a savoury finish.

Viticulture Cabernet Franc has two main advantages over Cabernet Sauvignon – it doesn't need quite as much warmth and ripens earlier. It best suits New Zealand's warmer North Island regions. Like all reds Cabernet Franc performs best on low-vigour soils.

Yields A moderate cropper, averaging about 5–10 tonnes per hectare.

New Zealand plantings New Zealand's fifth most widely planted red variety. Concentrated mainly in Hawke's Bay and Auckland.

Winemaking Receives gentler treatment (less aeration during 'pump overs' and not as much time on skins) than Cabernet Sauvignon because it has fewer tannins.

New Zealand history One of the red-wine varieties Romeo Bragato recommended as most suitable for New Zealand in his 1895 report, it nonetheless remained obscure until the 1980s.

Origins A genetic parent (along with Sauvignon Blanc) of Cabernet Sauvignon.

Worldwide plantings Heavily planted in the middle Loire Valley, and also planted in St-Émilion (France) and north-east Italy.

Syrah

Hawke's Bay Syrah

Syrah or Shiraz

What's in a name? Style. Syrah and Shiraz may be one and the same grape variety, but there are definite differences in the bottle between the two.

Grown in New Zealand, France and California, where it produces typically earthy, spicy wines, this classic red variety is called Syrah. Grown in Australia and South Africa, where it usually makes bolder, more fruit-driven wines, it is labelled Shiraz – the name you'll come across most often on New Zealand shop shelves. That's because we're big fans of Australian Shiraz, importing more of it into the country than any other red-wine style.

Our Australian cousins have big stakes in Shiraz. It's their most heavily planted red variety and the cornerstone of their greatest red wines. Here in New Zealand, until recently most producers had come to the conclusion that our landscape was too cool for the variety's liking. But now Syrah is the subject of rekindled interest. Plantings have steadily climbed since the 1990s and, although Syrah is still a rarity (occupying only three per cent of the country's plantings of red varieties), the warmest sites in districts such as Hawke's Bay and Martinborough are producing good cool-climate, classic styles – ripe, spicy yet nevertheless elegant wines.

Say it right
For Syrah say 'see-rah', for Shiraz say 'shi-rahz'

Styles
Everything from approachable light wines, quite close to Rosé in style and designed to be drunk young, to

full-bodied styles that take years to develop fully in the bottle. New-generation Australian Shirazes tend towards the younger, sweeter, light-bodied styles and are chock-full of fruitiness and less tannic than traditional styles. Fewer Australian examples now follow classic French-style Syrah with its characteristic structured palate, soft, full tannins and long life expectancy. The best long-living versions, wherever they come from, need at least five years' ageing and, indeed, may continue to evolve favourably for decades.

Flavours and aromas
New Zealand examples show attractive varietal characters of white/black pepper, tobacco, coffee and tight tannins without the warm, concentrated berry flavours common in Australian examples. Also rich flavours of black fruit and sometimes chocolatey flavours.

Food matches
Great with strong-flavoured foods such as beef, peppered steak (without being too heavy on the pepper), casseroles and roast game.

Syrah blends Australian versions often blended with Cabernet Sauvignon to improve balance, tannin structure, texture and aftertaste.

Viticulture Shiraz craves hot, dry conditions. The better local examples tend to come from warmer sites (in either the North or South Islands) and are grown on shingly, low-vigour soils which produce low crops of intensely flavoured and coloured fruit. A relatively late-ripening variety. Syrah is prone to botrytis.

Yields Mostly managed for yields of 7 tonnes per hectare or less.

New Zealand plantings Represents a tiny three per cent of New Zealand's red-grape plantings. More than 70 per cent of New Zealand's Syrah grows in Hawke's Bay.

Winemaking Some predominantly Australian styles are fermented in open-top concrete vats.

New Zealand history One of the earlier vines introduced to New Zealand in the 19th century, Syrah was being produced under the name Hermitage in the 1880s by pioneer winemaker William Beetham of the Wairarapa. On the strength of viticulturist Romeo Bragato's recommendation that Syrah would 'give heavy yields and wine of first quality' and 'should compose at least one half of the [red wine] vineyard', by 1914 it was one of the main varieties planted in Hawke's Bay. It declined in popularity thereafter, until it started making a comeback in the 1990s.

Origins One of the world's classic red grapes, it was long thought to have originated in ancient Persia or Syracuse in Sicily, but recent DNA testing has traced its parentage to two French grape varieties. Syrah is the cornerstone variety of classic French reds such as Hermitage and Côte Rôtie.

Worldwide plantings Wines from the granite soils of the northern Rhône Valley are pre-eminent. In Australia, it is the base wine for what is widely regarded as the country's finest red, Penfolds Grange. Australia's Barossa Valley, McLaren Vale, Hunter Valley and Victoria are especially well regarded for their Shiraz. Also produced in California, South Africa and Italy.

Barossa Shiraz bunches.

Popular clones New clones are improving the ripening performance of Shiraz in New Zealand.

Malbec

Malbec brings its dark, blue-black colours, big tannic structure and sweet aromas to a number of red-wine blends.

This highly tannic variety has slowly become more prominent over the last decade, particularly in Hawke's Bay, although it still only represents a tiny proportion of the national vineyard area. Malbec ripens well and it ripens early. What's more, it doesn't produce the unripe herbaceous flavours that can ruin Cabernet Sauvignon in cooler vintages, hence it serves as an understudy for Cabernet in difficult years.

As a stand-alone wine, however, New Zealand Malbec may lack balance, which is why you'll rarely come across it. Rather, local winemakers almost exclusively reserve Malbec for adding structure to Bordeaux-style red-wine blends. Malbec's tannins are often even stronger than those of Cabernet Sauvignon – so powerful, in fact, the variety typically makes up only a small proportion of a blend.

By contrast, Argentinian Malbec is usually bottled as a single varietal wine and has a deserved reputation for quality.

Say it right
Mol-beck (goes by a number of other aliases too, including Cot)

Styles
Rarely seen as a stand-alone wine, winemakers mainly use highly tannic Malbecs to build structure into Bordeaux-style blends.

Flavours and aromas
Violets, dark plums, chocolate, spice and sweet prunes.

Food matches
Steak, barbecue meats, grilled venison, roast duck, stews with black pepper, tomato or mustard.

With its rich blue-purple-black colours, Malbec adds colour density to red-wine blends.

Malbec blends When used in Bordeaux-style blends, Malbec typically comprises no more than between three and 20 per cent of the wine.

Viticulture An early-ripening variety, Malbec performs best in warmer climes, such as those of Hawke's Bay. It has a nasty habit of 'setting' (self-pollinating) poorly, which means it doesn't crop reliably. Some newer clones are more dependable, however. Malbec is also prone to significant variation in berry size, even on the same bunch.

Yields Yields can fluctuate markedly – capable of producing very high or very low crops, the latter due to poor setting as a result of cool, wet weather over flowering.

New Zealand plantings A minor bit player on the New Zealand wine scene, Malbec accounts for only about three per cent of red-grape plantings. Almost 70 per cent of plantings are in Hawke's Bay. Some new, relatively small-scale plantings are projected.

Winemaking Handled in much the same way as that other high-tannin variety, Cabernet Sauvignon. Winemakers must take care not to over-extract it when 'pumping over' the cap (see page 254). Winemakers may circulate the wine beneath the skins if tannin levels start to climb excessively.

New Zealand history Romeo Bragato recommended the variety for Hawke's Bay at the turn of the 20th century. By 1917, S. F. Anderson, who managed Henry Tiffen's Greenmeadows Hawke's Bay winery, mentioned it as one of the proven and reliable red varieties for the area.

Origins One of the traditional grapes of Bordeaux, but of less importance in that region today. Plantings have dropped markedly in the last 40 years.

Worldwide plantings Chiefly Argentina, Chile and south-west France. Relatively minor plantings in Australia, California and north-east Italy.

Pinotage

A South African immigrant to New Zealand, Pinotage's parents are Pinot Noir and a variety little known in New Zealand called Cinsaut.

Pinotage was bred in South Africa in 1925 with the express purpose of combining Pinot Noir's elegance with the resilience and higher yields of Cinsaut (elsewhere spelt as Cinsault). When it arrived here in the 1960s, Auckland winemakers in particular took a shine to it and even today a large slice of the country's tiny Pinotage plantings are still clustered in the Auckland region.

Pinotage can make deeply coloured, richly textured wines, full of raspberry-like characters and, when oak-aged, also smoky characters. Alas, these wines are often underrated. Early styles of New Zealand Pinotage were sometimes thought of as 'coarse' and prejudiced some people against the variety, even though today's well-made styles bear little resemblance to them. Now that the wine is of much better quality, its popularity can only increase.

Say it right
Pee-no-taj (taj pronounced as in Taj Mahal)

Styles
Soft, rounded reds, either oaked or unoaked, boasting fewer tannins than Cabernet Sauvignon. Made either in a more full-bodied style or in a lighter, fresher, fruitier Beaujolais style. Well-made wines boast a smooth finish. Generally, an early-maturing wine, although a few years of ageing can serve the fuller-bodied styles well.

Flavours and aromas
A rather gamey bouquet and smooth, berry-flavoured palate. Its raspberry flavours tend to be stronger than those of Pinot Noir. When aged in oak, smoke flavours are evident. Also shows peppery notes.

Food matches
Very good with game meats, roast lamb, salami and jerky.

Pinotage blends Usually produced as a stand-alone wine, although it sometimes comprises one of the varieties used in New Zealand sparkling wines.

Viticulture Pinotage ripens well and retains firm acidity. Grown in New Zealand's relatively cool climate, it has the ability to produce wines with good acid backbone.

Yields Pinotage has a tendency to crop heavily. To make the better-quality wines from the variety winegrowers need to peg yields to under 10 tonnes per hectare.

New Zealand plantings Plantings have increased but still only account for two per cent of the national vineyard area. Mostly centred in Auckland/Northland, Hawke's Bay and Gisborne.

Winemaking Long skin contact and oak maturation produces a fuller-bodied, more complex style.

Origins South Africa.

Worldwide plantings South Africa and Zimbabwe.

The carbon dioxide bubbles in méthode traditionnelle form as the wine undergoes a secondary fermentation inside the bottle.

Sparkling wines

Whatever its guise – be it a fresh, vibrant New Zealand méthode traditionnelle, a French Champagne or a cheap 'n' cheerful con-gas cousin – somehow a glass of effervescent wine brings one's love of life bubbling to the surface.

Everyone knows France is synonymous with Champagne, the jealously guarded name for sparkling wine produced in the Champagne region. Yet a few New World producers are now making serious dents in France's reputation as maker of the world's best sparkling wines. For evidence, look no further afield than Marlborough, where most of this country's finest méthode traditionnelle (sparkling wine made in the traditional bottle-fermented manner of Champagne) comes from. Marlborough's cool climate supplies just the right conditions for growing the crisp, low-sugar, high-acid grapes necessary to craft a quality méthode traditionnelle.

New Zealand's first widely available quality méthode traditionnelle, Lindauer, arrived on the wine scene a little over 20 years ago. Since then, Kiwis have gone on to develop such a penchant for sparkling wine that we drink more of it per capita than any other nation on earth – thanks in no small part to the enduring popularity of Lindauer. In New Zealand alone, Montana sells more than five million bottles of Lindauer each year: that's the equivalent of almost two bottles for every man and woman aged 18 or over in the country. Moreover, Lindauer remains the country's single biggest export brand.

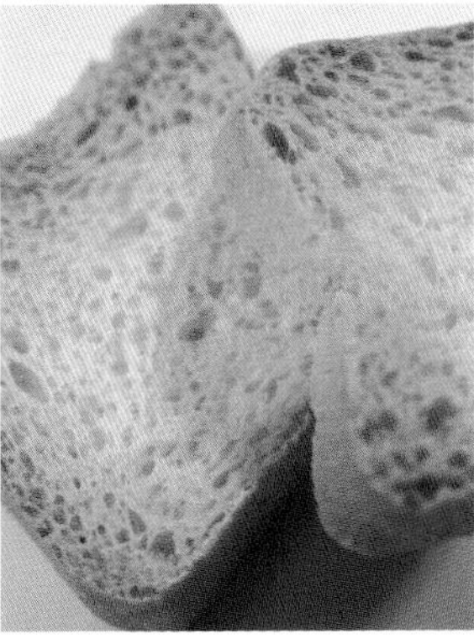

Champagne wines and méthode traditionnelles made in their style traditionally comprise three main varieties: Pinot Noir for fullness and length; Chardonnay for finesse and balance; and a little Pinot Meunier for extra bouquet, fruitiness and roundness. The better New Zealand sparkling winemakers replicate the true Champagne method (see page 274). Hence, you can expect a premium méthode traditionnelle to bear all the hallmarks of Champagne – intensity of flavour, softness of texture, great length, complexity and balance. Every producer's style is different, of course, but they often share some common nuances of flavour, such as fruity characters from the Pinot Noir perhaps, or toasty, mealy, nutty flavours from the Chardonnay and biscuity, yeasty flavours reflecting the wine's prolonged contact with lees (yeast sediment). Each style's flavour profile echoes the wine's place of origin – carries a regional fingerprint, if you like – and is usually crafted into a distinctive, recognisable 'house style'.

Food matches

Sparkling wines make excellent apéritifs as well as accompaniments to a range of different dishes. They team well with salty dishes and deep-fried foods, including humble fish and chips since the wine's acidity and carbon dioxide bubbles cleanse the palate of oil. Lightly spiced Oriental dishes, including sushi and sashimi, and seafood work well with sparkling wines, too. And be sure to serve those firm friends, strawberries and méthode traditionnelle, in summer. The sweetness and acidity in the strawberries marry with the natural sweetness and acidity of the wine. On the other hand, if you're planning to trot out the time-honoured Champagne and caviar combination sometime soon, think again. Not everyone believes they make a good team because the fish's intense flavours overpower the wine.

Sparkling wine styles

Non-Vintage (NV) sparkling wines
The classic French style of sparkling wine. Usually made from the latest vintage, blended with reserve wine from previous vintages to achieve consistency of quality and wine characteristics. This way, each Champagne house produces a distinctive, recognisable 'house style' year after year.

Vintage sparkling wines
Made from the very best fruit, harvested in exceptional vintages. Normally aged longer on yeast lees than Non-Vintage wines, they tend to be more full-bodied and have very fine flavours. Cellar for at least three years after purchase if you want to enjoy their developing biscuity, toasty characters.

Blanc de Blancs
Literally means 'white of whites' and made entirely from Chardonnay. A delicately flavoured, refined style with less fullness than traditional Champagne, it comes in vintage and non-vintage versions. Rather pricey, it makes a good apéritif to serve with the delicate flavours of seafood and fish. Of all the sparkling wine styles, Blanc de Blancs possesses the greatest potential for ageing, developing a toasty richness and mouth-filling fruit intensity as it matures.

Rosé or pink sparkling wines
Mostly made by adding a little red wine to white, but whatever the means of production Rosés have lower acidity because of their Pinot Noir content. Drink them while young. This delicate, floral-perfumed style gains nothing from ageing.

Blanc de Noirs
Means 'white of blacks'. A white wine produced from black grapes, such as Pinot Noir and/or Meunier, with fullness and strength. The gold-standard Blanc de Noirs is probably Bollinger's very expensive Vielles Vignes Françaises.

Sparkling facts

Méthode traditionnelle gets its carbon dioxide bubbles – or mousse – while undergoing a secondary fermentation in the bottle. The gas remains dissolved in the wine until the bottle's seal is removed (see page 274 for more on sparkling winemaking).

Take care when opening sparkling wine – see how to do it safely on page 97.

It takes almost a kilo of glass to make a sparkling wine bottle strong enough to withstand the six-times-atmospheric pressure inside.

Who's counting? There are said to be about 250 million bubbles in a bottle of méthode traditionnelle or Champagne.

Sweetness in sparkling wine

Extra Brut
Bone-dry sparkling (also known as Ultra Brut or Brut Sauvage).

Brut
Off-dry, Brut is by far the most popular sparkling wine. It makes a fine apéritif and great partner for seafood and fish.

Extra Sec (medium-dry), Sec (medium) and Demi Sec (medium-sweet)
Even though sec means dry in French, paradoxically, in wine it means noticeable sweetness. These wines have real appeal for people looking for slightly more sugar.

Doux (or Riche)
A termed used to refer to the sweetest méthode traditionnelles. Although rarely available in New Zealand, they make a fine complement to soufflés, meringue and parfait desserts.

Sparkling wine words

Cuvée
A word frequently seen on bottles. In terms of sparkling wines it refers both to the first and best juice to flow from the wine press as well as the blend of base wines assembled for secondary fermentation in the bottle.

Cuvée de Prestige (or tête de cuvée)
The very best wines, made from the best-performing vineyards during the best vintages. Little wonder they're unrivalled for fullness of flavour and complexity. Usually made from the first pressings only, hence quantities are small, while demand and prices are correspondingly high. Every Champagne house makes one: Cuvée William Deutz from Champagne Deutz; Mumm de Cramant from Mumm; Belle Epoque from Perrier-Jouët, Dom Pérignon from Moët et Chandon; and La Grande Dame from Veuve Clicquot to name a few key examples.

Grande Marque
Literally means a great or famous brand.

Lindauer (named as a tribute to the painter Gottfried Lindauer) has won many top international awards for quality. It's New Zealand's most popular wine and the country's biggest export brand.

The history of sparkling wine

The unofficial history of sparkling wine stretches way back to biblical times, when bubbles slipped into bottles by accident and unexplained fizziness in wine was no doubt the bane of many an ancient winemaker. Stories often credit French monk and history's first celebrated winemaker, Dom Pérignon, with deliberately putting the bubbles into wine back in the late 1600s. Yet, surprisingly enough, sparkling wine was already a popular drink in England about two decades beforehand.

Back then, wine was shipped from France to Britain across the English Channel in casks. Before it departed France's shores, winemakers added a little sugar to the casks which, quite by chance, triggered a secondary fermentation and a build-up of carbon dioxide bubbles in the wine. When it came time for the British to bottle the wines, they had two objects at their disposal which the French did not then possess – toughened glass and cork seals. British coal-fired furnaces (which burned at higher temperatures than wood-fired furnaces) produced glass strong enough to withstand the mighty pressure that builds inside a bottle of sparkling wine. And the English airtight corks sealed the bottles properly and trapped the wine's effervescence inside. The French, meanwhile, were still using leaky wooden bungs, wrapped in hemp, to stopper their wines. News travelled at an escargot's pace back then and it wasn't until a couple of decades later that the French latched on to strengthened glass-making and corks. Dom Pérignon, however, still takes the credit for inventing the classic Champagne blend.

New Zealand's sparkling wine history is comparatively young. The Mission Vineyard produced one of New Zealand's first classic Champagne-style wines, called Fontanella, in the 1960s. It was a very good wine and inspired Montana Wines' then chief winemaker, Peter Hubscher, to make Lindauer, which was launched in 1981. By 1988 Montana put New Zealand méthode traditionnelle on the world map when it enlisted the help of Champagne Deutz to produce the award-winning Deutz Marlborough Cuvée. Now New Zealand's sparkling wine industry is one of the most innovative and successful in the New World.

Dessert wines are more versatile than their name suggests. They make excellent apéritifs, too. Alternatively, you can serve them instead of dessert at the end of a meal.

Sweet dessert wines

The colour of liquid gold, velvety smooth and creamy, the best dessert wines are synonymous with luxury. Somehow their wonderfully luscious, intensely concentrated, ripe-fruit flavours have an uncanny ability to stir memories of summer turning to autumn, in all its mellow fruitfulness.

Yet many people give dessert wines no more than a passing glance because the very mention of the word 'sweet' conjures up best-forgotton memories of their misspent youth supping cheap, sickly-sweet, watery wines. In fact, in New Zealand quality dessert wines are as misunderstood today as you probably were back then, even though they have nothing in common with the shallow stuff of your salad days. Indeed some of the all-time great – and most expensive wines – ever produced are sweet dessert wines. Devotees of classic French Sauternes dessert wines are not averse to splashing out $500 for a premium-quality bottle.

Generally made from either Sémillon, Riesling, Sauvignon Blanc or Muscadelle grapes, dessert wines range from medium to very sweet in style. Traditionally, they hail from France and Germany, with those made in the Bordeaux region of Sauternes, France, being the most famous. Today, however, under the right climatic conditions New Zealand and other New World producers are making first-class Sauternes-style botrytised wines, too, as well as crafting delicious late-harvest wines and, very occasionally, true ice wines. (See page 282 to find out how each of these styles is made.)

Dessert wines usually age well, but check the back label for an accurate cellaring guide. Serve them either lightly chilled or well chilled. As a rule of thumb, New Zealand and New World Sauternes-style dessert wines, with their slightly higher acidity, are best lightly chilled. French Sauternes wines, on the other hand, tend to have a little less acidity and so respond better to a little more chilling.

Food matches

Serve dessert wines with any sweet, ripe fruit or fruit tart. They harmonise brilliantly with crème brûlée, too. What's more, they're brazen enough to partner strong blue cheeses and foie gras or duck terrines.

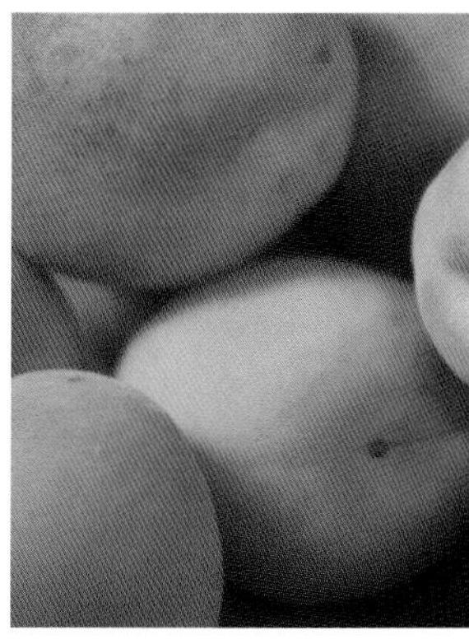

Fortified wines: Sherry

Seriously underrated, thanks to the less-than-distinguished reputations of many Sherry-style wines produced outside Sherry's native home, Spain, good Sherry and Sherry-style wines deserve a lot more credit.

Sherry suffers from an old-fogey image in New Zealand – memories of cheap, mass-produced 'sherries' made and sold here by the flagon in the 1950s and 1960s still put people off drinking it today. But why judge Sherry by that old paradigm when it is such a delicious, versatile wine and, what's more, there are some very good styles available locally? Serve Sherry as an apéritif, match it with food, or enjoy it after dinner with dessert or cheese.

Like Champagne and Port, Sherry takes its name from the place where it's made – Jerez de la Frontera, in the Andalucia region of south-west Spain, Sherry being an English corruption of Jerez. Within the European Union, only fortified wines produced in the demarcated Jerez winegrowing region have a right to bear the name Sherry, although a number of New World countries do turn out fortified wines modelled on the Spanish original and label them as Sherry. In France the wine is known as Xérès, hence you may find all three names, Jerez-Xérès-Sherry, on the label.

There are just two main branches of the Sherry family – the Fino and Oloroso styles. All the rest are simply variations on these twin themes. The making of delicate, pale Fino-style sherries hinges on a type of naturally occurring yeast, called flor, meaning 'flower' in Spanish, which in Jerez' rather humid weather conditions forms a crusty layer or film over the fermented wine as it matures in oak barrels (see making Sherry, page 286). This film prevents the wine from oxidising and imparts it with delicate nutty characters. Oloroso Sherry develops without a protective layer of flor and hence oxidises more, becoming a darker, richer and more full-bodied creature than Fino. In their natural conditions, both Fino and Oloroso

Fortified wines include Sherry and Port. Each is 'fortified' with spirit which boosts their alcohol content. In New Zealand, fortified wines usually contain somewhere between 15 and 23 per cent alcohol.

wines are dry, but may be sweetened to produce sweet-style versions at the final blending stage.

True Spanish Sherries contain one or more of three permitted grape varieties. Palomino (Fino or de Jerez clones) grapes now account for the vast majority of Sherries produced, while Pedro Ximenez and Muscat of Alexandria are sometimes raisined and pressed to produce the dark brown, concentrated juice used to sweeten the sweeter styles.

Food matches
Serve Amontillado, Oloroso and cream sherries with nuts (especially walnuts) and dried fruits. Olives are the perfect match for Fino and Manzanilla sherries.

Styles of Sherry
Sherry styles fall into two main camps: pale, delicate Fino sherries, influenced by flor yeast and fermented to about 15.5 per cent alcohol; and Oloroso sherries, fortified to 18 per cent alcohol and increasing to up to 23 per cent alcohol as the wines age, evaporate and thus concentrate in oak barrels. Virtually all sherries are blends of several vintages. (See page 286 for details on making Sherry.)

• **Fino** Elegant, pale, straw-coloured sherry, delicate, light in body and dry.

• **Manzanilla** A type of Fino, pale, straw-coloured, light, crisp, tangy, almost apple-like and dry in style.

• **Amontillado** An aged Fino that lost its flor before being fortified to 18 per cent alcohol. It has a deeper amber colour than Fino and is rich, dry and nutty, with hints of flor character and toast.

History

Jerez' winemaking heritage probably stretches as far back as 1110 BC and has survived the setbacks imposed by Spain's long, chequered history of conflict and war.

But since the 1980s, the size of the Sherry industry has had to down-size in response to the sidelining of its wines by other, more fashionable styles of wine.

• **Oloroso** Dark gold to deep brown, full-bodied, complex and, in its natural condition, dry with rich, concentrated flavours. Ferments without assistance from flor yeast.

Sweet sherries
These come in various guises and are mostly made from the above styles with the addition of sweet wines made from raisined Pedro Ximenez or Palomino grapes:

• **Medium sherry** Light brown and made from a slightly sweetened blend of Amontillado and light Oloroso.

• **Pale Cream sherry** A slightly sweetened blend of Fino and light Amontillado which accounts for about one quarter of all Sherry produced.

• **Cream sherry** Oloroso sweetened with the addition of sweet concentrated juice from Palomino or Pedro Ximenez grapes, a style pioneered by Harvey's Bristol Cream in the 1880s.

• **Brown sherry** A very dark, rich and sweet dessert-style Sherry.

• **Pedro Ximenez** (often abbreviated to PX on labels) An extremely sweet, syrupy, low-alcohol dessert wine full of rich raisin and Muscatel flavours.

BARROS
1997
VINTAGE
PORT

Fortified wines: Port

Port is the one style of wine that still somehow conjures up images of a bygone era – upper-crust, dinner-jacketed men retreating to dark, wood-panelled smoking rooms to puff cigars and drink what was then a men's-only drink, leaving the women to tittle-tattle around the dining table.

Well, forget all that nonsense. Port is shaking off its fuddy-duddy image and enjoying a modern-day renaissance. It now features on the after-dinner menus at good restaurants everywhere and is served by the glass – giving you every excuse to go ahead and taste the many different styles. In fact, there are so many styles of Port that over the centuries a hierarchy has evolved. Vintage Port (which sells for exceptionally high prices) is the pinnacle Port style; Tawny Port the style aged in barrels long enough to lose its fruity freshness; and Ruby Port the younger, fresher mainstay of Portugal's proud Port industry.

Locally produced Port-style wines were, along with other fortifieds, Sherries, Madeiras and liqueurs, the public's wines of choice between the 1930s and 1970s. Today, only a few producers in west Auckland specialise in Port and make serious styles of very good quality.

The true home of Port is Portugal, of course, specifically the demarcated wine region of Douro which starts about 100 kilometres inland from Oporto (the city from whence British merchants first began shipping Port more than 300 years ago) and stretches all the way to the Spanish border. Most of the vineyards are planted on the steep slopes of the hills beside the Douro River, no more than 500 metres above sea level, shielded from Atlantic winds by the high hills on the seaward side and mountains to the north and south. The further away from the coast, the more extreme the climate: temperatures soar in summer, frequently passing the 35°C mark and rain rarely falls. Near the Spanish border rainfall is barely 150 millimetres a year.

Port takes its name from the city of Oporto in Portugal, from where merchants shipped the wine to Britain in the 17th century. Today, Portugal still makes the world's best Port. It's rich, vigorous and, when nurtured to full maturity, extraordinarily complex in flavour and aroma.

The Douro divides into three sub-regions: the comparatively cool and wettest zone, Baixo (Lower Corgo), which tends to produce Ruby Ports and Tawny Ports; the warmer, drier Cima (Higher Corgo), where most of the Vintage Port, Late Bottled Vintage and high-quality Tawny Port flows from; and the hot, arid, only relatively recently planted Douro Superior zone in the east.

Strictly speaking, the name Port belongs to Portugal. On the Continent, European Union laws restrict the use of the word Port to Douro-produced wines. But outside the EU some countries still borrow the term, if only for the reason that substitute words don't adequately describe Port-style wines. In New Zealand, wineries are allowed to use the term, however, on the proviso they have used it in the past.

Food matches

Serve port with strong-flavoured cheeses, dried fruits, nuts, rich chocolate or toffee desserts.

Styles of Port

Ruby Port The original-style Port, a fresh, youthful, ruby-coloured wine with ripe, fruity, grapey flavours and little evidence of oak. The backbone of the Port industry, Ruby Port is ready for drinking as soon as it is bottled, usually after about two years of maturation in large oak cuves.

Tawny Port Aged in barrels long enough to lose its fruity freshness and ruby colour, Tawny Port takes on a brown or tawny hue which lightens further with age. As a rule, they're complex, smooth, silky, nutty-flavoured wines. Standard Tawny Ports comprise blends of various wines of different ages – the age stated on the label means the wine tastes as if it's 10 years old, but doesn't necessarily accurately

reflect the age of the wines in the blend. The most highly prized are the 10-, 20-, 30- and 40-year-old versions.

Vintage Ports The King of all Ports, these are Ruby Ports made only in the best years, defined by Portugal's Instituto do Vinho do Porto (IVP) as 'of one harvest produced in a good year of recognised quality and having exceptional organoleptic characteristics, dark and full-bodied, with a very fine aroma and palate'. Blended and bottled after two years' barrel ageing, whereupon it ages further in the bottle, normally taking at least 15 years, sometimes many more, to reach its peak. Decant before serving (see page 96). The most recent vintages are 2000, 1997, 1995, 1994, 1992 and 1991. However, not all producers make Vintage Ports in declared years.

Single Quinta Port Like Vintage Port in colour, aroma and flavour, most Single Quinta Ports come from an individual vineyard (or quinta) and are usually made in the years that just miss out on being granted full vintage status by the IVP. The year of vintage is declared on the bottle.

Colheita Port A Tawny Port from a single vintage, aged in wood for at least seven years and often for considerably longer. Colheita (meaning 'crop' or 'harvest' in Portuguese) is often confused with Vintage

Port because it's vintage-dated and shows the harvest and the final bottling dates on the label.

Late Bottled Vintage (or LBV) Made in a similar style to Vintage Port, it is highly concentrated and comes from a single vintage (which is not always declared on the label). LBVs spend between four to six years in barrels and vary significantly in flavour and style between house producers. Those that spend longer in barrels are ready to drink when bottled, others take a further four to six years to fully mature. Good LBVs offer excellent value.

Crusted Port Named after the sediment deposits that precipitate in the wine. Crusted Port is the product of two or three vintages and is aged in barrels for two years before bottling. Of higher quality than Vintage Character Port, it is perhaps the closest style to Vintage Port and ages well in the bottle.

Vintage Character Port Blends of several years' wines. A difficult style to pin down, perhaps best described as having more fruit and body than a Tawny Port and an extra helping of nutty, woody flavours from ageing for four to six years in barrels. It first arrived on the scene in the 1950s under the name Reserve Vintage, a nom de plume a few Port houses still use today.

White Port Range in style from the bone-dry to the unctuously sweet ('lagrima' meaning 'tears'). Made exclusively from white grapes in much the same way as other Ports from red grapes, except that maceration is shorter. Cask-aged for two to three years in much the same way as Ruby Port, White Port becomes darker in colour as it grows older.

History

The British serendipitously stumbled upon Port in the 17th century. In 1678, two Liverpudlian wine merchants despatched to Portugal in search of wine supplies met with an abbot in a Douro monastery who offered them smooth, sweet wines, quite unlike the dry, more aggressive styles they were acquainted with. The abbot's secret was to add brandy to the wine during fermentation, rather than after it (as was customary to preserve wine before shipping it to Britain). The practice stopped fermentation prematurely and thus preserved some of the wine's natural sugars, creating a medium-sweet, fortified wine by, essentially, the same means used to make Port today.

Before long, shipping agents were ferrying Port to British shores where it soon became the subject of ritual. A decanter of Port was always passed clockwise around a table and offered only to men. (Women were expected to stick with Sherry, on account of its lighter, presumably more suitably feminine style.)

No such protocol surrounded the drinking of the typical, locally made Port-style wines in this country, however. New Zealand-produced Ports, along with Sherries, were our most popular wines throughout the 1940s, '50s and '60s, celebrated, 'more for their alcohol content than their finesse,' observed New Zealand wine writer, Frank Thorpy in 1970. Local wine producers found New Zealand's climate simply too cool to ripen the grapes sufficiently to make naturally sweet wines, so they added cane sugar to ferments and fortified the wines with grape spirit made from marc (the spent lees, grape skins and stalks) mixed with sugar – a practice outlawed in Portugal. The result was New Zealand Ports and Sherries tasted artificially sweet on the palate and had a 'kick like a mule in the stomach,' reported Thorpy.

Rest assured, however, that those local winemakers who still work in this area today now produce wines of good quality.

Making the most of wine

For all the rituals, rules and insider jargon surrounding wine, learning to appreciate it need be no more complicated than trying lots of different styles and seeing which ones you enjoy. The ultimate test for any wine is: 'Do I like it?' Only you can be the judge of that.

Buying wine

In New Zealand, we drink most of the wines we buy within 48 hours of purchase. But that doesn't give us licence to treat soon-to-be-opened bottles with disrespect. Avoid leaving wine sitting in a hot car and as soon as you arrive home stow the bottles away in a cool, dark place – not on top of the fridge or in the firing-line of direct sunlight. If you do decide to keep the wine for a few months or longer, store it under as close-to-ideal conditions as you can (see cellaring, page 121).

Reading the label

Know how to read the label on a wine bottle properly and you'll have a pretty good idea of what to expect from the wine when you open it.

Brand name
Usually the most prominent name on the bottle.

Grape variety (or varieties)
If only one variety is mentioned then it comprises at least 75 per cent of the wine. The producer is not obliged to name the varieties that make up the balance. Where two or more varieties are named, the first-mentioned dominates the blend. Since most European countries stipulate that wine identified by a single variety must compose at least 85 per cent of that variety, the majority of New Zealand (export-focused) producers label their wines according to the 85 per cent rule, no matter where they sell the wines.

Producer's name and address
As required by law.

Bottle size
Usually expressed as millilitres or centilitres. Standard bottles hold 750 ml, half bottles (usually dessert) hold 375 ml.

Alcohol content
As a general rule, the riper the grapes used to make the wine, the higher its alcohol content. Most table wines' alcohol content ranges between 10.5 and 14 per cent by volume; Chardonnay and red wines tend towards the higher end of that scale.

Food match suggestions
Use as a general guide only.

Standard drinks
The number of standard drinks (containing 10 g of pure alcohol) contained in the vessel. (See responsible drinking, page 120.)

Region of origin
The region that produced the grapes may also give more than a few clues about the wine's style.

The individual vineyard
Where the grapes grew, sometimes named on the more expensive labels. Usually implies the vineyard consistently produces good wines.

Vintage
The year in which the grapes were harvested. It offers clues about the quality of the wine. Vintages vary, for better or worse, according to weather patterns during the growing season and harvest. Law does not require producers to state the vintage.

Preservatives
New Zealand law says these must be stated on the label, whereas in some countries (the UK, for example) it's illegal to declare them. Wine preservatives commonly include:
- Preservative 300 (vitamin C or ascorbic acid)
- Preservative 220 (sulphur dioxide), used since Roman times for its anti-oxidative and anti-microbial properties; aside from its main role of preventing oxidation, it neutralises any stray yeast cells that could ferment the wine in the bottle. Reds contain 15–25 parts per million, whites 20–35 parts per million.
- Preservative 202 (yeast-inhibiting potassium sorbate), used in cask wine.

Cellaring suggestions
Recommendations about how long the wine can be stored or 'cellared'. Use as a general indication only.

① **'Reserve' or 'Private Bin'**
Words like 'Reserve' or 'Private Bin' mean wine producers consider the wine of higher quality (on account of special winegrowing or winemaking methods) and produce it in smaller quantities and sell it for higher prices. But since no rules define how such words may be used, they're not necessarily a reliable indication of quality. Rather than put too much store in them, look to brand names you trust first and foremost.

Other descriptors
Words referring to winemaking techniques, such as 'barrique matured' (wine fermented in 225-litre oak barrels) often rate a mention on labels. See the glossary at the back of this book for explanations of words you don't understand.

③ **Brix degrees**
The ripeness of the grapes at harvest is expressed as Brix degrees (sugar levels). 20–24°Brix, the average sugar level of grapes harvested in New Zealand, produces a 12–14 per cent alcohol wine when fermented to dryness. 25–30°Brix is standard for sweet late-harvest wines; and 30–55°Brix for ultra-sweet botrytised dessert wines.

Residual sugar
The sugar present in the wine, measured in grams per litre (which can be retained by stopping the fermentation before it is fully completed).

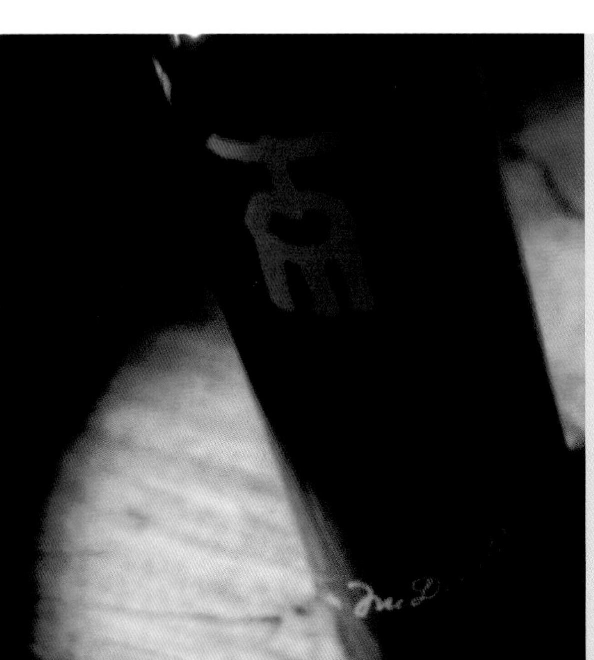

Not all New Zealand wines are named after the grape varieties from which they are made.

Take Tom, one of New Zealand's finest red-wine blends. The blend of Bordeaux-variety grapes used to craft this wine varies from vintage to vintage so it's known simply by its brand name.

Wine style words
4 Words which describe the wine, such as fortified wines (Ports and Sherries, usually 23 per cent alcohol) or table wine (non-fortified wines with typically 15 per cent alcohol or less).

More wine style words
5 Words like Vintage Port or Fino Sherry – see page 81 for descriptions of Port styles and page 79 for Sherry styles.

NV: stands for Non-Vintage
6 Meaning the wine inside the bottle may be a blend of several vintages of wine.

Wine style
7 Words which describe the wine, such as méthode traditionnelle (bottle-fermented sparkling wine); Extra Brut or Brut de Brut (meaning totally dry) or Brut (meaning off-dry). See page 74 for descriptions of méthode traditionnelle and Champagne styles.

Old World European wine countries, such as France, Italy, Spain, Portugal and Germany...

label their wines according to their own individual wine-classification systems. See Imported wines chapter, page 290, for explanations of label terms.

Sizing up the bottle

Tradition isn't the only reason why most wines are still sold in glass bottles. Glass is an inert material so it cannot affect wine in any way.

Dark-coloured glass has the added advantage of protecting the wine against ultraviolet light, hence wines with the potential to age well usually come in dark bottles. The use of clear glass often signifies that the wine makes better drinking when young. Either that, or it has a particularly appealing colour worthy of showing off.

Wine bottles turn up in countless different guises, of course, as anyone looking at the array of artful shapes and designs gracing today's shop shelves can see at a glance. Yet most share a few features in common: the vast majority hold 750 millilitres (ml), the standard volume agreed to by both the European Union and North American producers in the late 1970s. The bulk of them are more or less cylindrical in shape, meaning they can be cellared (or stored) on their sides, thus keeping cork closures moist and elastic.

Certain Old World winemaking regions and individual vineyards are synonymous with specific bottle shapes. New Zealand and other New World producers have adopted some of these standard shapes for themselves:

1. The German (Hock) bottle A tall, elongated bottle, generally used for aromatic styles of wine, such as Riesling and Gewürztraminer.

2. The Bordeaux bottle A bottle with high shoulders: a very popular shape for red wines.

3. The Burgundy bottle A bottle with low-slung, sloping shoulders: a large number of Chardonnays come in Burgundy bottles.

4. The dessert wine bottle A clear glass bottle containing 375 ml of wine – half that of the other standard 750 ml bottles pictured here. Since dessert wines have the potential to age well, by rights you would expect their bottles to be made of dark glass, but tradition dictates otherwise.

5. The sparkling wine bottle A thick, heavy bottle, designed to withstand the high pressure within. It takes about 900 grams of glass to manufacture a standard 750 ml sparkling wine bottle, compared to approximately 600 grams to make a standard-sized still wine bottle. Note how the sparkling wine bottle always has a deep punt (an inverted, bell-shaped impression in its base for added strength) which serves as a convenient place to rest your thumb when pouring the wine. (You may also come across punts on still wine bottles, too.)

Bigger bottles

- The magnum: 1.5 litres (equivalent to two standard bottles).
- The Champagne and Burgundy regions' Jéroboam: 3 litres (equivalent to four standard bottles). Known as the 'double magnum' in Bordeaux.
- The Bordeaux region's Jéroboam: 4.5 litres (equivalent to six standard bottles).
- The Bordeaux Impériale: 6 litres (equivalent to eight standard bottles).

Wine bottle and label designs make a visual statement about the wine inside the bottle. Wine producers know them to be persuasive marketing tools. This Corbans Private Bin Sauvignon Blanc label, with its embossed New Zealand fern and stylish metallic copper foiling, conveys both the wine's New Zealand heritage and its high quality.

Montana Wines was the first wine producer in Australasia to achieve the quality standard ISO9002 certification for its bottling process.

The earliest winemakers in Mesopotamia and Egypt stored their wines in amphorae—large clay flasks stamped with the name of the producer, the style of wine and the vintage. The Romans went on to invent glass blowing and soon found glass to be an excellent medium for storing wine. Yet for many centuries no one had the technology to manufacture bottles in standard sizes, so wine drinkers took their own glass bottles to their merchants who filled them with wine sold by the measure. In Britain, it was illegal to sell wine in glass until the 1860s. By that time manufacturers had developed the technical means to produce uniform-sized bottles. Today, glass bottles remain the best medium in which to store finished wines.

Wine stoppers

Cork closures currently remain the most common means of stoppering wines, but the proportion of wines sealed with screwcaps is growing fast.

méthode traditionnelle

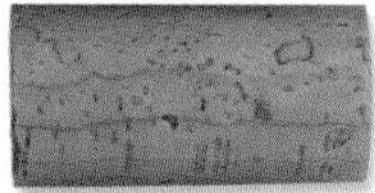
quality 49 mm cork

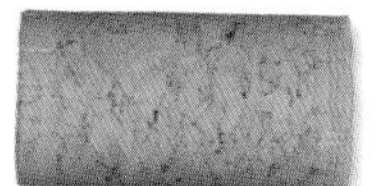
twin-top 44 mm cork

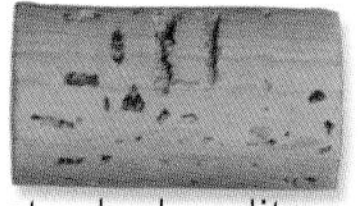
standard-quality 44 mm cork

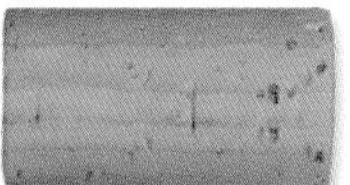
quality 44 mm cork

38 mm twin-top composite cork

synthetic cork

The most common length for a cork is 38–45 mm. Longer corks tend to be reserved for top-quality wines with potential for cellaring. Poorer-quality corks have greater numbers of pits (or lenticels) on their surface.

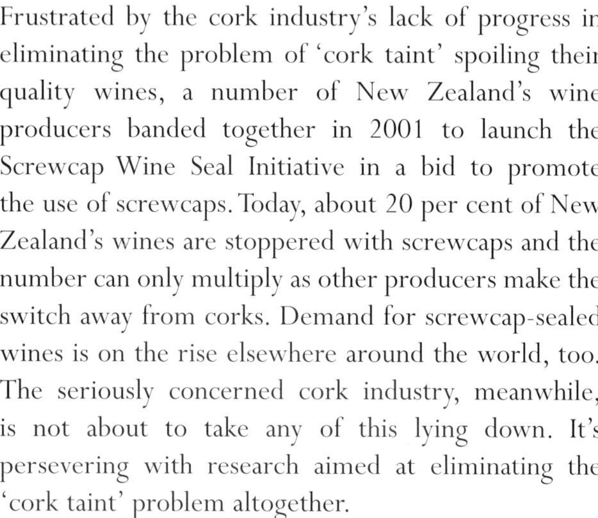

Frustrated by the cork industry's lack of progress in eliminating the problem of 'cork taint' spoiling their quality wines, a number of New Zealand's wine producers banded together in 2001 to launch the Screwcap Wine Seal Initiative in a bid to promote the use of screwcaps. Today, about 20 per cent of New Zealand's wines are stoppered with screwcaps and the number can only multiply as other producers make the switch away from corks. Demand for screwcap-sealed wines is on the rise elsewhere around the world, too. The seriously concerned cork industry, meanwhile, is not about to take any of this lying down. It's persevering with research aimed at eliminating the 'cork taint' problem altogether.

Besides removing the risk of 'cork taint' screwcaps have another major advantage. They are user-friendly: both easy to open and equally easy to reseal. And without the need to keep a cork moist, screwcap-sealed bottles can be stored upright. Yet, when all is said and done, the act of twisting the cap on a bottle of wine doesn't quite replace the ritualistic romanticism of pulling a cork, does it?

The facts about screwcaps

- Apart from removing the risk of 'cork taint', the screwcap eliminates the possibility of the wine oxidising under a faulty cork.
- The screwcap has inert, food-grade polymer at the base of the cap which means it doesn't affect the taste of the wine.
- Early-drinking wines bottled under screwcaps are said to retain their freshness for longer.
- Cellar-worthy wines will age when bottled under screwcaps, since there is sufficient oxygen in both the wine and head space inside the bottle to allow maturation to occur. However, screwcap-sealed wines may take longer to age than those under cork closures.

The ins and outs of cork

- Cork is the thick, yet lightweight outer bark of the imposing cork oak *Quercus suber*, a species of oak which grows mainly in Portugal, Spain, southern France, Italy and north-west Africa. Most cork used in New Zealand comes from Portugal's extensive cork forests.
- Cork is harvested by stripping the bark from the tree every nine years. The process doesn't harm the trees: each cork oak can yield an average of 16 harvests over its lifespan of about 150 to 200 years.
- Cork is unique: it is elastic as well as biodegradable.
- Cork shouldn't adversely affect the taste of the wine (see corked wine, page 109).
- The cork closure doesn't provide an absolute seal, therefore it allows micro-quantities of oxygen to slowly enter the wine over time and facilitate bottle ageing (see cellaring, page 121).

Waiheke Island's Goldwater Estate boasts its own cork oak tree.

If corks become too dry they may crumble when you try to remove them from the bottle. When cellaring (or storing) a wine for longer than two months, lie the bottle on its side to keep the cork moist and elastic.

Stripping the cork oak of its bark once every nine years does not harm the tree. Cork bark is dried for about six months after harvesting before being processed into sheets. It's then sorted and graded according to quality. Wine closures are punched out of the sheets.

Common corks

Cork closures come in a variety of grades. The best corks – such as the 49 millimetre-long cork pictured opposite – are earmarked for similarly top-quality, cellar-worthy wines and are punched out of sheets of the bark. At the lower end of the cork scale are composite corks, made out of tiny cork particles laminated together and used to seal wines intended for early drinking. 'Twin-top' corks are those made from two slices of cork glued to the top and bottom ends of composite cork material. Plastic corks are reserved for less-expensive styles of early-drinking wines.

The history of cork

- The Ancient Greeks probably were the first people to seal their wines with corks. Yet knowledge of cork closures became 'lost' to wider civilisation and wooden bungs wrapped in cloth were used to stopper wines for many centuries.
- Shakespeare's work makes mention of cork closures, but only since the beginning of the 17th century has cork became the most common means of stoppering wine bottles.

Serving wine

If you've spent a lot of time – and money – carefully choosing a wine, then of course you want to serve it at its best. The key is to bring it to the right temperature.

Serving temperature

How often have you pulled an icy-cold white wine straight from the fridge and served it straight away? It's a common mistake. Over-chilling a wine suppresses its aromas and flavours, makes it taste less sweet, appear to have less body (or viscosity) and gives it a more acidic or more tannic impression on the palate. (What's more, where Chardonnay is concerned, over-chilling can exaggerate any oak characters.) Even a high-quality, pricey wine can taste quite ordinary if you drink it too cold. Serving wine at too high a temperature won't do it justice either. Once a wine hits 20°C or more, it starts to lose its delicate aromas.

Take note of the room or air temperature in which the wine has been stored prior to serving – it gives a good indication of whether you need to chill or warm a wine. Better still, keep a thermometer in your wine storage area.

During a New Zealand winter, you probably won't need to chill whites so long as they've been stored properly in a cool place. But during the coldest months you may be advised to warm red wines a little by briefly running hot water over the unopened bottle. Cupping a glass of red wine in your hands helps warm it as well.

Medium- to full-bodied red wines don't normally need chilling – even in the middle of a hot New Zealand summer – if they've been stored somewhere cool. Lighter-style Pinot Noir and Beaujolais are also best served at room temperature, but can be lightly chilled to 14–15°C if you wish, since they are less tannic than other red wines.

Temperature guide

Serve well chilled (8–10°C)

- Sparkling wines: méthode traditionnelle and Champagne. You can serve sparkling wines straight from the fridge after a couple of hours' chilling, but allow the more expensive styles to stand at room temperature for 20 minutes afterwards to bring out their full flavours.
- Middle-of-the-road, inexpensive, light, fruity white wines.

Serve lightly chilled (11–14°C)

- Medium- to full-bodied white wines and more expensive white wines.
- Light red wines such as Pinot Noir, Rosé and Beaujolais.
- Sweet dessert wines.
- Fino and Manzanilla sherries.
- Ruby Port, light Tawny Port and White Port served as apéritifs.

Serve at room temperature (15–18°C)

- Medium- and full-bodied red wines, such as Merlot/Cabernet Sauvignon blends and Shiraz.
- Expensive Tawny and Vintage Ports, Late Bottled Vintage (LBV), Vintage Character and Single Quinta Ports, sweeter sherries and Oloroso sherries.

Quick temperature tips

To chill a bottle of wine quickly...

Stand it in a bucket filled with a mixture of half water and half ice and a large handful of salt. The ice-and-water combination chills the wine quicker than ice alone.

To warm a bottle of wine in a hurry...

As a last resort, remove any metallic capsules/foil from a 750 ml bottle and microwave on high for a 10-second burst to increase the temperature by 2°C. And don't tell anybody! Microwaving wine is an oenological sin as far as some wine buffs are concerned. It alters flavours and is definitely not recommended for more interesting, complex wines.

Screwpull 'automatic'
Clever engineering makes this recent design one of the most effortless cork removers yet.

Screwpull with detachable lever
A very reliable style of corkscrew with a long, sharp, Teflon-coated screw.

Traditional wine knife
The most popular device, often known as the 'waiter's friend'. Some versions come with a capsule-cutter on the handle end.

Dual wire opener
Often called the 'butler's friend'. Excellent for retrieving a stubborn or broken cork.

Air pump with hollow needle
The hollow needle punches through the cork, pumping air into the space below and pushing the cork out with air pressure.

Opening wine

Take a firm hold of the screwcap and turn anti-clockwise – those are the only instructions necessary to open the ever-increasing number of New Zealand wines sealed with screwcaps. Alas, removing corks can be a little more trying.

You can buy any number of gadgets to do the job but – don't we all know it – some work better than others. If, despite all your best efforts, the cork crumbles, either push the cork inside the bottle – it won't affect the taste of the wine – and then strain the wine, or use a dual wire opener to retrieve the cork. What key features does a good corkscrew possess? The screw should be wide enough to allow a match to pass up through the centre; the end of the screw should always be sharp; the shank (which joins the screw to the handle) should be rectangular in shape, not rounded; and ideally the corkscrew comes with a foil cutter.

Breathing and decanting

Whether or not you choose to decant a wine into another vessel before serving is mostly a matter of personal taste. Decanting aerates the wine, altering its impression on both the nose and the palate. It can also remove any sediment from the wine. Not all styles benefit from decanting, but some do – particularly red wines and Port.

One of the great myths that still persists about red wine is it needs to 'breathe', or aerate, in the bottle to improve its flavour after opening. It doesn't work. Leaving an opened wine to stand for an hour or so won't aerate it because only the wine sitting in the bottle's narrow neck comes into contact with air. If you want to aerate a wine thoroughly, you need to decant it into another vessel.

So why would you bother? Well, if you open a young red wine to find its mouth-puckering tannins all too obvious and coarse, decanting will go some way towards softening and mellowing the offenders in a relatively short space of time. Pour the wine into another vessel (and if you wish, back into the original

There are literally hundreds of different styles of corkscrews – so many that they have become a serious collector's item. The best corkscrews are those that remove corks quickly and efficiently. Pictured are a few of the types available.

bottle), then wait 20 to 30 minutes before serving. (Some wines may require a little longer, but it is better to err on the side of caution unless you have had previous experience with the wine.) Expect decanted wine to show fresh fruit flavours when first poured, but for those flavours to become less intense after half an hour or so. And see how the wine becomes a softer, smoother model of its former self. On the other hand, if you delay drinking a decanted wine for several hours its aromas and flavours dull significantly.

The other reason why you may want to decant a wine is if you see some sediment lurking in the bottom of the bottle. It's entirely over to you whether to remove it or not. In no way do these natural deposits (usually a combination of tartrate crystals, destabilised tannins and natural colouring agents) signal a faulty wine. Many of the world's finest, most expensive reds and all premium Vintage Ports are bottled without filtration and likely to carry at least a little sediment. This can give the wine a coarser mouth-feel, which you personally may not like.

You have two options to remove sediment. The traditional method has all the ritual of a religious ceremony. Stand the bottle upright for a day or two, so that the sediment pools in the bottom. Next, remove the cork and, disturbing the sediment as little as possible, pour the wine off slowly into a decanter or glass container. Have a candle (if you want to do things the old-fashioned way) or torch lit behind the bottle. As soon as you see the sediment sliding up the neck of the bottle, like a dark, slippery eel, it is time to stop pouring. Tip away the sediment and any remaining wine.

If all that sounds too fiddly for your liking, try pouring the wine through a paper coffee filter. Not only does the filter do a thorough job of removing the sediment, it's not wasteful of the wine and catches any crumbly bits of cork that may have dropped into the bottle.

Either serve the wine from the decanter or pour it back into the rinsed-out wine bottle.

Sediment is generally only found in older wines, whose tannins are usually soft, so serve them immediately as they won't benefit from aeration.

Opening sparkling wine

Sorry to sound like a killjoy, but popping the cork on a bottle of sparkling wine is a potentially hazardous business. The cork's impact can cause serious injury so you'd best forget jiggling the bottle about in excitable, Formula One-winner fashion. The pressure inside a bottle of sparkling is about six times greater than normal atmospheric pressure – greater again in hot weather. Shaking or dropping the bottle disturbs the carbon dioxide and causes the internal pressure to climb even higher. Bottles have been known to explode on rare occasions. If you do drop a bottle, put it in the fridge and wait a couple of hours before opening it. Only ever open sparklings when they're chilled.

Step 1

Remove the foil after tearing or cutting it. Drape a napkin over the cork to catch the foam and the cork (should it unexpectedly fly off). Hold the bottle at a 45° angle to minimise foaming. Point the bottle away from yourself, other people and fragile objects.

Step 2

Grip the top of the bottle, keeping your thumb on top of the cork. Loosen (but do not remove) the wire cage by undoing the twist tie with six half turns. Hold the cork and wire cage through the napkin with one hand, while gently twisting the bottle with the other. You should hear a faint sigh rather than a loud 'pop' as the cork comes out. (Popping the cork tends to destabilise the bubbles and increases the risk of the wine 'foaming over'.) Never completely remove the wire cage and then leave an unopened bottle unattended.

Splendour in the glass

Does the glass play a part in one's appreciation of a wine? Absolutely. And not just from an aesthetic point of view. Now science backs long-held claims that the glass can affect how the wine tastes.

If you want to show off a wine from every angle, stick with simple, clear, tulip-shaped stemmed glasses. And forget arty coloured glasses, tumbler-style glasses, patterned glasses and weird and wonderful-shaped glasses, especially those that curl outwards at the top, like elegant lilies. They may bring ornamental appeal to a table setting, but they'll detract from the enjoyment of the wine itself.

From a wine purist's point of view, glasses should be clear – not coloured or opaque – so one sees the wine's colour clearly. They also require reasonably long stems – long enough to fit several fingers around – so the drinker's hands have no need to hold the bowl of the glass and inadvertently warm the wine. As for their shape, the best, all-purpose profile is the tulip style, with its slightly tapered top that concentrates the wine's aromas in the bowl. (Flared, lily-like bowls allow the aromas to dissipate too quickly.) Size-wise, wine glasses need to be big enough to hold a generous amount of wine when filled half to two-thirds full, the usual filling heights. The wine's aromas can then gather in the head-space between the wine and the top of the glass and the wine drinker can swirl the wine around before tasting it without spilling any. Some serious wine lovers add another requirement to the list of criteria for a good glass – that it be made from thin glass, although this isn't necessary.

Glassware care

Detergent residues can mar the flavour of a wine and reduce a sparkling wine's effervescence. Always rinse glasses well after washing. If you don't, the detergent leaves a slippery, invisible film behind. Sparkling wine bubbles can't cling to this film and so evaporate too quickly. Either leave glasses to air dry or dry them with a lint-free cloth – linen tea towels are good. Always store glasses upright. Avoid putting them away in cardboard boxes, otherwise you may taint your glasses with a papery smell.

Can the shape of a glass affect a wine's chemistry?

Yes, discovered a study reported in the *New Scientist* recently. Kari Russell of the University of Tennessee in Knoxville measured the concentration of phenolic compounds in a flute glass, a martini glass and a (large, tulip-shaped) Bordeaux glass.

After pouring wine into each of the three glasses, Russell found the concentration of a phenolic compound called gallic acid (stemming from gallic tannins) increased in all the samples. But 10 to 20 minutes later, the gallic acid in the Bordeaux glass had fallen, while in the flute and martini glasses it remained high. Russell believed this happened because the Bordeaux glass exposed a higher surface area of the wine to air.

So what's the significance? Oxygen and gallic acid form catechin-gallate esters which, when they pass one's lips, precipitate proteins in saliva and make the wine taste dry.

To seriously evaluate a red or white wine, fill glasses no more than one-third full. And when pouring the wine to drink, fill the glasses two-thirds full.

With countless different styles of glasses to choose from, how many are an absolute must to own? Only three: a generous-sized, all-purpose glass for both reds and whites; a longer, narrow flute for sparkling wine; and a largish copita for Sherry and Port.

An all-purpose glass for both reds and whites

It's not essential to serve red and white wines in different-sized glasses, although traditionally red wines are served in larger glasses than white varieties.

Champagne flute

The narrow surface area of the tulip-shaped Champagne flute concentrates aromas, helps the bubbles last longer and the wine stay lively. Some Champagne flutes have a spot of roughness ground into the bottom of the glass to give the bubbles something to 'seed' off. Crystal is said to be best because its (microscopically) rougher surface gives the bubbles something to cling to, thus the carbon dioxide releases more slowly. Pour a little sparkling wine into the flutes, then go back and top them up to between two-thirds and three-quarters full. The saucer-shaped Champagne coupes favoured in the 1960s and 1970s are a thing of the past – bubbles and aromas dissipate from them too quickly.

The copita

The traditional, tulip-shaped glass for Sherry and Port, the copita is smaller than the average XL5 tasting glass. These glasses can be filled almost to the top, since the alcohol present lifts the flavours to the wine drinker. Older and/or special ports can also be served in slightly larger glasses. Brandy is traditionally served in a larger glass still, called a brandy balloon. Brandy balloons are only partially filled, thus allowing the wine's aromas to concentrate in the bowl of the glass.

The XL5 tasting glass

Smaller than the average wine glass and designed to facilitate professional examination of a wine. Wine tasters use these at tastings and competitions. Made from very clear and uncut glass, the XL5 doesn't distort the wine's colour and is stemmed so the taster can swirl the wine without warming it with his or her hands.

Tasting wine: the art and science

Swirling, sniffing, sipping, gargling and spitting – tasting wine the way the professional wine buffs do is an ugly business. You don't have to engage in quite as many sucking noises or facial contortions as the pros do to fully appreciate a wine's character – but unfortunately it does help.

LOOK...
...at the colour of the wine against a white background. Colour gives clues about a wine's age and origin, as well as its varietal composition.

SWIRL...
...to aerate the wine and release its aromas into the glass.

SMELL...
...inhale deeply and try to identify the wine's aromas – with practice you'll soon get the hang of it.

Montana Wines' wine education manager Mark Polglase demonstrates the tasting procedure.

Learning how to taste and assess a wine is part and parcel of learning how to appreciate wine. There's no real mystery to it. The more wines you taste, the sooner you develop a palate memory – a mental library of wine memories – with which you can compare new wines and begin to understand why you like or dislike certain ones. Serious wine tasters, who taste thousands of wines each year do exactly this, but on a vastly bigger scale than the rest of us. The sniffing-gargling-spitting ritual they use neither looks nor sounds attractive, but it does help focus attention on each separate aspect of a wine.

Professional wine tasters and judges insist that the only way to evaluate a wine objectively is to taste it 'blind', with the label hidden. That way, they cannot be swayed by any preconceived notions they may have about the wine. (Try hosting a blind tasting with friends. Hide wine bottles in brown paper bags if you don't want to go to the trouble of pouring the wines out of sight of your guests into numbered glasses.)

If your impression of a wine differs from someone with a more experienced palate, don't feel you've read a wine wrongly. Right and wrong don't enter into it – wine tasting is an entirely subjective affair.

SIP...
...the wine and make mental notes about its flavours and textures in the mouth.

CHEW...
...move the wine around inside the mouth, sucking a little air in as you do so, again making mental notes about flavours and textures.

SWALLOW OR SPIT...
...if you're tasting a succession of wines, you need to keep a clear head so spit the wine into a spittoon.

Tasting guide

Use this step-by-step guide to taste wine – write down your impressions as you go, using the tasting sheet opposite. If tasting sparkling wine, read page 107 first.

Step 1: Look

Look closely. A wine's colour gives clues about its regional origins, grape variety(ies), age and general health. Pour a little wine into the glass and then tilt it away from you at a 45° angle. Hold the glass up to the light or, even better, look through the wine against a white background (such as a piece of paper) with the light either above or behind you. Natural light is best. Fluorescent lighting tends to make red wines look a little brown and thus older than they really are.

Note the colour. As a wine matures it changes colour (see opposite below). Expect wines to be bright and clear, but there's nothing wrong with a slightly hazy, unfiltered red wine. Usually, the haziness signals that sediment has been disturbed. Lack of clarity won't detract from the quality of the wine.

The vinous rivulets – known as 'legs' – that swim down the sides of the glass after the wine has been swirled about are indicative of a wine's alcohol content. The higher the alcohol content, the 'skinnier' the legs.

Colour: the measure of a wine's development. The colour of a wine reveals much about where it comes from and how old it is. Cool-climate whites and reds are paler than their counterparts grown in warmer regions. All white wines develop deeper colours as they age and eventually turn brown when over the hill. The reverse is true of reds. They lose colour as they mature and take on more brick-coloured hues before finally fading to tawny tones when well past their best.

White wine		
Youthful	**Early Maturity**	**Late Maturity**
Green/white colour. Fresh fruit aromas along with wine-making aromas (oak, yeast and malolactic charac-ters). Crisp acid.	Straw/yellow colour with greater depth. More nutty flavours are now evident.	Yellow/gold colour. Strong bouquet with maximum apparent complexity and minimal fruit. Soft acid.

Red wine		
Youthful	**Early Maturity**	**Late Maturity**
Purple or ruby colours. Strong fruit and oak (if used) aromas. Rough tannins.	Red, plum, cherry colours. Flavours integrate and devel-op new and more complex flavours. Firm tannins.	Lighter colour with brick tones. More complex, savoury, masculine flavours rather than fruit. Soft tannins.

Tasting sheet

	Wines to compare			
	#1	**#2**	**#3**	**#4**
Colour **Intensity: pale, light, medium, deep** The colour of white wine deepens with age and tends to be deeper in sweeter wines. Thick-skinned grapes such as Cabernet Sauvignon tend to have a deeper colour than thin-skinned grapes like Pinot Noir. **Hue: whites – green-tinged, yellow/green, yellow/gold** White wine loses its youthful green tones with bottle age or during barrel maturation. **reds – purple, ruby, brick, brown** Red wine can be purple when young and may become brick-coloured with age.				
Aroma **Intensity: shy, medium, intense, + / –** Stronger aromas may result from more intensely flavoured grapes. Flavour intensity can be a quality factor when comparing wines from the same grape variety. **Characteristics:** Use terms that describe the characteristics detected. These are usually based on floral, fruit, vegetable, caramel and wood descriptors. Use everyday words that other people can relate to and understand.				
Taste **Apparent dryness: dry, off-dry, medium, sweet** dry – no perceptible sweetness off-dry – a hint of sweetness medium—moderate sweetness sweet – very sweet **Body: light, medium, full-bodied** The body is the weight or viscosity of wine. Sauvignon Blanc tends to be lighter than Chardonnay. **Acid: soft, balanced, acidic, tart** Some wine styles such as Gewürztraminer tend to be soft, while others like Sauvignon Blanc and Riesling can be more acidic. **Tannin (for reds): soft, well-structured, grainy, rough** Thick-skinned grapes such as Cabernet Sauvignon and Syrah tend to be more tannic compared to thin-skinned varieties such as Pinot Noir. **Aftertaste: short, average, long** The length of time that the flavour stays in the mouth. A measure of intensity.				
Comments For other general comments, such as value, food match, cellaring potential and quality assessment.				

Writing up your impressions of a wine

Using a pre-formatted tasting sheet helps organise your thoughts about a wine. In wine competitions, wine judges usually score wines out of 20, with up to three points going to colour, brightness and clarity, up to seven for bouquet or aromas, and up to 10 for general taste and impression. Gold medals go to wines that score at least 18.6 points, silvers to wines that score between 17 and 18.5 and bronzes to those that score 15.6 to 16.9. You, of course, are at liberty to come up with your own scoring system.

Don't confuse your nose

Taste wines in a smell-free room with good lighting. Cooking smells, perfumes, tobaccos and, indeed, any strong odours, as well as lingering aftertastes interfere with our senses of taste and smell.

Smell it, taste it

Our tongues can distinguish four basic tastes – sweetness, sourness, bitterness and salt. It's left up to a mucus membrane lining the top of the nasal sinuses, called the olfactory mucosa, to detect the thousands more. When food or wine enters the mouth, aromas travel up the back of the throat into the nasal cavity where the olfactory mucosa distinguishes them. Our brains, in turn, recognise these as both smells and flavours. So, for example, the tongue picks up the sweetness in honey, but the olfactory mucosa identifies the honey's manuka or bush flower flavours. All of which explains why anyone with a heavy head-cold loses not only their sense of smell but also their sense of taste. Once the wine is in your mouth you may get a stronger, more vivid impression of its aromas. That's because as the mouth warms the wine, the wine releases yet more aromas.

The wine world makes a distinction between aromas and bouquet:

Aromas refer to a wine's fruity and (occasionally) botrytis smells which are grown in the vineyard; a wine's bouquet refers to the smells that originate from the winemaking process, such as oak, yeast or malolactic fermentation-derived smells. Bottle age can give rise to another set of smells – nuts, toast and caramel.

Step 2: Smell

With the exception of sparkling wine (see page 107) swirl the wine rapidly for about three seconds, making a mini-whirlpool. Forcing the wine onto the sides of the glass in this way exposes more of it to the air and helps it release aromas. Expert wine tasters swirl wine with a few deft flicks of the wrist – you may want to start out by keeping the glass on a flat surface and rotating it in tight circles. Next, put your nose into the glass, inhale deeply and withdraw it. Have a short break to refresh your sense of smell, then go back for a second whiff. Swirl the wine again before smelling it.

The nose identifies two key characteristics in a wine: its aromas and the intensity of those aromas (meaning how pronounced or 'lifted' they are). Fix these aromas in your mind. Can you remember where you may have smelt them before? Try putting names to them, no matter how odd-ball they may sound (after all, how else did some bright spark come up with the name for the 'wet dog' aroma sometimes present in wine). Are the aromas fruity or spicy, earthy or floral, for instance? Are they shy and delicate or, at the other end of the spectrum, intense or heavily perfumed? Novices probably find fruit aromas the easiest to pick. For help with naming aromas, use the 'Aroma Wheel' (pictured opposite) or refer to the Grape varieties and wine styles chapter, beginning on page 20, which outlines the key characteristics of each variety. You may detect a wine fault at this point, too (see page 109).

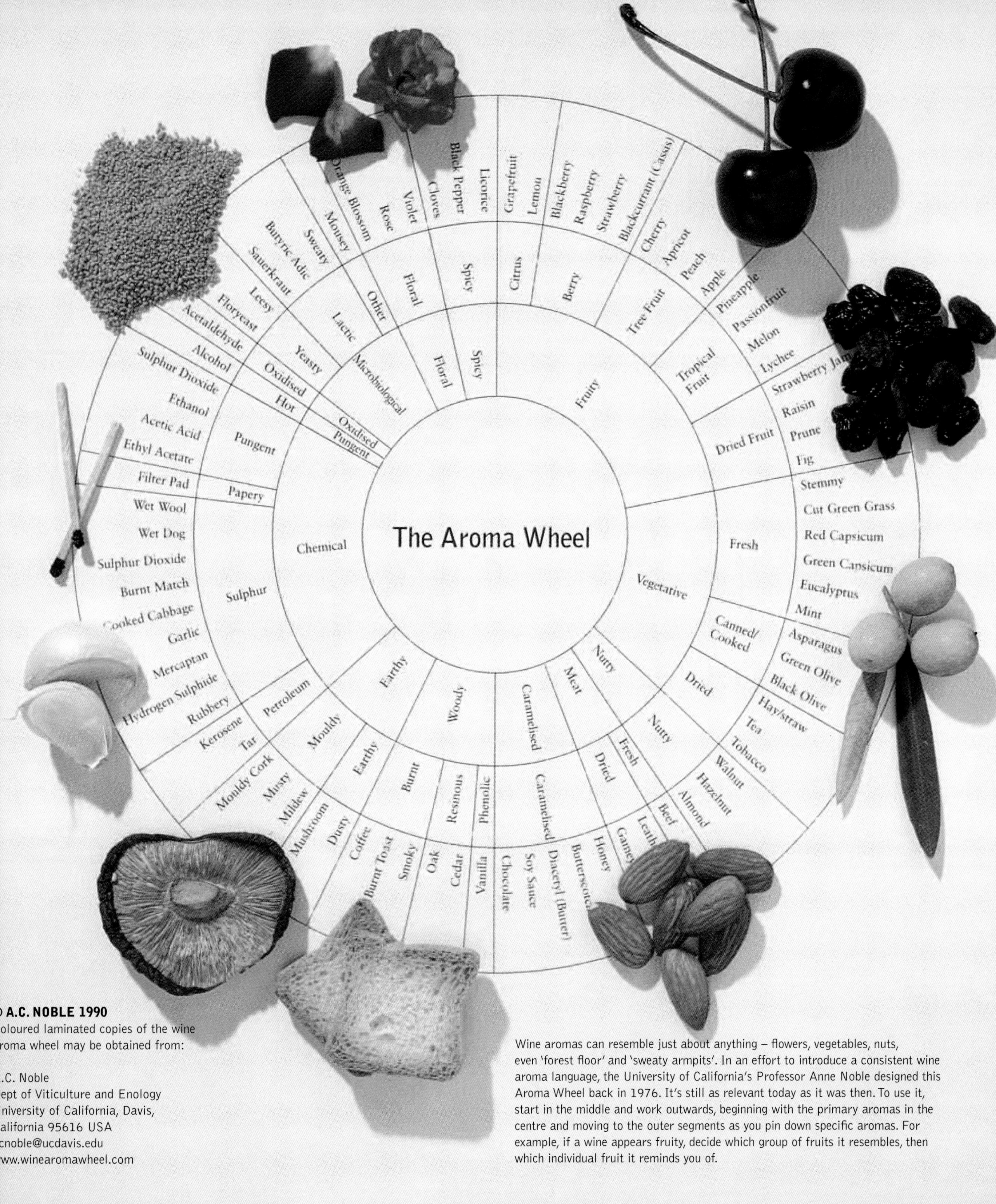

Coloured laminated copies of the wine aroma wheel may be obtained from:

A.C. Noble
Dept of Viticulture and Enology
University of California, Davis,
California 95616 USA
acnoble@ucdavis.edu
www.winearomawheel.com

Wine aromas can resemble just about anything – flowers, vegetables, nuts, even 'forest floor' and 'sweaty armpits'. In an effort to introduce a consistent wine aroma language, the University of California's Professor Anne Noble designed this Aroma Wheel back in 1976. It's still as relevant today as it was then. To use it, start in the middle and work outwards, beginning with the primary aromas in the centre and moving to the outer segments as you pin down specific aromas. For example, if a wine appears fruity, decide which group of fruits it resembles, then which individual fruit it reminds you of.

Step 3: Taste

Now sip the wine, swirling it around in your mouth, coating the tongue, roof of the mouth and gums. 'Chew' the wine as if it were a piece of steak. Practised tasters suck a little air into their mouths and gurgle air through it. (Agitating the wine in this way, called aspiration or trilling, helps heighten aromas.) Now swallow some or all of the wine or, alternatively, spit it out if you've several others to sample.

Taste buds (receptor cells) concentrated in sections of the tongue pick up sensory information about the wine, especially in terms of sweetness and acidity. (See the tongue diagram opposite.) Make mental notes about the tastes: they'll reflect the aromas you smelt earlier, but you may notice their intensity has changed because now you're experiencing them alongside other flavours and textures. Now think:

• **Is it dry, medium or sweet?** Don't confuse fruitiness with sweetness. A wine can be fruity and dry at the same time. (Indeed, it may help you better assess sweetness if you dip the tip of your tongue in the wine before taking a sip.)

Sugar levels in different wine varieties and styles

Residual sugar	Classification	Varieties
Less than 5 g/litre	Dry	Chardonnay, Sauvignon Blanc, Chenin Blanc, Sémillon, Pinot Gris and all red wines
About 10 g/litre	Off-Dry	Riesling, Gewürztraminer
About 15 g/litre	Medium-Dry	Riesling, Gewürztraminer, Müller-Thurgau and dry white cask wines
About 25 g/litre	Medium	Most white cask wines
30 g/litre and over	Sweet	Late-harvest and dessert wines including Sauternes

• **Is the wine soft and round (low acid) or fresh, crisp, even tart (high acid)?**

• **Is the acidity and any sweetness in the wine in balance, or does one dominate the other?**

• **What does it feel like in the mouth – light, medium or full bodied?** Using your tactile sense, judge the wine's body (or viscosity) in your mouth as you would to distinguish between the feel of skim milk, whole milk and cream. Body can range from light to heavy, thin to oily. Another term used to describe body which may help you pinpoint it is 'fleshiness'.

Acid levels in different wine varieties and styles

Acid levels	Variety and Style
Higher	Riesling, Chenin Blanc, méthode traditionnelle
Average	Chardonnay, Sauvignon Blanc, Sémillon, Pinot Gris
Lower	Gewürztraminer, red wines

• **Notice any drying, mouth-puckering sensation in the inside of your mouth when drinking red wine? What does that sensation feel like?** Tannins, the astringent substances found in many fruits, tea and red wine (see page 250) are responsible for this sensation. Tannins lock onto the insides of the mouth, more so at the front than the back, but also around the sides, the gums and the roof of the mouth. The further the drying sensation travels, the more tannins in the wine. They range in feel from harsh and coarse to silky smooth. In young red wines tannins can be overbearing, but with age they soften and mellow. Because New Zealand's red wines are now made from riper fruit than in the past, the tannins are riper too and as a result the wines softer and more approachable.

• **What does the alcohol level feel like?** Alcohol has a slightly sweet taste. Fuller-bodied wines with higher alcohol and glycerol have a smoother, sometimes slightly oily texture. Fortified wines such as Sherry and Port feel warm and fiery on the back of the palate. Overly alcoholic wine tastes 'hot'.

• **What are your lasting impressions of the wine?** How long do the flavours and the 'feel' of the wine linger in your mouth after you swallow a little of the wine? Wines whose characteristics linger longer in the mouth are described as having 'good length' – the mark of a quality wine. But the aftertaste may be short or long. Older wines and those that mature in oak barrels usually have a longer aftertaste.

• **Record your impressions of the wine for future reference.** The tasting sheet on page 103 is a good format to work with.

Mouth-feel

When wine experts talk about 'mouth-feel' they mean how the wine's body, tannins and alcohol feel in the mouth.

Acidity

Acidity is the principal agent that gives white wine structure and helps to preserve it. Note a wine's acidity softens as a wine becomes older.

Tactile tannins

Tannins give red wines that drying, mouth-puckering sensation on the palate. They're responsible for both the structure of reds and have important preservative qualities.

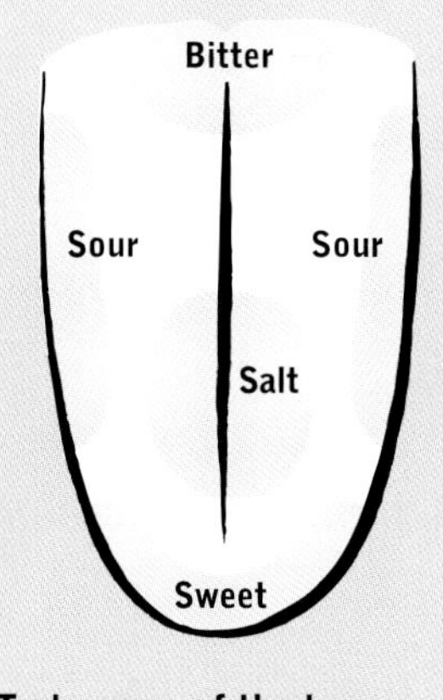

Taste areas of the tongue

On the tip of your tongue

Sweetness is detected on the tip of the tongue. Sweetness in medium- to sweet-style wines comes from the sugars fructose and glucose. In drier wines, alcohol and to a lesser extent glycerol can add an impression of sweetness. In méthode traditionnelle, carbon dioxide bubbles can erase some of the impression of sugar.

Acidity comes across as sourness in the mouth and registers itself most strongly on the sides of the tongue. Cool-climate wines and younger wines tend to have higher levels of acidity. Whites are generally more acidic than reds. Riesling, méthode traditionnelle and Chenin Blanc are high-acid wines; Chardonnay, Sauvignon Blanc, Sémillon and Pinot Gris typically medium-acid varieties; and Gewürztraminer and red wines typically lower-acid wines (although some Pinot Noirs and Italian varieties show more than a little acidity). Note that acidity can cancel out to some degree the impression of sweetness in a wine with residual sugar. Wines contain many types of acids: tartaric acid in the main, as well as sometimes 'green', unripe malic acid and lactic acid (the last produced during malolactic fermentation).

Bitterness, detected as an unpleasant sensation at the back of the tongue, is considered a wine fault, usually caused by either oxidation or very hard pressing.

Saltiness, not a taste normally associated with wine, is detected most strongly in the middle of the tongue.

Tasting sparkling wine

No need to swirl a sparkling wine before tasting it – the carbon dioxide bubbles give off the wine's aromas. Otherwise, when seriously assessing sparkling wine, follow the step-by-step tasting guide beginning on page 102, paying close attention to the wine's mousse – the bubbly, beaded froth that sits atop the glass. The mousse is an important measure of the wine's quality. Tiny, high-pressure, slow-release, long-lasting bubbles are the hallmarks of a wine with an excellent pedigree. The smaller and more plentiful the bubbles, the finer the mousse. But since our eyes can't always accurately judge bubble size, assess the quality of the mousse in the mouth as well. It's not as tricky as it may sound. Take a sip and roll the wine around the inside of your mouth. You should be able to detect the difference between a high- and low-pressure mousse by the way it feels. The degree of fizziness indicates the strength of the mousse, which varies from firm to soft/gentle depending on the style. Decide if the bubbles are coarse or fine. Larger bubbles feel coarser, whereas the smaller, most sought-after bubbles give the mousse a silky, creamy feel.

Judging a wine's quality

How good is the wine you are drinking? The only way to make your mind up is to see how it measures up against great wine.

Great wines are the yardsticks by which we can judge the quality of all other wines. So what makes a wine very special? The finest wines display all the following characteristics:

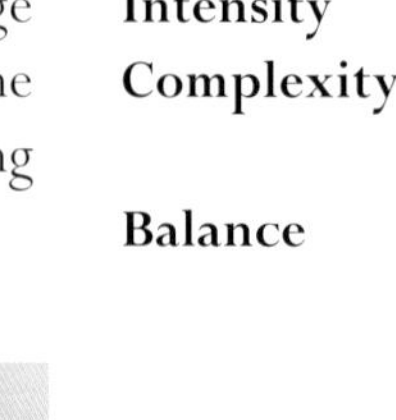

Intensity pronounced flavours and richness
Complexity many different flavours in harmony with one another
Balance harmony between the wine's main structural components (acids, sugars, tannins and alcohol)
Texture smooth and seamless
Aftertaste long and pleasant

By definition, an out-of-balance wine is an inferior-quality wine. Hence the key question to ask yourself is, 'Is this wine in balance?' In other words, do all its structural components (acids, sugars, tannins and alcohol) add up to a harmonious whole? It should show enough acidity to cleanse any sugar from the palate, but if the acidity appears high, it's a sign the wine may benefit from cellaring. Is the balance between the fruit and any oak correct? In overly oaky wines, the oak dominates, even swamps, the fruit flavours.

Wines typically have three character levels:

- **Primary characters**, derived directly from the grape such as the herbaceousness of a Sauvignon Blanc.
- **Secondary characters**, which come from or are enhanced by winemaking techniques, such as buttery characters which come from malolactic fermentation.
- **Tertiary characters**, the complex characters induced by ageing – that kerosene character that some aged Rieslings take on, for example.

Wine faults

Good producers do their utmost so their wines meet strict quality-control standards. Occasionally, however, you may come across a wine which, irrespective of its age or value, is suffering from a fault or two.

In restaurants, when the wine waiter opens the wine and pours a dash into your glass for you to approve, it's not necessary to taste it. Simply inhale the wine's aromas and look for problems that suggest the wine is spoiled – such as odours reminiscent of mouldy wet paper, vinegar or burnt matches – each a sign of the wine faults explained on this page. If you're unsure about the quality of the wine, invite the wine waiter's opinion.

If you suspect something is wrong, return the wine to the retailer or wine waiter for replacement. Most wine faults are easy to identify if you know what you're looking for:

Corked wine Dank, musty odours, reminiscent of wet cardboard or old books, suggest the wine is 'corked'. Cork taint can turn up indiscriminately in any wine, young or old, sealed with a cork; red, white or sparkling. The culprit is 2,4,6 trichloroanisole (TCA), a naturally occurring chemical – most likely an intrinsic element of cork itself – which turns up at random in about two to five per cent of cork-sealed wines. TCA is a very powerful chemical: it only needs one or two parts per trillion to create a negative impact on a wine.

Oxidised wine If exposed to the air for too long the wine may have brownish hues and taste dull and flat. Poor storage, a poor cork or old age are the usual reasons for oxidation.

In the same way an apple browns after peeling, wine left exposed to air browns, too. You may notice dusty, boiled sweet or apple-skin flavours in white wines, or stewed, dull smells in red varieties. In truly 'over the hill' examples, white wines become more like Sherry and reds more like Port. Red wines, however, resist oxidation better than whites because they contain higher levels of tannins, natural antioxidants that guard against browning. Check the size of the gap between the bottom of the cork and the top of the wine – it should be no more than two centimetres in a young wine. Any leakage from the cork is a likely sign that high storage temperatures have expanded the wine, forcing it out of the bottle, and allowing air to fill the void.

Volatile acidity shows up as vinegary, nail-polish remover-like or glue-like characters. A rare problem which today's strict winery hygiene standards largely prevent, volatile acidity is sensed as a vinegary character on the back of the palate and caused either by bacteria or roguish yeasts in wine that convert alcohol to acetic acid (vinegar). Yeasts always produce small amounts of acetic acid in the normal fermentation process, but the acid shouldn't be detectable on the palate.

Overuse of sulphur dioxide as a preservative which may suck the colour out of a wine Used in judicious quantities, sulphur dioxide is completely undetectable by smell or taste (although it can be evident as a clean, chemical impression in the first month after bottling). But when too much sulphur dioxide is used, it gives off a pungent, irritating smell, similar to a freshly lit match. It is, however, a problem rarely seen today.

Rotten egg smell A symptom of hydrogen sulphide in the wine, generated during the yeast fermentation. Very uncommon, given the high standards of winemaking in New Zealand. When it does occur, it's more common in reds, where even small amounts can spoil aromas and flavours. Hydrogen sulphide can also develop into even smellier substances, called mercaptans, reminiscent of boiled cabbage or burned rubber. On the other hand, some Old World winemakers consider a little hydrogen sulphide attractive as it imparts what they call barnyard or farmyard character, but New World winemakers do not share their enthusiasm for it. If you find these aromas intrusive, try decanting the wine or leaving it in the glass for a while to reduce the odour.

Steamed or poached dishes – usually based around fish and seafood – are much easier to categorise. These cooking styles produce delicate, soft flavours that make the most of natural juices. Their aftertaste is short and their flavours subtle. Team them with light, young white wines, such as Riesling, Chenin Blanc, Pinot Gris and light styles of Chardonnay.

2: Match the sweetness levels in the food and wine

Match dry wines with savoury foods. Team slightly sweeter dishes with medium wines. And put sweet desserts with ultra-sweet late-harvest or botrytised wines. For example, a slightly sweet crayfish in a light sauce works well with a medium-dry, slightly sweet-styled Riesling. Sweetness in a dish can come from meat – especially pork, crab or crayfish – as well as from vegetables and sauces. Sweetness can also be disguised somewhere in the dish, buried under spices or curry flavours, for instance. Avoid putting a dry wine with a dish that has a hint of sweetness, no matter how well hidden, because the two will clash. And if you put a sugary sweet wine with a dry, savoury dish, the wine will probably taste even sweeter. There are a couple of exceptions, however: Ports and sweet dessert wines are so rich and intense that they can withstand the tangy, savoury characters of fine, strong cheeses. A wine's back label usually tells you about its sweetness level, but for a general guide see the table on page 106.

Seasonings, sauces, marinades and dressings can obviously introduce not only sweetness, but also any number of different flavours to a dish. Make sure that the richness of the sauce is in balance with the flavours of the meat or fish and that the sauce does not dominate.

Flavour intensity of different wine styles

Here's a simple, approximate guide to the intensity of flavours in our most popular wine styles. Flavour intensity varies, according to where, when and how a wine was grown and made, but as a general rule you can expect the more higher-priced wines and wines with higher alcohol content to have stronger, fuller flavours. As many wines age, their flavours become more complex, too.

Light white	Chardonnay, Riesling, Müller-Thurgau, méthode traditionnelle, Chenin Blanc, Pinot Gris, Sémillon
Medium white	Chardonnay, Riesling, Sauvignon Blanc, Gewürztraminer, Sémillon, Pinot Gris
Full white	Chardonnay, Gewürztraminer, late harvest and botrytised dessert
Light red	Rosé, lighter-bodied Pinot Noir, Beaujolais
Medium red	Cabernet Franc, Pinot Noir, cool-climate Cabernet Sauvignon, Merlot
Full red	Warm-climate Cabernet Sauvignon, Merlot, Syrah

3: Match one or two similar flavours in the food and wine

Pick one or two dominant flavours in the food – such as herbal or peachy tastes – and match these with like flavours in the wine. Here's a good example: mushroom soup pairs beautifully with the earthy, mushroom flavours of a more mature Pinot Noir. Varietal styles do vary considerably according to winegrowing and winemaking techniques so bear this in mind when choosing a wine to accompany a meal.

The Matchmaker's ABC: a quick guide to good food and wine matching

Asian food, lightly spiced: Young, zesty Rieslings often make a good match. A touch of sweetness in the wine provides a counterpoint for the spiciness in the food.

Asian food with rich but not burning-hot spices: Older Rieslings (such as Reserve Rieslings) and Gewürztraminer.

Asian noodle dishes: Try a flinty Riesling.

Asparagus: A vegetable that can produce metallic taste when served with wine. It is best matched with older Sauvignon Blanc which often has asparagus-like flavours.

Avocado: The obvious wine match is a rich, buttery (malolactic-fermented) Chardonnay. Both the avocado and wine have smooth textures and buttery flavours in common.

Avocado, guacamole: Team with Pinot Gris or Chardonnay. If serving as a pre-dinner nibble, sparkling wine is a suitable option.

Barbecued red meats: These marry well with Merlot, Cabernet Sauvignon, Shiraz or Malbec or blends of any of such fuller-flavoured red wines. The fats or oils in the meat coat the palate and serve to soften the impression of the wine's texture in the mouth.

Beef dishes, casseroles and stews: Merlot, Cabernet Sauvignon or blends of either; and Malbec or Shiraz. The pronounced flavours in the food beg for similarly powerful red-wine partners.

Beef steak: Merlot, Cabernet Sauvignon or blends of either make good companions. Rare steaks help soften the impression of the wine's tannins in the mouth.

Cajun-spiced dishes: Mouth-filling Gewürztraminer, Pinot Gris, Sémillon and older-style Rieslings work well with the types of spices used in this style of cooking.

Cheeses: The strong flavours in hard cheeses, such as aged Cheddar and Parmesan, harmonise well with heavier, full-bodied reds as well as Ports. Blue cheeses

continued overleaf...

cry out for a rich dessert wine or, once again, a Port. Team tangy-flavoured goats' cheese with Sauvignon Blanc or Pinot Gris.

Chicken or turkey, either fried or roasted: You can't go wrong with a richer, buttery-flavoured Chardonnay.

Chinese food: see Asian food.

Curries: Frankly, Indian-style curries are probably better accompanied with beer rather than wine. For Thai curries, see Thai food.

Desserts: A sweet botrytised or late-harvest wine would be the obvious choice for many desserts, especially dishes with strong fruit flavours, honeyed or caramel flavours and those made with dried fruits. That said, apple desserts team beautifully with Gewürztraminer, while a soft, tropical fruit-flavoured Chardonnay makes the perfect partner for peach, apricot or nectarine desserts. Rich chocolate desserts, on the other hand, need a very powerful, concentrated companion. Serve them with Tawny and Vintage Ports or be bold and try them with a young Cabernet Sauvignon.

Duck, roast: A moderately flavoured dish that responds to the company of a soft, gamey-flavoured Merlot or Pinot Noir.

Eggplant or moussaka: Merlot or Cabernet Sauvignon or blends of either have the power to cut through the oiliness in these dishes.

Fish: Delicate white fish, such as snapper, calls for subtle-flavoured wines, like the lighter styles of Chardonnay or Pinot Gris. Sémillon is another good option. When serving stronger-flavoured oily types of white-fleshed fish – kahawai or kingfish for example – why not plump for a fuller-bodied, fuller-flavoured style of Chardonnay or a tasty Gewürztraminer? Put pink-fleshed fish – the likes of trout, salmon, tuna or marlin – with either a Rosé méthode traditionnelle or a lighter style of Pinot Noir. Not only do the colours in the fish and wine complement one another, more importantly both share similar intensities of flavour.

Fish and chips: This humble traditional meal marries nicely with méthode traditionnelle. The wine's clean, fresh, crisp acidity and carbon dioxide bubbles cut through the heavy oils in the dish.

Fruit cake: A sweeter-style Sherry or Port never goes amiss with rich fruit cake. Often though, we enjoy fruit cake at celebratory occasions, such as weddings or christenings, when a glass of méthode traditionnelle makes a more appropriate companion.

Ham: Baked ham has more than a hint of sweetness and is often glazed with fruits such as pineapple. So pick a wine that mirrors the meat's sweet and fruity flavours. Try an off-dry or medium Riesling, Pinot Gris or Gewürztraminer.

Italian food: see Tomato-based dishes.

Japanese sashimi and sushi: You may prefer beer with these dishes, but if you have a liking for a bit of wasabi on the side, a spicy Gewürztraminer makes a fitting partner.

Lamb, roast with rosemary or mint: Merlot and Cabernet Sauvignon or blends of either are the obvious choices because they flatter the lamb's flavours while their tannins slice through any fat. A fuller-bodied style of Pinot Noir is another excellent option.

Mushroom-flavoured dishes: The earthy flavours in mushrooms find a highly compatible companion in the earthy flavours of some styles of Pinot Noir. Make Merlot another alternative to put on your list of matches.

Nuts: Both mixed and roasted nuts served with Flor Fino Sherry create a great twosome since the wine has nutty characters of its own.

Olives: Black olives pair well with Cabernet Sauvignon, while green olives are better suited to Sauvignon Blanc. In each case, there's a marriage between similar flavours.

Pesto-flavoured dishes: Perfect with the herbal flavours of a cool-climate grown Sauvignon Blanc.

Pork: Delicious with medium-dry Riesling. When served with pork, the wine's sweeter, lightish apple and honey flavours combined with citrus flavours create a harmonious partnership.

Salads, green leafy: Served as entrées with a herbal-flavoured dressing, Sauvignon Blanc is a sure-fire match.

Seafood: Put crab, crayfish or scampi – all of which are slightly sweet – with a Riesling that boasts a subtle sweetness. For shellfish, such as mussels, pipis and

continued overleaf...

tuatuas, fresh-flavoured Chenin Blancs and lighter styles of Chardonnay make reliable partners. But whatever varieties you choose to put with them, always aim for subtle-flavoured wines so as not to overpower the flavours in shellfish. Where scallops are concerned, soft subtle Pinot Gris or, once again, lighter-style Chardonnays offer some of your best options. Their delicate flavours, moderate acidity and light oak influences offer good matches of flavour and intensity. Oysters served with a squeeze of lemon and Brut méthode traditionnelle are guaranteed to be a success. Put them together and you have a two-way match of flavour intensity and crispness between the food and wine. Then again, who can go past the traditional coupling of Bluff oysters and New Zealand Sauvignon Blanc? Simply delicious.

Thai food: Sémillon or Gewürztraminer and Müller-Thurgau are worthy options. Other suitors include off-dry Pinot Gris and Riesling.

Tomato-based dishes: Merlot and Cabernet Sauvignon or blends of either complement tomato-based dishes (such as traditional pizza) and sauces, especially where stronger-flavoured cheeses comprise a key part of the recipe. Don't overlook the classic Italian varieties of Chianti and Sangiovese either.

Veal: Try Pinot Noir or buttery (malolactic-fermented) Chardonnay. The comparatively subtle flavours in veal better suit the lighter-style reds or fuller-bodied white varieties. Pick a wine which mirrors the dominant flavours in the sauce or garnish.

Venison: The gamey flavours found in Merlot and certain styles of Pinot Noir make a good match for venison. Both varieties boast well-structured tannins which suit lean cuts of meat well.

Vietnamese food: Sémillon, Gewürztraminer, off-dry Pinot Gris and off-dry Riesling are some of the better wine options.

Whitebait fritters: Marry the delicate flavours of this classic New Zealand delicacy with Pinot Gris, a lighter-style Chardonnay or a crisp méthode traditionnelle.

And chew on these food and wine matching titbits...

Not sure what wine to serve with chocolate? A sweet, fortified, high-alcohol wine, such as an older Tawny Port, makes a perfect companion.

Red wine with fish is seldom a good idea. Not only are most red wines too strongly flavoured to serve with fish, but for around a third of the population the tannins in reds react with the oils in fish to produce an unpleasant, metallic taste in the mouth. If you do want to put red wine with fish, opt for a low-tannin red, such as Pinot Noir or Rosé, and stick with a less oily variety of fish.

• Very hot, mouth-burning curries go better with beer or fruit juice than wine. In fact, the only wine that stands a chance of contending with a hot curry's intense flavours is sweet dessert wine, either botrytised or late-harvest in style. These wines may soothe the mouth, but even they're not an ideal match.

• Globe artichokes and asparagus contain a naturally occurring chemical called cynarin which can make wine taste bitter.

• Very acidic foods – such as vinegary dishes and pickles – can be tricky to match with wine. Try them with high-acid wines such as young Riesling, South Island Sauvignon Blanc or a crisp méthode traditionnelle.

Balancing the intensity of flavours in food and wine for best results

	White wine			Red wine		
	light	**medium**	**full-bodied**	**light**	**medium**	**full-bodied**
Shellfish shrimp, crab, scallops	★★★	★★	★★	•	•	•
Fish light sauce	★★	★★★	★★	•	•	•
Fish heavy sauce	★	★★	★★★	★	•	•
Chicken, turkey	★★	★★	★★★	★	★	•
Pork	★	★★	★★★	★★	★	•
Ham	★	★★	★★	★★★	★★	•
Lamb	•	•	★	★★★	★★★	★★
Duck, game	•	•	★	★★	★★★	★★
Beef	•	•	★	★★	★★★	★★★
Red meat stews with heavy sauces	•	•	★	★★	★★★	★★★

★★★ Obvious first choice
★★ Very good matches possible
★ Very good matches possible, but need to consider cooking method and sauce
• Much reduced chance of success

Entertaining

When planning an important celebration or special event, take time before the big day to taste the food and wine matches you have in mind to make sure they work well together. If you've any doubts about a match, talk to your specialist wine supplier or the sommelier (wine waiter) helping you organise the event.

Wine with a sit-down menu

• **What styles of wine?** As guests arrive, serve a dry, Brut-style New Zealand méthode traditionnelle or Champagne. Or try Fino Sherries with tapas, olives, nuts and hard cheeses.

• **How to chill the wine...** See page 95.

• **How many glasses?** One tulip-shaped wine glass and one water glass per table setting suffices, but if you wish, put one larger-style red wine glass at each setting as well.

• **With the dinner menu...** Follow the food and wine matching guidelines on page 113. Allow two glasses of wine for each food and wine match.

• **With the toasts...** See toasts under Wine and food for buffet-style occasions.

• **After dinner...** Offer guests a glass of Port or cream Sherry – or even a glass of dessert wine served with ripe fruit, such as peaches, and nuts.

Wine for large buffet-style occasions

• **How much wine?** This depends on how long the big occasion is set to last, but as a general rule allow up to half a bottle per person to drink over the meal and up to half a bottle extra if there's a party afterwards. Most wine merchants will gladly enter into 'sale or return' arrangements whereby they credit returns of unopened, undamaged cases and bottles – check your supplier's policy before you buy.

The majority of New Zealanders still prefer white wine over the fuller-bodied reds (although red wine's popularity is growing rapidly). Catering professionals usually recommend supplying about two-thirds white wine and one-third red, allowing for some seasonal adjustment to take account of weather-dependent changes in tastes. In summer, wine drinkers heavily favour whites and the lighter-style reds, whereas in winter they often turn to more full-bodied reds. Always have plenty of non-alcoholic drinks on hand – allow at least 500 ml per person.

• **How to chill the wine?** See the temperature guides for wine on page 95. If you're hiring a cool-store, stow unopened cartons in the chiller for two days prior to the event. Or hire large plastic bins and fill them with a mixture of ice and water (and put wines in for half an hour before the event).

• **How many glasses?** You'll need glasses galore as your guests move from table to table, leaving glasses in their wake. If hiring glasses, order at least two Champagne flutes, two standard stemmed wine glasses and one water glass per person, plus plenty of extras for beer and juice. It's not necessary to offer different styled glasses for white and red wines.

• **What styles of wine?** Upon your guests' arrival, offer a glass of lightly chilled New Zealand méthode traditionnelle or Champagne to freshen their palates. If you're offering only one style, choose a Brut: it's drier than the sweet Sec style and so makes a better aperitif for savoury finger foods. Allow two glasses per person.

What to do with those leftovers in the bottle?

Once opened, wines soon lose their fresh fruit flavours and tastes flatten. Old red wines, especially, go into a rapid decline. Look after them properly if you want to enjoy them at a later occasion:

• Stopper opened wines and store them in the fridge. (Before serving, remove them from the fridge, allowing enough time for the wine to return to its ideal serving temperature.)

• Aim to keep opened wine for no longer than three days. Exceptions include Fino Sherries which, although they're ideally consumed within two to three days of opening, can be kept for a week or so; and sweeter Sherries which can last longer on account of their higher alcohol content.

• If you want to keep opened wine for longer than three days, freeze it and thaw as required. Should you notice crystals on the bottom of the thawed bottles don't be alarmed – they're completely harmless tartrate crystals and won't affect the wine's flavour. Carefully pour the wine from the bottle, leaving the crystals in the bottle.

• The Portuguese are happy to keep Tawny Ports for up to a year after opening, but all other styles of Port, including Ruby Port, Vintage Port, LBV Port are all best enjoyed soon after opening, before they start losing delicate flavours. If you must keep them for a week or so, pour leftovers into a smaller bottle and stopper.

• Using a vacuum stoppering device removes dissolved carbon dioxide from the wine, but also may remove some of its delicate flavours, particularly in tank-fermented wines such as Sauvignon Blanc, Gewürztraminer and Riesling.

• **To drink with the pick-and-mix buffet...** Choose from among New Zealand's most popular wine styles. Chardonnay and Sauvignon Blanc remain the favourite whites, while blends of Merlot/Cabernet Sauvignon are our favourite reds. But don't overlook the lighter-style reds, such as New Zealand's delicious Pinot Noir. They're ideal drinking for red-wine fans during summer and at lunch-time gatherings.

• **With the toasts...** Whether you choose to hold the toasts before or at the end of the meal is a matter of personal preference. But if several speeches and toasts are planned, spread them at intervals throughout the meal. Offer each guest a glass of méthode traditionnelle or Champagne just prior to the first toast, then offer to top up their glasses before each subsequent toast.

Responsible drinking

The Alcohol Advisory Council of New Zealand (ALAC) has developed a set of general guidelines about the safer upper drinking limits for men and women. But everyone is different and so even these upper limits may not be safe for everyone – certainly not pregnant women or those with some specific medical problems.

In any one week, drink no more than:
21 standard drinks for men
14 standard drinks for women

On any one drinking occasion, drink no more than:
6 standard drinks for men
4 standard drinks for women

A standard drink contains 10 g of pure alcohol – that roughly equates to either one measure of spirits or fortified wine; or one average-sized (100 ml) glass of table wine; or one 250 ml glass of beer.

Remember: Do not drink and drive.

Cellaring

All the wines for sale on New Zealand shop shelves are ready to drink. That said, most wines do benefit from ageing – but only on the proviso that they are stored, or 'cellared', under the right conditions.

Few homes boast custom-built, subterranean wine cellars, so for most of us 'cellaring' simply means putting aside some wine to age – be it in a cool, dark cupboard somewhere or temperature-controlled wine storage cabinet – out of harm's way.

Very often, personal taste dictates whether we prefer a wine when it is in the full flush of youth, or enjoy it better when it has a little more maturity on its side. Many of us would rather drink, say, Gewürztraminer or Müller-Thurgau when the wines are young, at which time their fresh, fruity flavours are at their peak, rather than wait for them to mellow over time.

It is true, nonetheless, that although all wines are ready to enjoy as soon as they are released onto the market, a number of them do improve with age. They include quality white wines as well as almost all red varieties and, in particular, premium red wines, such as Montana's Tom and Te Mata Estate's Coleraine.

Red wines take longer than white wines to reach their best and as such make the most obvious candidates for cellaring. Even so, fewer New Zealand reds than ever before reward cellaring. Nowadays local winemakers are increasingly moving away from making the robust, tannic, red-wine styles that require long-term ageing, and in their place are producing reds with softer, riper tannins, such as Merlot-dominant blends and Pinot Noir.

By all means check the back label for the producer's cellaring guide, but unless you follow good cellaring procedures, the wines won't live nearly as long as the label says. Wine ages prematurely when exposed to light and heat.

Despite the fact that only a tiny proportion of wines are ever cellared, the subject of cellaring remains one of the most talked-about and debated aspects of wine.

What happens to wine when it's cellared?

Even wine scientists don't yet fully understand the processes that alter wine as it matures, but we can either see or taste the key changes that occur. In white wine, the colour turns deeper and more golden. Most importantly, though, the wine's acids lose their crispness and soften over time. Fresh fruit flavours fade, but new, more complex flavours, often reminiscent of honey, cold tea, nuts and caramel, rise in their place.

With reds, the wines assume lighter, brick-coloured hues with age. Tannins evolve and produce a softer, silkier mouth-feel. New flavours form, too, among them tobacco, liquorice, smoke, spice, pepper and cedarwood.

There are about 500 different chemicals in wine, many of which interact with one another to bring about change. Among them, short-chain tannin molecules work with each other to form long-chain tannins which have a smoother mouth-feel, while micro quantities of oxygen (entering the wine slowly through the 'breathable' natural cork or already dissolved in it) also react with tannins to soften them further. (Note that wines sealed with synthetic corks or screwcaps will mature over time, although they may take longer to do so.)

Wines to drink young

Most méthode traditionnelles and Champagnes

These are best enjoyed within two years of going on sale, while the wine is fresh, fruity and in full possession of its effervescence. By the time expensive vintage Champagne reaches the shelves, it's often already about eight years old and all set for drinking.

Fortified wines: Sherries and Ports

Sherries and Ports have a reputation for longevity and yet, with the exception of Vintage Port, aren't good candidates for cellaring. They do change over time, but not necessarily for the better. Fino and Manzanilla sherries must be drunk when young.

The majority of fruity wines

Most Müller-Thurgau, Gewürztraminers and Rosés are best enjoyed when young, before their fresh, fruity flavours fade. Even so, some of the more intense Gewürztraminers may develop favourably over a period of about three years.

Drink now or cellar: you decide

Should you or shouldn't you cellar a Sauvignon Blanc, Chenin Blanc or Chardonnay, for instance? The answer comes back to personal taste. When Sauvignon Blanc is young, its aromas are pronounced and it has a fresh, crisp finish. Yet short-term cellaring for up to two years integrates Sauvignon Blanc's many different components and takes the edge off its acidity without compromising many of the wine's fresh, fruit flavours. Any longer than this, though, and asparagus-like flavours – not to everyone's liking – may creep into the wine. The crisp acidity of Chenin Blanc also softens with age. Lighter-style Chardonnays are best enjoyed within two or three years of vintage, but fuller, more generous examples can be cellared for up to five years.

Wines to cellar

Vintage Port

A safe bet for long-term cellaring. Stow away a bottle or two to bring out at 21st birthdays or a 25th wedding anniversary. Vintage Port, with its steep alcohol and tannin contents (which together preserve the wine in the bottle), is a long-living creature – so long as we're talking about the real thing from Portugal, of course.

The Bordeaux varieties and blends (Merlot, Cabernet Sauvignon, Cabernet Franc and Malbec) and Syrah

Whether or not to cellar today's Bordeaux varieties and Syrah is again a matter of personal taste. Invariably these wines are ready for drinking upon purchase, but they may benefit from ageing. Cabernet Sauvignon can last for up to a decade, though younger examples taste softer when you drink them with fatty, oily foods or rarer cuts of meat.

Riesling

One of the best varieties to cellar for two or three years, Riesling becomes increasingly luscious and more balanced with age.

Botrytised sweet dessert wines

With their extra acidity, sugars and concentrated fruit flavours, dessert wines can mature nicely for between six to eight years, the best even longer. What's unusual about the way these wines age is that they don't lose their fruit flavours with time. Rather, the flavours may become more complex and the perception of dryness on the palate may increase. Drink them when you believe them to be at their best.

How to cellar wine

Wine has a delicate constitution. It doesn't like light, temperature fluctuations or movement. Such is its sensitivity that if you cellar a wine with an expected life span of 10 years under poor conditions it might only keep for a year or two. So even though your wine cellar needn't be a grand affair – indeed it may be as humble as a cupboard set aside for your favourite labels – it needs to provide your wines with a good home.

Constant temperature and dark

• A constant temperature setting. A temperature of 12–15°C is ideal. A wine stored at 12°C will long outlive an identical wine stored at 20°C. Fluctuations in temperatures shorten wines' lives, while temperatures in excess of 25°C bring about rapid decline.

• A dark place, or at the very least a storage area away from direct sunlight. (Light, especially ultraviolet light, ages wine prematurely.)

• An area as free from movement and vibration as possible. (Hence, that cool, dark cupboard under the stairs isn't such a good idea after all!)

• A relatively humid area. If the atmosphere is too dry, it dries out the cork. On the other hand, if the storage area is too moist, mould may grow on the bottle. In humid storage conditions, wrap the label in plastic cling wrap to keep it looking good.

Organise your wine cellar

• Lie the bottles on their sides to keep the corks moist and elastic (for a good seal) with the bottle necks facing towards you. Always store sparkling wines upright.

• Store label side up for easy identification.

• Avoid moving or turning the bottles. Contrary to popular belief, there's no need to periodically turn them.

• Catalogue the wines so you have no need to go rummaging around for them.

The helicave, a commercially available wine cellar built around a spiral staircase sunk into the ground.

Right: Temperature- and humidity-controlled wine cabinets, available from whiteware stores, are a good, reliable, reasonably priced cellaring solution.

Check your wine cellar

• Keep a thermometer in your wine-storage area so you can monitor its temperature and know what temperature adjustments to make to the wine before serving.

• Periodically check the wines for leaks around the corks. If you spot any mould, drink the wine sooner rather than later because it is at risk of oxidising.

• Ideally, taste the wine at intervals of 12–18 months to assess its maturation. You probably need to keep at least four bottles of a particular wine to do this. So if, for example, you're putting a case of Merlot away, plan to drink one bottle per year after the first 18 months' cellaring. Make notes so you can chart how the wine is developing. And don't keep the wine past its best.

Cellar timekeeper

Use this timekeeper as a general guide only. How long a wine can be safely cellared depends on the storage conditions in your cellar and your personal taste.

Keep (if you must) for up to 3 years

- Fresh, crisp Sauvignon Blanc.
- Most Pinot Noir.
- Champagne and méthode traditionnelle.
- Light, fruity white wines, such as lighter-styled Chardonnay and crisp Chenin Blanc and Sauvignon Blanc.
- Light red wines such as Pinot Noir, Rosé and Beaujolais.

Keep (if you wish) for up to 5 years

- Medium- to full-bodied whites, such as generous Chardonnays and the more expensive whites.
- Merlot.

Keep for up to 8 years

- Riesling.
- Very good Pinot Noir.
- Medium- and full-bodied reds, such as the Bordeaux varieties.
- Syrah (or Shiraz).

Keep for up to 10 years

- Bordeaux reds or blends from exceptional vintages.
- The best botrytised or late-harvest dessert wines.

If you're enjoying a wine now, don't cellar it.

Instead, keep a supply of the wine on hand for short-term drinking. It's better to enjoy a wine young, rather than keep it until it starts to dull with age.

Wine regions

Why does a Sauvignon Blanc grown in Marlborough, New Zealand taste different to one grown in the Loire, France? And why does the typical Marlborough model burst with fresh, zingy, grassy-green qualities when another one grown in Hawke's Bay exudes riper, rounder characters? The answers to these questions and more lie within the fabric of New Zealand's winegrowing regions – each unique in its own way.

New Zealand's climatic suitability

Vines are temperate-climate plants. They prefer a cold winter in which to lie dormant and prepare themselves for bud burst in spring, followed by a warm but not overly hot summer to grow and ripen their fruit. It helps if autumn – harvest-time – stays dry so fungal diseases have less chance of taking hold.

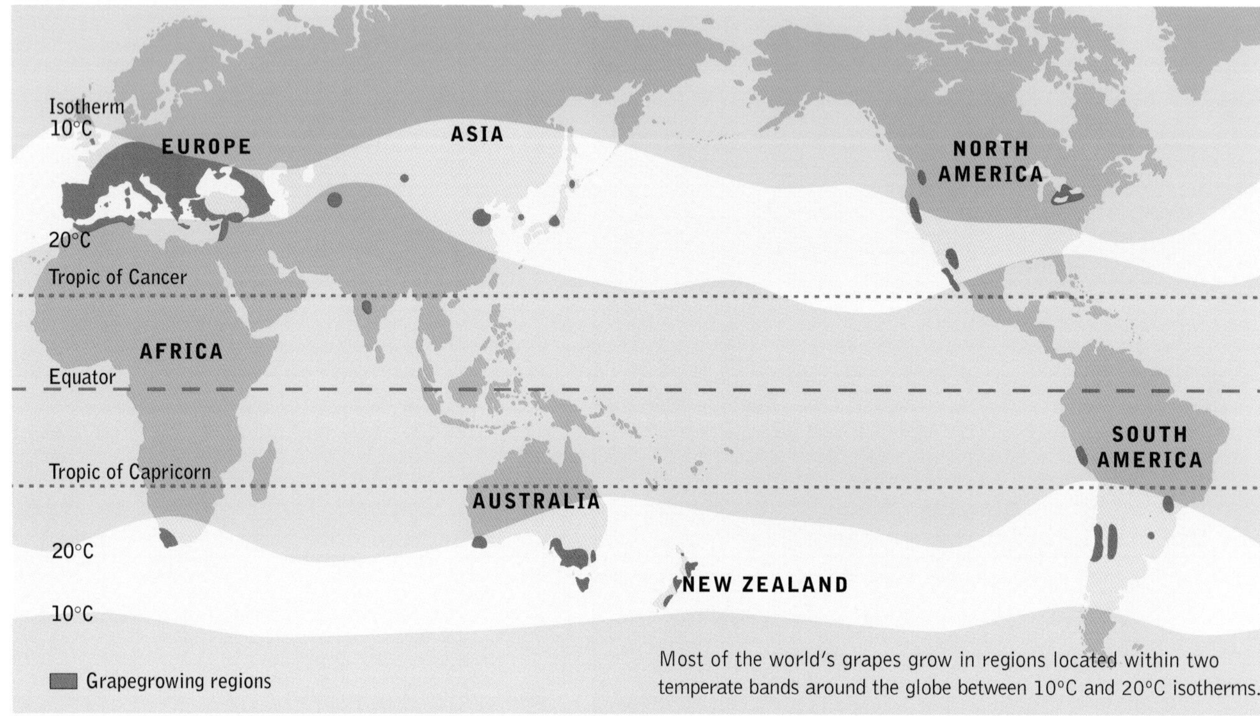

Most of the world's grapes grow in regions located within two temperate bands around the globe between 10°C and 20°C isotherms.

Look at a map of the world's grapegrowing regions and you'll see most vines grow within two temperate bands that span the globe to the south of the Tropic of Capricorn and to the north of the Tropic of Cancer. Northern-hemisphere Europeans can grow grapes further away from the equator than we can in the southern hemisphere, thanks to the warming effects of the Gulf Stream ocean current and the hot air masses that hang over the continent's interior.

New Zealand's climate, on the other hand, is a maritime one – cooler during summer than the northern-hemisphere regions situated in comparable latitudes. Being more than 1 000 kilometres from the nearest land mass, the temperatures of all our large-scale weather systems are influenced (or moderated) by their passage over the ocean. Our predominantly westerly winds pick up moisture from the seas on their journeys here. Upon their arrival over land, the long, narrow mountain 'spine' that runs the length of the country from the south to East Cape intercepts them, causing most mountain-generated rain to fall in the west and drying air to the east. The end result is relatively cool-climate easterly regions with low rainfall and high sunshine hours – exactly the kind of conditions in which New Zealand grapes retain the fresh, crisp qualities and build the intense fruit flavours for which they are renowned.

Little wonder then that by far the majority of New Zealand grapes are planted in the comparatively dry, sheltered belt that extends down the east coasts of both the North and South Islands. Vines can't stand around like pukekos in soggy soils, not for long anyway. Most vineyards sit on either old stony river terraces or alluvial plains, protected by mountain ranges.

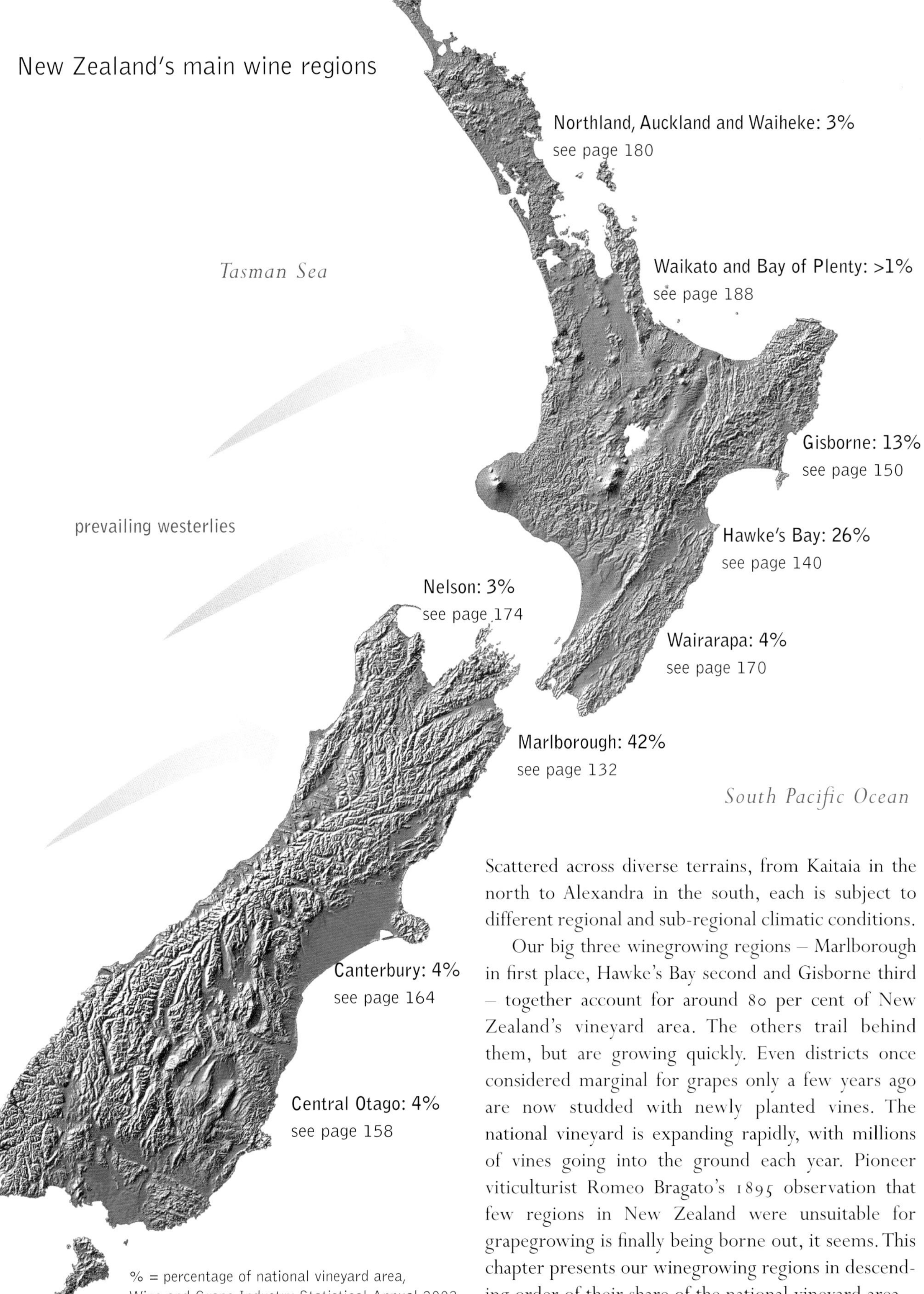

Scattered across diverse terrains, from Kaitaia in the north to Alexandra in the south, each is subject to different regional and sub-regional climatic conditions.

Our big three winegrowing regions – Marlborough in first place, Hawke's Bay second and Gisborne third – together account for around 80 per cent of New Zealand's vineyard area. The others trail behind them, but are growing quickly. Even districts once considered marginal for grapes only a few years ago are now studded with newly planted vines. The national vineyard is expanding rapidly, with millions of vines going into the ground each year. Pioneer viticulturist Romeo Bragato's 1895 observation that few regions in New Zealand were unsuitable for grapegrowing is finally being borne out, it seems. This chapter presents our winegrowing regions in descending order of their share of the national vineyard area.

Location, location, location

The catch-phrase of the real estate agent can just as easily belong to the winegrower.

Each of New Zealand's wine regions has its own specialities. Knowing at least a little about those regions helps you choose from the many styles of New Zealand wine available.

Many of the best wines are fluid expressions of their birthplace – not only their region of origin, but also the vineyards which give them their start in life. A Sauvignon Blanc from the Rapaura side of Marlborough's Wairau Valley, say, cuts a different figure to a wine grown a few kilometres south, even though both may have been made in the same way by the same person. It's as if there's some sort of elemental alchemy at work in the vineyard, shaping the wines' identities long before they reach the winery.

The French put a name to it centuries ago. They call it terroir (pronounced 'tair-wah'), a simple little word articulating the complex synthesis of site-specific environmental influences which nature brings to bear, not only on each individual vineyard, but also on the discrete areas within it and, ultimately, the grapes themselves. It is this interplay of every imaginable environmental factor peculiar to a parcel of land that holds the key to its grapegrowing potential and predetermines many of the flavour characteristics that distinguish one wine from another.

That is not to underestimate the enormously influential role of the winegrower (or viticulturist) who must coax the terroir into yielding the best

After variety, the second most important factor that shapes the character of a wine is where its grapes came from.

Unlike the winegrowing regions of the Old World, there are virtually no demarcated boundaries within New Zealand winegrowing regions (the exceptions being the Gimblett Gravels area in Hawke's Bay and the Martinborough Terraces in Wairarapa). The main winegrowing districts referred to in this chapter are those identified as such by local producers.

possible quality grapes, drawing upon any scientific understandings and tools-of-the-trade that can lend a hand along the way. As you'll see in the viticulture chapter, the winegrower manipulates the natural environment and in doing so becomes, if not another environmental influence within the terroir, then at the very least an appendage to it.

New Zealand viticulturists are free to plant whatever and wherever they choose. Not so French winegrowers, who must abide by their country's time-honoured Appellation Contrôlée system which imposes strict rules on demarcated winegrowing regions, governing which varieties and styles of wine each can produce as well as laying down maximum crop levels. It's a proven system, based on centuries of working and scrutinising individual plots, identifying the grapes that have special affinities with each appellation and prescribing the roles they play in the national scheme of things.

New Zealand viticulturists, by comparison, have barely scratched the surface of this country's winegrowing regions. Older areas and vineyards have proven themselves better suited to some varieties than others, but winegrowers admit they still have much to learn about the newer ones. They must make decisions their Old World counterparts need no longer trouble themselves with – where to plant, what to plant and how to plant? And finding out is half the fun, they say.

'Terroir' is a French term that refers to the unique combination of soils, climate and topography that influence a vineyard and the areas within it.

The growing season in the southern hemisphere occurs between 1 October and 30 April. The term Growing Degree Days (GGD) referred to under each region in this chapter is the sum of the average daily temperatures above a 10°C threshold during that period. So, if the average daily temperature is 21°C, the GDD for that day is 11 (21 minus 10 equals 11).

It takes about eight years for a grape variety to prove its suitability for a vineyard.

Montana's Brancott Estate is almost as renowned for its east/west rather than north/south row orientation as for its famous Sauvignon Blanc. One side of the vines lives in the sun, the other in the shade. The shaded side's grapes retain higher levels of methoxypyrazine, the substance that gives Marlborough Sauvignon Blanc its characteristic grassy-green herbaceousness.

Marlborough

Internationally, it's the most recognisable name in New Zealand winegrowing – a little place synonymous with something quite monumental: the world's most revered Sauvignon Blanc.

The Awatere Valley vineyard terraces, Marlborough.

When Montana Wines planted New Zealand's first commercial Sauvignon Blanc vineyards here in 1976, no one could have foreseen that Marlborough would yield a zesty, zingy style of Sauvignon so wonderfully individual it would outshine those from the variety's homeland – the Loire Valley, France.

Today, Marlborough is New Zealand's wine capital – the beehive that produces almost half our wines and home to some of the most highly acclaimed labels in the land. Sauvignon Blanc's hegemony continues to grow stronger by the day. Come 2005 it will comprise almost 60 per cent of the region's plantings. Soon to become its second most planted variety is Pinot Noir – tipped to grow into Marlborough's, and the country's, signature red.

Marlborough is a small area – the entire Wairau Plain on which most of its vineyards sit comprises only 20,000 hectares – yet its terroirs are diverse. Winegrowers know they can plant identical rootstocks and clones in vineyards barely a couple of kilometres apart and still produce parcels of fruit with contrasting flavour profiles for winemakers to work with. Any attempt to make generalisations about Marlborough's separate districts' wine styles, then, is bound to generate controversy, but there are those who maintain wines grown on the northern side of the Wairau Plain tend to exhibit more tropical fruit flavours, while those grown on the slightly cooler southern side (where soils generally have higher clay content) have more of a herbal edge and tighter structures. Some go so far as to say the best Marlborough wines are blends of both sides – a delicious balance of fruit and structure.

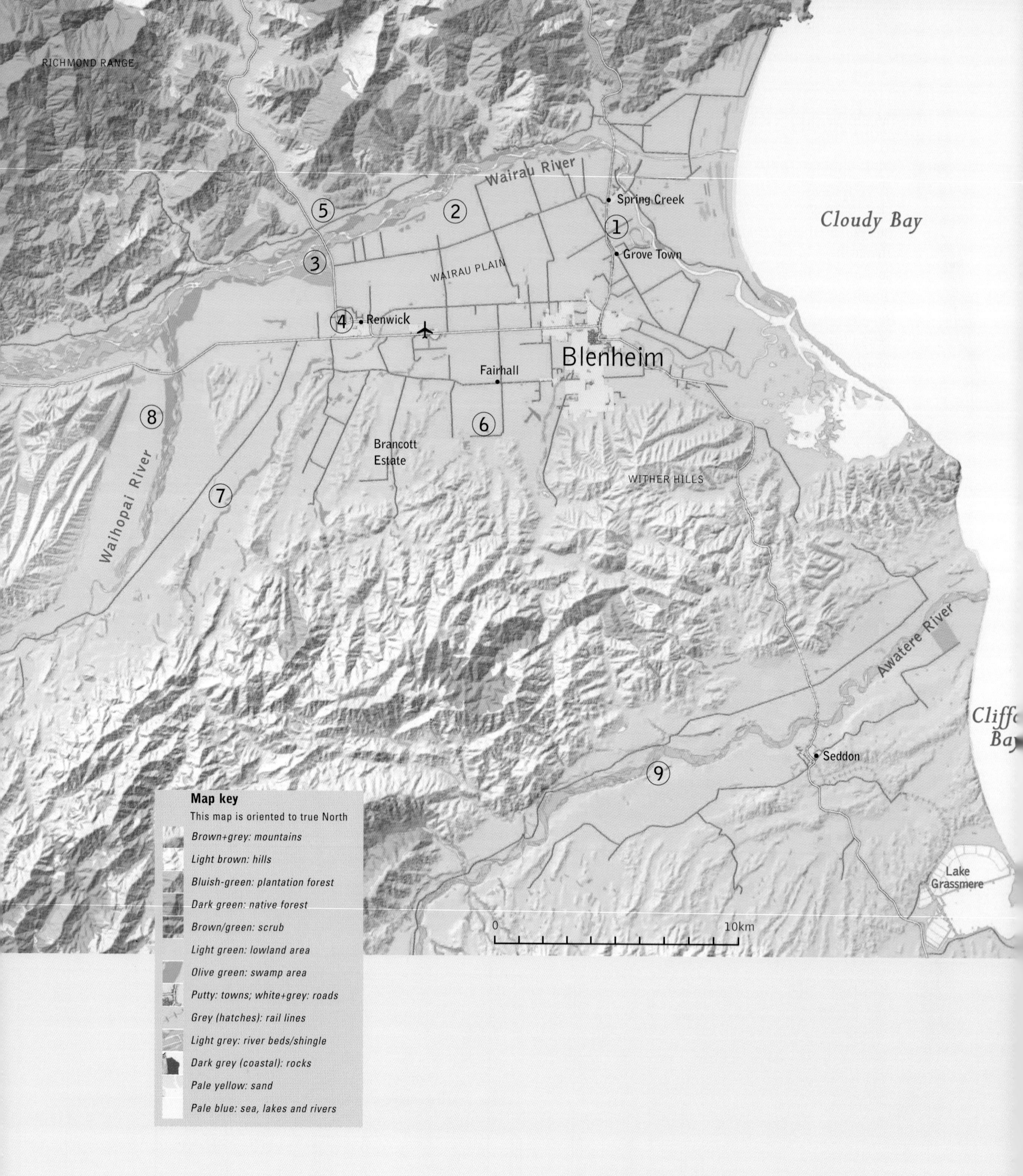

RICHMOND RANGE
Wairau River
Spring Creek
Cloudy Bay
Grove Town
WAIRAU PLAIN
Renwick
Blenheim
Fairhall
Brancott Estate
WITHER HILLS
Waihopai River
Awatere River
Seddon
Lake Grassmere
0
10km
1
2
3
4
5
6
7
8
9
Map key
This map is oriented to true North
Brown+grey: mountains
Light brown: hills
Bluish-green: plantation forest
Dark green: native forest
Brown/green: scrub
Light green: lowland area
Olive green: swamp area
Putty: towns; white+grey: roads
Grey (hatches): rail lines
Light grey: river beds/shingle
Dark grey (coastal): rocks
Pale yellow: sand
Pale blue: sea, lakes and rivers

Main winegrowing districts

Most of Marlborough's vineyard plantings lie in the Wairau Plain, wedged in between the rugged, bush-clad Richmond Range in the north-west and the bare, dry Wither Hills to the south-east. The mountainous Inland Kaikoura Range shelters the valley from cold, southerly winds and the North Island shields it from north-easterlies. Just over the Wither Hills is the smaller Awatere Valley which in the last decade has been the focus of extensive new vineyard plantings. Marlborough holds 42 per cent of the national vineyard area, a figure tipped to increase to 46 per cent by 2005.

(1) **Grove Town/Lower Wairau/Spring Creek** Planted in mainly Sauvignon Blanc, Pinot Noir and some Chardonnay. Sauvignon Blanc grown on these mainly free-draining silty soils tends to have a herbal edge. Irrigation often isn't necessary.

(2) **Rapaura** Enjoys a warmer, wetter mesoclimate than on the southern side of the plain, hence the region's grapes are among the first to be harvested. Typically produces quite aromatic, fruit-forward white wines with hints of pineapple, passionfruit and melon as well as a number of riper-flavoured reds.

(3) **Conder's Bend** The site of recent Sauvignon Blanc and Pinot Noir plantings.

(4) **Renwick** All Marlborough's key varieties are grown here. The Chardonnays tend towards predominantly citrus and stone-fruit flavours. The Sauvignon Blanc is usually a cross between the Rapaura and Brancott styles.

(5) **Kaituna** An emerging grapegrowing district, planted mainly in Sauvignon Blanc.

(6) **Southern Valleys (including Taylor Pass/Ben Morven and Fairhall [also known as the Brancott Valley] and Montana's Brancott Estate)** Planted in Sauvignon Blanc, Pinot Noir, Chardonnay and Riesling. Whites grown here usually show citrus and stone-fruit flavours. Drier and cooler than Rapaura, grapes ripen later in these areas.

(7) **Omaka (or Hawkesbury) Valley and Omaka River Valley** An emerging area for Pinot Noir and also planted in Sauvignon Blanc.

(8) **Waihopai Valley** Planted in all the key Marlborough varieties. Has a relatively cool climate and later seasons.

(9) **Awatere Valley** Awatere wines show lifted fruit flavour concentration. The valley is cooler, drier and windier than the Wairau Plain – and grapes may take one to two weeks longer to ripen. The Awatere's coastal vineyards experience less diurnal (day/night) temperature fluctuations and their warmer winters induce an earlier bud burst, although the cooler autumns delay ripening.

Long-time Marlborough vineyard worker Ollie Hodgkinson.

Water, water everywhere nor any drop to drink

The ancient mariner's lament could have been that of the parched vines Montana planted in 1973 which perished during one of Marlborough's worst droughts. Not that Marlborough is a water-short region, many argue. It has enough for its needs, but the water is often in the wrong place, at the wrong time.

The Wairau Plain's main population centres, industries, agriculture and viticulture depend almost entirely on groundwater. No surprise then that Marlborough was the first New Zealand wine region to introduce irrigation and that today most of its vineyards have permanent drip irrigation systems installed. Yet the severe droughts of 1997/1998 and 2000/2001, when the region's groundwater reserves fell perilously low, reminded some producers of their vulnerability to water shortages.

Vineyards in the Wairau Plain mostly draw water from a huge Wairau River-fed aquifer – tens of metres thick and some 15,000 hectares in area – so big it acts as an enormous storage tank. Even in severe drought conditions, this aquifer flows to a certain degree. There are also smaller, but less reliable, ancillary aquifers known collectively as the Southern Valleys aquifers. The further one moves away from the Wairau River, however, the deeper one has to bore for water. Some wells in the south-west are 200 metres deep.

Most vineyards in the Awatere Valley have resource consent to draw water from the river.

The Awatere Valley has no large aquifer. Most vineyards have resource consent to draw water directly from the Awatere River, but all the reliable (class A) water permits have been allocated. A number of those holding less reliable (class B) permits are planning storage dams to collect higher winter waterflows from tributaries fed by the Awatere River which can be used to augment irrigation during winter months.

Access to Marlborough's finite water supply is a major issue affecting land prices and the direction of Marlborough's development. In the now extensively planted south-west Wairau Plain, located away from the main Wairau aquifer, water already runs short in summer. The Marlborough District Council is now funding a piped irrigation scheme from the Wairau River into the Southern Valleys, serving 4500 hectares.

Climate

In a nutshell, the Wairau Plain's climate is one of plentiful sunshine, warm days contrasted with cooler nights throughout the growing season and continual dry weather. Of key significance to the region's wine styles is the (diurnal) temperature variation between day and night. Temperatures typically drop by at least 10°C overnight during the growing season, allowing the grapes to retain higher levels of fruit acids and varietal flavours than their counterparts grown in climates where day/night temperature differences are less marked. What's more, since Marlborough enjoys reliably dry autumns, its grapes can stay on the vines longer (without increasing their risk of developing fungal diseases), giving them time to build ripe fruit flavours. Nonetheless, Marlborough's climate is a maritime one. Certainly, nights are cool, but temperature swings between day and night are nothing remarkable when compared to the searingly hot days and bitterly cold nights of continental climates such as Coonawarra in Australia.

Extended dry spells are common in Marlborough. During the parched 2000/2001 vintage, only 77.4 millimetres of rain fell during the growing season. The main northern side of the Wairau Valley and sub-valleys (located closer to the Richmond Range and the Wairau River) are a little wetter and warmer than southern areas of the plain, however. The Awatere Valley is drier again than the Wairau Valley. Fungal diseases, such as botrytis, are less prevalent in Marlborough than in the North Island.

Late spring frosts are a risk – the so-called Dr Müller Frost has the potential to swing by in the first or second week of November.

Annual sunshine hours (mean)	2448* (Blenheim Research)
Annual rainfall (mean)	696 mm* (Blenheim Research)
Growing degree days (mean)	1154 (Blenheim Research)

*1986–1995

Soil types

Two words sum up Marlborough's soils: very variable – and therein lie advantages and disadvantages (see soils, page 200). In areas such as Rapaura, soils can change within the space of a few metres from low-vigour, stony gravels to deep, fertile silts. As a rule, the region's younger, stonier, more variable soils tend to be found close to the Wairau and Waihopai rivers. Head south-west across the plain and the soil situation becomes more uniform, with older loess (wind-blown, fine-grained clay and silt soils) dominating. Further south still, in the Awatere Valley, the soils are a mixture of stony gravels and loess. On the northern side of the Awatere Valley stony soils prevail, while in the southern, downwind side, loess soils dominate.

Typical vintage

On the Wairau Plain harvest generally lags one to two weeks behind Hawke's Bay. In the cooler Awatere Valley harvest runs about one to two weeks behind the Wairau Plain's picking schedule.

Early March: Pinot Noir and Chardonnay for sparkling wine. Late March: The first of Sauvignon Blanc and Pinot Noir for varietal wines. Early April: Table wine Chardonnay and most of the Sauvignon Blanc. Mid-April: Riesling. Late April: Riesling, Merlot, Sémillon, Pinot Gris and Cabernet Sauvignon.

Trends

Anyone visiting Marlborough after only a few months' absence cannot fail to be astonished by the pace at which its wine industry is growing, as hectare upon hectare of newly planted baby vines march across the landscape. New Zealand Winegrowers estimates Marlborough's vineyard area will increase by 43 per cent between 2002 and 2005. Enormous local and overseas investment is pouring into the region. It's getting crowded here – and very expensive. Winegrowers are looking further afield for potential sites. New vineyards now appear in areas once considered marginal, out in the cooler, wetter south-west and also south – districts located further away from known aquifers and where the incidence of frosts is greater. A few are establishing vineyards in the heavier, more fertile soils of Spring Creek and the Lower Wairau Plain, areas which will demand expert management to keep a tight rein on vine vigour. Some say these new ventures are risky – but then Marlborough's stellar winemaking reputation has been built upon pluckiness. Doubting Thomases are not about to deter anyone.

Pronounced fruity flavours coupled with a crisp, at times tart, edge characterise Marlborough white wines.

Marlborough – key varieties and styles

Sauvignon Blanc Characteristics include red capsicum, passionfruit, gooseberry, cut-grass and asparagus. Wines grown on the warmer sites exhibit more tropical passionfruit and melon flavours; wines grown on cooler sites more stone-fruit, citrus and green olive and green pepper characters. Awatere Sauvignon Blanc may have distinctive tomato stalk aromas (as in the award-winning Saints Sauvignon Blanc) as well as green pepper and herbal notes.

Chardonnay Generally crisper than Chardonnays grown further north as the cool Marlborough nights keep the grapes' fruit acid levels higher. Zingy, citrus flavours are the key characteristics, while peaches, apricots, melon and passionfruit are more evident in wines grown on warmer sites.

Pinot Noir Fragrant wines, with bright cherry and strawberry flavours. More structural examples tend to hail from the southern side of the Wairau Plain.

Riesling Aromatic and zesty, with lime, grapefruit, ripe pear and tropical fruit flavours. A few deliciously rich, honeyed, botrytised sweet Rieslings are made here, too.

Méthode traditionnelle Most of the country's premium sparkling wines are born in Marlborough where the cool climate produces the crisp, high-acid grapes necessary to produce quality styles.

History

One hundred years before Montana Wines planted its first vines in Fairhall and ushered in the brave new world of Marlborough winegrowing, two 19th-century pioneers – gentleman landowner, Charles Empson, and his Scottish farm manager, David Herd – established the region's first commercial vineyard, Auntsfield, in the Fairhall district. They yielded their first vintage of red muscatel in 1875. Five years later, in 1880, George Freeth, of Mount Pleasant just south of Picton, set up the region's second winery. Romeo Bragato (who in 1895 advised the government about New Zealand's wine-producing prospects) failed to mention Marlborough, but there were early indications that the region could produce wines of good quality for the day. Auntsfield won prizes at local wine exhibitions and Freeth's collected commendations in American, English and French exhibitions.

Nevertheless, during the first half of the 20th century, wine production in Marlborough was confined to the trickle of wines coming out of Auntsfield, Freeth's and the small-scale winemaking endeavours of Harry Patchett and Mansoor Peters.

Then in early 1973 Montana's head Frank Yukich arrived on the scene. Eager to expand the company's vineyard holdings, Yukich was convinced of Marlborough's viability for viticulture on the strength of a DSIR report by scientist Wayne Thomas. At the time, North Island producers believed the South Island too cold for commercial grapegrowing – and so too did Montana's board. Rejecting Yukich's bold scheme for wine production in Marlborough, the board labelled the DSIR report inconclusive. It was only after a letter from Professor H. W. Berg, of the University of California, Davis' viticulture department reiterated the region's suitability that the board reversed its decision and gave Yukich's plans belated approval.

Montana began planting its first 2000-acre vineyard on 11 August 1973, on what is today called Fairhall Estate. Almost overnight Marlborough had became the country's largest wine region. But disaster was soon to follow. Around 80 per cent of the cuttings withered for want of water and 20,000 replacement vines, each grown in little terracotta pots, had to be trucked to Marlborough from Montana's Avondale, Auckland, nursery the following March. The first light, 15–20 tonne

On top of the world
The wine world was soon enamoured with Marlborough Sauvignon Blanc and in 1990 Montana Marlborough Sauvignon Blanc 1989 won the Marquis de Goulaine trophy for best Sauvignon Blanc at the International Wine and Spirit Competition. Montana's Peter Hubscher (centre) receiving the trophy from Peter Drouhin (left) and the Marquis de Goulaine.

harvest of Müller-Thurgau (then called Riesling Sylvaner) and Cabernet Sauvignon was harvested in March 1976, packed into apples crates and shipped across Cook Strait in Maté Yukich's truck, the Champagne Lady, and then driven through the night to Montana's Gisborne winery. Two years later, Montana built the region's first large-scale winery (now known as the Brancott Winery and visitor centre).

Emboldened by Montana's success, other producers arrived in the late 1970s, including Penfolds, Corbans and smaller, boutique-style winemakers, such as Ernie Hunter of Hunter's and, in 1980, Daniel Le Brun.

It hasn't all been plain sailing since – the phylloxera aphid had appeared by the mid-1980s and during the wine glut of the same period, several contract growers for Penfolds were paid to pull vines and end their contracts (although the region didn't lose as much of its vineyard area during the government-funded vine-pull of 1985–86 as other areas). But, given the scale of Marlborough's success today, in retrospect these events were nothing more than minor hiccups.

In the days before Marlborough winegrowers installed modern drip-feed irrigation, the Montana Marlborough vineyard worker would water young vines from a seat on a tractor-towed trailer. A foot-pedal opened a valve which released gravity-fed water through a hose.

Standing over vineyard workers with a shotgun? No, the man on the tractor was using a rifle sight to line up the rows for these Montana workers planting Marlborough's first modern-day vineyard in 1973.

In 1973, Montana workers trialled placing 800,000 waxed cardboard cones over the vines to protect them from wind and to conserve moisture around the plants. But it didn't work. Marlborough's strong north-westerly winds promptly uplifted the cones, scattering thousands of them across the landscape.

The Montana Brancott Winery and visitor centre just outside Blenheim is one of the country's foremost wine tourism attractions.

Hawke's Bay

Wend through the stark, rough-hewn mountain ranges and gaping gorges that lead to Hawke's Bay on the isolated south-east coast of the North Island and you cross into a seemingly sovereign wine state. Sun-crested road signs stationed at its borders declare the region 'Wine Country' – the name locals use to market its long, illustrious winemaking tradition.

Today, there are more than 50 wineries in Hawke's Bay, mostly smaller boutique-style producers, crafting wines as diverse as crisp sparklings to full-flavoured Bordeaux-style reds – and everything in between. They can grow almost any variety here, but the wine-drinking public knows Hawke's Bay best for its rich, well-rounded Chardonnays, soft Sauvignon Blancs and, above all else, those classic robust, red Bordeaux-style blends we so revere.

How does Hawke's Bay – New Zealand's second largest winegrowing region – produce such a miscellany of fine wines? With vineyards spread along cool coastal plains, warmer inland flats and high country foothills in the west, it is as varied a winegrowing region as any in the country. Subject to a raft of climatic influences and blanketed in scores of different soils, it's little wonder so many varieties find a good home here.

The annual Harvest Hawke's Bay festival held in early February celebrates wine, food, music and art. Each year, thousands of wine and jazz devotees attend the Church Road Winery Jazz Concert. Opposite: The Tukituki River looking south toward the Havelock Hills with Te Mata Peak in the centre.

Main winegrowing districts

Situated on the eastern side of the North Island, Hawke's Bay extends from Cape Kidnappers in the south to Mahia Peninsula in the north-east. Apart from the large, relatively flat, vineyard-studded Heretaunga Plains and the inland Takapau Plain to the south-west, most of Hawke's Bay is rolling hill country, bounded on the west by steep, wind-shielding mountain ranges. Hawke's Bay occupies 26 per cent of the national vineyard area.

Vineyard worker Duncan McPhail, at Montana Terraces.

① **Esk Valley** Close to the coast, sea breezes bring this relatively fertile area cooler daytime and warmer night-time temperatures as well as a little more rain than inland on the Heretaunga Plains. An area renowned for producing both reds and whites.

② **Dartmoor Valley** Based around the Tutaekuri River (with silty, sandy soils on one side and loams over gravels on the other) these districts grow reds and whites. Some sheltered sites in the Woodthorpe and Moteo areas on the southern banks experience some of Hawke's Bay's highest growing-season temperatures and particularly suit Merlot and Chardonnay.

③ **Korokipo and Fernhill** The warmer conditions and silt loam soils produce especially good Chardonnay. The fertile coastal plains grow mainly Sauvignon Blanc as well as Pinot Noir and Chardonnay for méthode traditionnelle.

④ **Havelock Hills and Te Mata** A historic wine-producing region and now designated a 'special character zone'. Its north-facing slopes number among the warmest sun-traps in Hawke's Bay. Produces excellent reds and whites.

⑤ **Gimblett Gravels** Situated on the inland edge of the Heretaunga Plains, Gimblett Gravels is the marketing name given to wines produced within the designated boundary of the area's free-draining alluvial gravels. Known particularly for late-ripening reds, such as Cabernet Sauvignon, as well as Chardonnay.

⑥ **The Red Metal Triangle** So-called after its silt over red metal soils which retain a little more moisture than the Gimblett Gravels and particularly suit earlier-ripening reds, such as Merlot. In some vintages Cabernet does very well.

⑦ **Mangatahi** An elevated district, cooler than the plains overnight. It produces mainly white varieties, including excellent Chardonnay. Winegrowers have high hopes for their newer plantings of Pinot Noir destined for table wine.

⑧ **Crownthorpe (sometimes called Matapiro)** A new winegrowing district, it may prove better suited to early-ripening varieties.

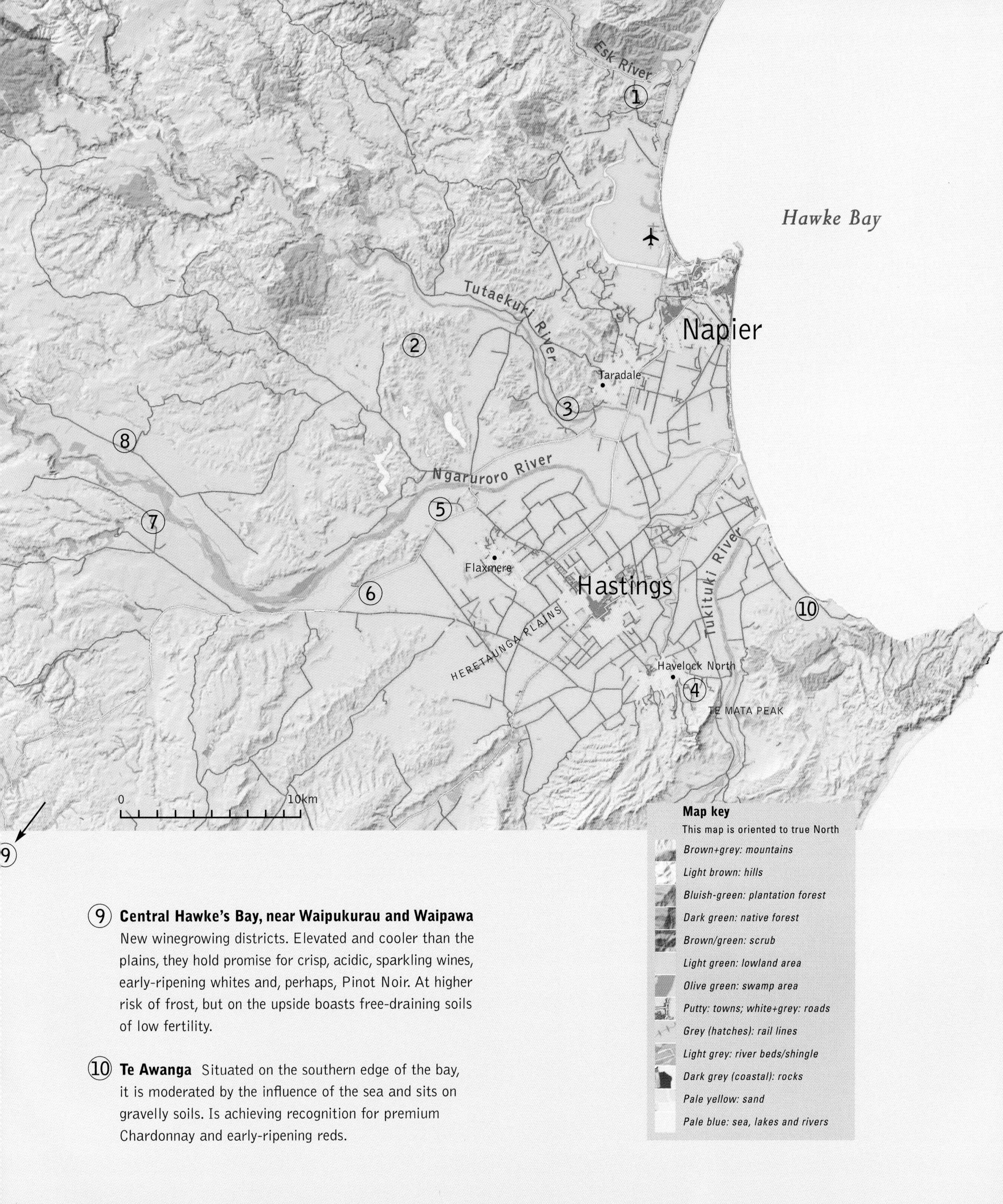

⑨ **Central Hawke's Bay, near Waipukurau and Waipawa** New winegrowing districts. Elevated and cooler than the plains, they hold promise for crisp, acidic, sparkling wines, early-ripening whites and, perhaps, Pinot Noir. At higher risk of frost, but on the upside boasts free-draining soils of low fertility.

⑩ **Te Awanga** Situated on the southern edge of the bay, it is moderated by the influence of the sea and sits on gravelly soils. Is achieving recognition for premium Chardonnay and early-ripening reds.

Gimblett Road, in the Gimblett Gravels winegrowing district of Hawke's Bay.

Climate

It may be one of New Zealand's sunniest, warmest regions, yet low-lying areas of Hawke's Bay are frost-prone in the cooler months, usually experiencing about eight to 10 frosts in spring. Late-spring frosts on the Heretaunga Plains have been known to wipe out some areas at bud burst on occasions.

Hawke's Bay is less windy than many other coastal areas of New Zealand, on account of towering mountain ranges to the west which shelter the Bay when westerlies blow and induce hot, dry (and often drought) conditions on the plains. In annual terms, Hawke's Bay experiences moderate rainfall, thanks to its drier, east coast location. During summer, most of its rain comes from the south or south-east, while in March/April it may receive light, misty rains from the north-east, the latter being tail-ends of tropical cyclones that sweep through places such as the Coromandel during autumn. Water supply is not a problem for the region. If winegrowers do need to irrigate (as they may do in Ngatarawa or Gimblett Gravels) one major aquifer emanating from the underground path of the Ngaruroro River supplies water for Heretaunga Plains' viticultural and horticultural needs.

With its warm, sunny climate and moderately fertile soils, Hawke's Bay produces some of the finest red wines in the country.

Because Hawke's Bay's nights are typically warmer than those in the south, its grapes are generally lower in fruit acids than Marlborough's.

Annual sunshine hours (mean)	2297* (Napier Nelson Park)
Annual rainfall (mean)	741 mm* (Napier Nelson Park)
Growing degree days (mean)	1476 (Napier Nelson Park)

*1993–2002

Soil types

Look at a soil map of Hawke's Bay and you can count almost as many soil types as wines grown in them, including stony gravels, sandy silt loams over gravels, sandy loams, sandy loams on clay pans ... the list goes on. If any generalisations can be made, they are these: Hawke's Bay's winegrowing districts sit on mainly alluvial flood-plain soils with moderate fertility. Geologically speaking, they're young soils and highly variable due to three meandering rivers (Tukituki, Ngaruroro and Tutaekuri) having laid down separate deposits over eons. As a rule of thumb, the further away from the old riverbeds, the more fertile the soils become. Soil variability can be a plus – it's one reason why Hawke's Bay grows such a wide spread of varieties with great success, but it can also pose viticulture management problems (see soils, page 200).

Typical vintage

Begins in early March with Pinot Noir for sparkling wine; mid-March to early April for Chardonnay for table wine; early April to mid-April for Merlot, Cabernet Franc, Malbec, Sauvignon Blanc and Chenin Blanc; mid-April to end of April for Cabernet Sauvignon.

Trends

You'll see a few newer developments on the Heretaunga Plains, but not many. Land suitable for quality winegrowing is increasingly hard to come by, hence the hunt is on for new pastures. The bulk of the newer plantings are situated directly west of Napier in promising districts such as Crownthorpe and in central Hawke's Bay, near Waipukurau and Waipawa.

As for new varietal trends, a number are growing in significance. Malbec ripens well here. Interest in Syrah is gaining momentum, with the Hawke's Bay style being more akin to Northern Rhône Valley Syrah than the rich, robust Shiraz of Australia. Increasingly popular Pinot Gris yields good, expressive fruit in Hawke's Bay and may in the future become an important variety. Gewürztraminer produces fragrant wines with refined, elegant palate structures, although Hawke's Bay styles show a little less opulence than those of Gisborne. But as Church Road's winemaker, Tony Prichard, cautions, 'Maybe the lesson for Hawke's Bay is to not try to become a "fruit salad" region, but instead concentrate on what it does best – the Bordeaux reds and, to a lesser extent, Chardonnay.'

Hawke's Bay – key varieties and styles

Chardonnay Ripens well in Hawke's Bay, producing robust wines with aromas and rich flavours of peach, grapefruit and citrus. Softer than South Island Chardonnay, but a little crisper than those grown further north.

Merlot Rich, vibrant fruit flavours which marry well with careful use of French oak. The best exhibit a gamey complexity. Plantings of Merlot in Hawke's Bay are tipped to increase significantly over the next two years.

Cabernet Sauvignon Intense, ripe, concentrated berry fruit flavours and often a hint of mint.

Sauvignon Blanc An increasingly important variety for Hawke's Bay as winegrowers facing escalating land prices in the South Island look elsewhere for potentially good Sauvignon sites. Hawke's Bay Sauvignon Blancs are generally softer than Marlborough's and a little more likely to have been oak-aged. Notice their nectarine, peach and melon flavours married with a touch of herbs.

Pinot Noir General consensus is that many parts of Hawke's Bay are too warm to produce premium stand-alone varietal Pinot Noir. The region's relatively warm nights deny Pinot the opportunity to ripen slowly and build colour and varietal flavours. But more temperate areas, usually near the coast, yield good Pinot Noir for sparkling wine, harvested at a crisp 19°Brix (sugar level).

Sweet dessert wines Another regional speciality, made in either the botrytised Sauternes-style or late-harvest styles. Special growing conditions at Korokipo can produce excellent botrytised fruit (see page 283).

Sparkling wines Cooler parcels of land lend themselves to the production of good méthode traditionnelle.

Harvest

(for Church Road)

A small church – wooden,
dark – pews and kneelers rich
with oiled grain.
Late summer, in that third
season, we'd celebrate the harvest
with hymns, parade
produce from our gardens
down the central aisle.

Church Road from
All Saints Anglican
now harvesting. It's a full-
bodied kind of day. Te Mata
Peak and Ruahines
gleam as Pellenc, Braud
and Gregoire shake
down the rows. Grapes
roll from bandy trunks.
They're reaping water
from the Ngaruroro – its gravel, shingle
silt – children swimming,
all that sun from north
to south. The Bay shines
para-gliders ride
the lift. In it goes. Staff
of '49; grape-pickers of '61 in
floral prints, formal, with hats
and bags; the old gear – Bradford Mangle,
Paddle Grape Clusters, the Great
Torrent Filler and the Purdey
Labeller, commonly known as
'Flapping Annie' – all
gathered up, heaped
on backs of trucks
headed for town, to
the winery, to the road
with the church, to cuves,
barrels, the dark wood
waiting.

by Jenny Bornholdt

On 3 February 1931 a massive earthquake felled Hawke's Bay's capital city, Napier, and the surrounding countryside. Legendary red winemaker Tom McDonald was inside his Taradale winery on that fateful day and later recalled what he saw: 'There was the most terrific noise and constant shaking. Eight hundred wine barrels rose up and then fell down, smashing into matchwood. The wine went all over the floor. I looked up at the hills and saw the top of the Sugar Loaf [mountain]. It went right up in the air and down again. Must have been about seven feet. Nobody believed me when I told them.'
Reprinted from *Taradale: The Story of a Village* by Janet Gordon.

History

Marist missionaries brought the first vines to Hawke's Bay in 1851 with designs on making sacramental wine and, no doubt, table wines as well to lessen the hardships of pioneering life. They built a mission at Pakowhai, where lay brothers tended the vines. (Subsequently, the religious order moved once more before finally settling at the present Mission Vineyards site in Greenmeadows.) A succession of relatively wealthy landowners later put down vinous roots in the region, too – among them Bernard Chambers of Te Mata Station and Henry Tiffen of Greenmeadows Station. By 1900 Hawke's Bay could lay claim to being the most important wine producer in the land. As a region founded upon the enthusiasm of devout missionaries and comfortably-off 'gentleman farmers' – rather than the economic necessities driving winemakers in the North – Hawke's Bay had garnered a reputation as the country's most elite winemaking enclave.

Spanish immigrant Anthony Vidal, whose name lives on today in Vidal Estate, became the region's first commercial winemaker in 1905. But harsh social and economic realities were to hinder Hawke's Bay's wine industry for most of the first half of the 20th century. The strong anti-drink prohibition movement (echoed in the 1918 Sale of Liquor Act's infamous 'closure [of wineries] without compensation' provision should the government have introduced the alcohol ban) alarmed the district's winegrowers; the catastrophe that was World War I interrupted the industry's progress; and then, as if things couldn't have gotten worse, the Great Depression of the 1930s dried up much of what was left of the market. Winemaking did continue, but only on a tiny scale. Winegrowers hedged their bets and

Mr Mortimer Scott atop Sugarloaf (or Pukekura) Mountain shortly after the 1931 earthquake.

Tom McDonald pictured with his winery staff in 1949. Back row, left to right: Charlie Green, Bill Harrison, Harry Buchanan and Jack Swift. Front row, left to right: Tom McDonald, Oliver McCutcheon, Arthur McCutcheon, Gordon Smith, Albert Foster, Doug Prue, Jim Browne and Keith Hickey.

pulled out the classical *Vitis vinifera* varieties that had until then proliferated the Bay's vineyards, replacing them with European/American hybrid wine grapes that would also double as table grapes – varieties, alas, which made inferior wines. Quality winemaking was, for the most part, put on hold.

Then the advent of World War II, which saw duties imposed on overseas wines and the arrival of American servicemen, reversed the fortunes of local wines somewhat. Fortified wines – Sherries, Ports, Madeiras and liqueurs – became the preferred styles and remained such until the 1970s, not so much for their quality, but for their steep alcohol levels. Still, most New Zealanders would rather drink beer. Throughout those relatively undistinguished years, Hawke's Bay winemakers did, however, manage to craft tiny quantities of classic Claret, Burgundy and Sauternes-style wines. Take how in 1949 Tom McDonald made a Cabernet Sauvignon which was tasted 15 years later by visiting international wine expert André Simon who declared it, 'rare and convincing proof that New Zealand can bring forth table wines of a very high standard of quality'.

But it wasn't until the 1960s that the classical *Vitis vinifera* varieties began to make a proper comeback, in the form of a trickle of encouraging Chardonnays and Cabernet Sauvignons. The area of land under vines in Hawke's Bay more than doubled between 1960 and 1970, from 157 to 327 hectares. McWilliams, then the dominant Hawke's Bay player, was busy mass-producing three wines still etched in a generation of Kiwis' memories: sparkling Marque Vue, dry white Cresta Doré and dry red Bakano.

The 1970s saw the emergence of more table wines, including boxed Müller-Thurgaus. But canny wine-growers had begun putting more emphasis on site selection in a bid to lift wine quality and price returns. Vineyard holdings continued to climb, along with land prices. The total Hawke's Bay vineyard area expanded two and a half times between 1970 and 1975. In the 1980s, Müller-Thurgau was still the region's most planted variety, but increasing hectares of Cabernet Sauvignon and Chardonnay were making their presence felt. During the 1990s, the region more than doubled again, and other classical varieties – Sauvignon Blanc and Merlot for example – became entrenched.

Pioneering Hawke's Bay winemaker and the founding father of quality red winemaking in New Zealand, Tom McDonald (1908–1986), is pictured here leaning on the vineyard horse in 1929, on the site of what is today Church Road's Tom McDonald Cellar. Note how he grew low and bushy vines, like those of the old European vineyards, unlike today's taller, slimmer, trellis-trained vines around which vineyard machinery manoeuvres. Taradale resident Jim Gilmour, 92, who joined Tom McDonald in the late 1920s and remained in the winery's employ until 1976, recalls working life back then. 'It was damned hard work, day after day. Hand-pruning in winter. Sickle-trimming in summer. The vines were much lower in those days and you spent a lot of time kneeling. At the end of the day you could hardly stand up. We had a hand crusher which took half barrel-loads of grapes – stalks, leaves and everything – which made it ten times harder to operate. When you went down to the pub afterwards, you hardly had the strength to lift your beer.'

After making his first Cabernet Sauvignon in 1949, Tom McDonald went on to produce a string of benchmark Cabernets using much the same pumping over technique (see page 254) used by makers of Bordeaux-style wines today. The Tom McDonald Cellar at the Church Road Winery is named in his honour, as is Montana's pinnacle red wine, Tom.

Gisborne

Locals dub it the Chardonnay capital of New Zealand, but there's much more to beautiful, bountiful Gisborne than luscious Chardonnay.

A veritable wonderland for surf-casters, ocean divers and big-game fishermen, in New Zealand Gisborne is almost as famous for its abundant seafood as it is for its delicious wines.

But the world at large knows and loves this warm, sunny, pristine realm best for a definitive style of Chardonnay – soft, lush, tropical fruit-flavoured wines with what's called great 'approachability' (meaning they're ready to drink soon after they're made). Wines which, in one of those serendipitous accidents of nature, harmonise with the harvests locals haul from the sea – fresh scallops, crayfish and snapper.

Situated on the most easterly tip of New Zealand – where its vineyards are the first to feel the warmth of each new day's sunshine – Gisborne is New Zealand's third largest winegrowing region. Chardonnay reigns supreme, accounting for more than one half of all plantings. Yet look beyond the district's signature wine and you'll find exquisite aromatic, floral Gewürztraminers, intense limey, tropical fruit-flavoured Sémillons and honeyed, almonded Chenin Blancs, to name a few of its celebrities, as well as a sprinkling of vibrant, fruit-flavoured Merlots with warm, soft, drink-when-young palates. Some of Gisborne's wines are sold as 'East Coast' wines and many offer excellent value for money. What's more, lovers of New Zealand's single-biggest export wine, Lindauer, owe a debt of gratitude to Gisborne – it's here that much of the Chardonnay and Pinot Noir for the méthode traditionnelle grows.

Opposite: The Waipaoa River and neighbouring vineyards. Upfront fruity bouquets and soft, lush, tropical fruit flavours are the defining characteristics of Gisborne's wines.

Main winegrowing districts

The Gisborne Plains (or valley as locals prefer to call it) is shaped like a triangle, ringed by two converging mountain ranges and the coastline. Some maps refer to the valley as the Poverty Bay Flats, although a more inapt title one could not imagine for this plentiful region. Poverty Bay was the name Captain Cook lumbered the district with after he sailed away from its shores without procuring much-needed supplies for the *Endeavour*.

Gisborne occupies 13 per cent of the national vineyard area. Most of its vines are planted in the Ormond Valley and along the Waipaoa River plains stretching from the start of the valley to the north-west beyond Ormond, to the south reaching past Manutuke. Others are now climbing into some of the surrounding hillsides. There is a smaller vineyard area further north in Tolaga Bay, too.

1. **Patutahi** (pictured above) Home to more than one third of Gisborne's vines, Patutahi produces premium, richly flavoured, award-winning wines, particularly when grown on the region's Kaiti clay loam soils. Planted in mainly Chardonnay as well as Gewürztraminer. The source of the much-decorated and sought-after Montana Patutahi Estate Gewürztraminer.

2. **Ormond** Especially renowned for its impressive Chardonnays, such as Montana Ormond Estate Chardonnay and Corbans Winemakers Cottage Block Chardonnay. The Ormond Valley has a great track record of producing premium Chardonnays, dating back to the 1980s.

3. **Manutuke** Gisborne's oldest winegrowing region, grapes first flourished here in 1894 (see History, page 156). Today, it wins acclaim for its fine Chardonnay, Chenin Blanc, Malbec and varietal Muscat as well as good Pinot Noir for méthode traditionnelle. Home to the internationally renowned organic and biodynamic The Millton Vineyard.

4. **Hexton** Has a great track record for growing long-living, distinguished Chardonnays. Also enjoys success with Gewürztraminer, Merlot, Malbec and Viognier. Threaded with parcels of Kaiti clay soils. The Golden Slopes, renowned for producing fine Chardonnay, are situated here.

5. **Matawhero** The historic birthplace of New Zealand's first premium Gewürztraminer, crafted by Matawhero Wines. The area is now largely planted in Chardonnay

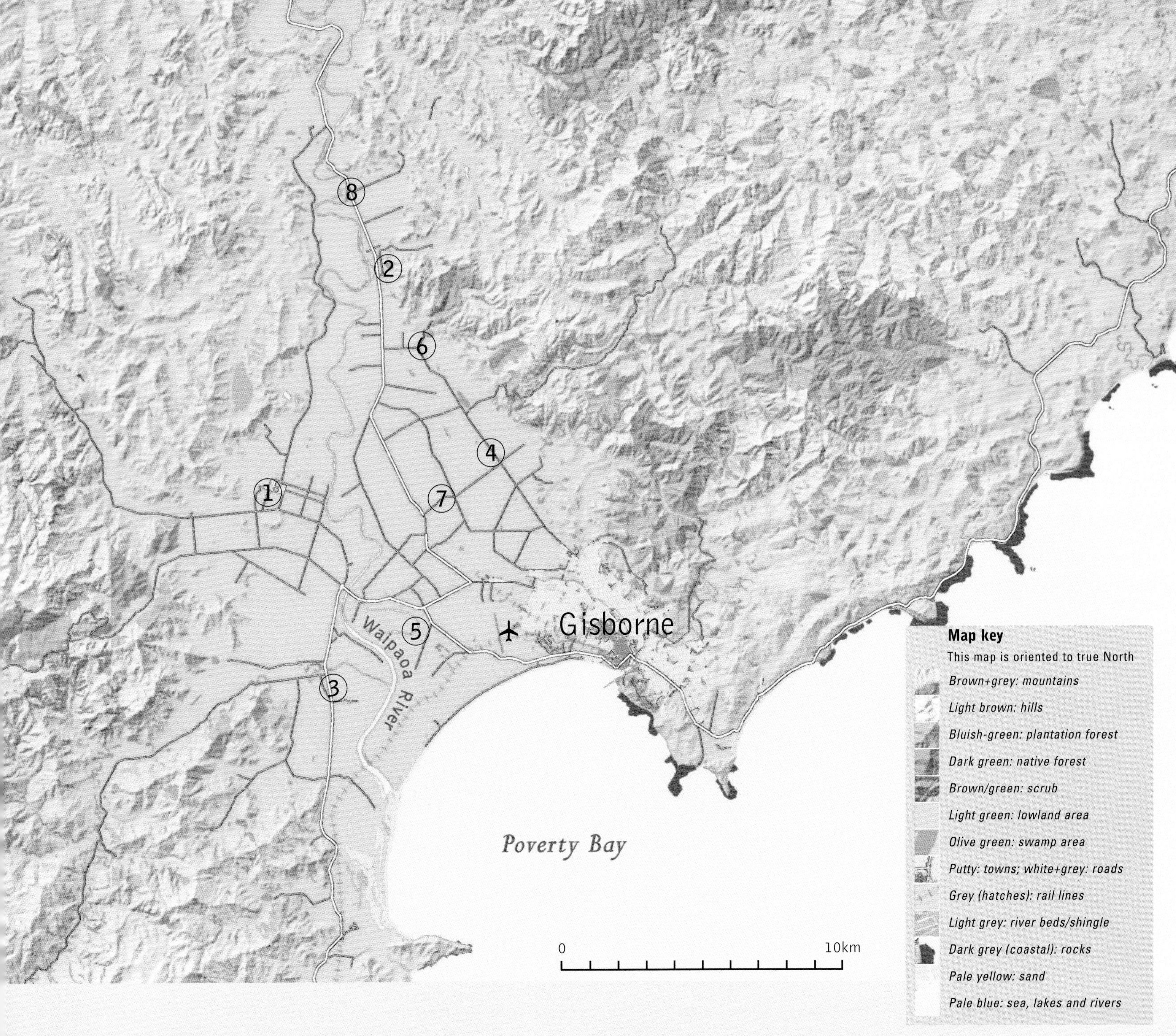

and Gewürztraminer, as well as some Bordeaux varieties. Afternoon sea breezes cool Matawhero's landscape, which in turn helps the grapes retain their crispness.

(6) **Waihirere** The district where Gisborne's first commercial winegrower, Friedrich Wohnsiedler, planted his vines during World War I. This small but highly regarded district with a reputation for producing award-winning wines is mostly planted in Chardonnay. It is the birthplace of the biggest-selling varietal wine in New Zealand, Montana Gisborne Chardonnay.

(7) **Makauri/Bushmere** The centre of the valley, this area takes credit for producing consistently high-quality, good-value wines from Chardonnay, Merlot, Sémillon, Muscat and Müller-Thurgau.

(8) **Waipaoa Valley** Populated with young vines yielding mainly Chardonnay and Sémillon as well as Pinot Noir for méthode traditionnelle. The vineyards are mostly situated on the edge of the Waipaoa River: generally, the closer they are to the river, the lighter and more free-draining the soils; the further away from the river the heavier they are in clay.

Many of the grapes produced in Gisborne are grown by contract growers, such as Billie Abbot.

Climate

One of New Zealand's sunniest, warmest regions, grapes ripen here on average two to three weeks before Hawke's Bay and Marlborough. While the summer winds are predominantly from the north-west, the region doesn't experience gusty north-westerly winds to the same extent as more southerly grapegrowing districts. During the heat of the afternoon sea breezes cool the coastal vineyards. In wetter autumns, botrytis bunch rot can be a problem.

Annual sunshine hours (mean)	2225* (Gisborne AWS)
Annual rainfall (mean)	905 mm* (Gisborne AWS)
Growing degree days (mean)	1413 (Gisborne AWS)

*1993–2002

Soil types

Gisborne's soils primarily comprise moderately fertile alluvial clay loams and silt loams. Since the soils don't vary markedly across the region, winegrowers tend to strategically plant different rootstocks and clones to produce fruit with a range of flavour profiles. That said, local winegrowers report that wines grown on predominantly clay soils have softer, broader mouth-feels, whereas wines grown on siltier soils are leaner and have a fruity elegance. The soils have good moisture-holding capability and irrigation is rarely required. On the best sites vines can achieve a natural balance between their canopy and root areas – one reason why Gisborne wines show such up-front fruit flavours and approachability, believes Montana Gisborne winemaker Steve Voysey. Off the valley floor, carefully selected hillside sites are now also producing wines of great complexity and subtlety. Where Gisborne's soils are fertile, modern viticultural techniques are used to keep vine vigour under control including the use of competitive cover crops and lower-vigour rootstocks. (See page 201.)

Typical vintage

Begins in February with Reichensteiner. Late February: the first of Chardonnay for méthode traditionnelle. First to third week of March: Chardonnay for still wine. Mid-March: Gewürztraminer. April: Sémillon and Chenin Blanc.

Gisborne – key varieties and styles

Chardonnay Soft, lush, tropical fruit-forward Chardonnay is Gisborne's signature wine, encompassing everything from excellent-value-for-money, very approachable (meaning they make good drinking even when young) styles to top-of-the-range, rich, complex award-winning styles. Although the region's Chardonnays have a deserved reputation for youthful appeal, many of those same wines also age extremely well.

Müller-Thurgau Gisborne Müller-Thurgau shows very distinctive floral, citrus characters and compares very favourably with the best wines produced in the variety's homeland, Germany.

Muscat Gisborne produces a handful of outstanding varietal Muscats – scenty, spicy, lush, fruit-flavoured wines with obvious grapey flavours and great mouth-feel. At present, most Gisborne-grown Muscat disappears into Montana's popular sparkling wine, Bernadino.

Sémillon One of Gisborne's fortes: delicious crisp lime and melon tropical fruit-flavoured varietal wines which make an excellent alternative to Sauvignon Blanc.

Gewürztraminer Arguably, the best winegrowing region in the country for Gewürztraminer, Gisborne produces a range of styles: among them elegant, floral-scented, rose-petal wines, through to super-rich, spicy, complex mouth-filling styles. Gisborne has a celebrated reputation for Gewürztraminer – it was here that the country's first benchmark wines were produced by Matawhero Wines in the 1970s.

Merlot Soft, plummy reds with vibrant fruit flavours which suit early drinking. In exceptional years, Gisborne Merlots rival some of New Zealand's more classic styles.

Pinot Noir Most Gisborne-grown Pinot Noir goes into sparkling wine. The variety yields well in the region, producing the ripe flavours at low Brix (sugar levels) necessary to craft quality méthode traditionnelle. But Gisborne also produces a sprinkling of exceptional, ripe-flavoured varietal Pinot Noirs, grown on carefully selected sites.

Whitmore vineyard, just north of Ormond.

Te Arai vineyard, Opou Road.

Chenin Blanc Ripe honeysuckle and quince aromas, with warm honeyed (slightly botrytised) flavours and clipped acid finishes are the hallmarks of the varietal Chenin Blancs crafted by Gisborne's leading producers, such as The Millton Vineyard.

People who are convinced they don't really enjoy wine probably find it too acidic and austere for their tastes. So try offering them Gisborne wines – their softer acidity and upfront fruity flavours have wide appeal.

Long-time Montana Gisborne winery manager Roger McLernon (left) and cellarhand Tom Stevens.

Gisborne is home to New Zealand's largest cooperage. Montana Gisborne winery holds more than 12,000 oak barriques, holding 2.5 to 3 million litres of wine. The region's coopering tradition began with Friedrich Wohnsiedler who crafted the region's early barrels from the native totara tree.

Trends

Conscious of Gisborne's reliance on Chardonnay, prudent winegrowers are always investigating and trialling new varieties. Based on their plantings, it looks likely that Pinot Gris will become the region's next big wine once winegrowers have identified the best clone for local conditions. So far, fruit harvested from newer plantings of Pinot Gris shows remarkable peach and strawberry fruit flavours, characters which bode well for the variety's future prospects in Gisborne. New plantings of fashionable nectarine-and-apricoty Viognier indicate it too suits Gisborne. Furthermore, Pinotage is making a comeback. It was once grown extensively in parts of Ormond and Patutahi during the so-called cask wine era, when its ability to crop well was exploited. Now Pinotage is on the rise again. A few local producers are already making excellent, well-balanced, up front fruit-flavoured Pinotage and wine lovers can look forward to seeing more of this delicious, spicy red wine on the shelves in future. Trial plantings of several Italian and Spanish varieties are under way also, but it will take another 10 years to properly evaluate their potential.

History

Gisborne's wine history begins in 1850, the year Marist priest Father Lampila and two other Marist missionaries set sail from Wellington bound for Hawke's Bay, carrying not only their prayer books, but also vines to grow grapes for sacramental wine. When their ship was driven off course and landed instead at Gisborne in Poverty Bay, the brothers stayed, began converting local Maori to Christianity and dug their vines into the region's rich soils. Only when the brothers' superiors discovered their whereabouts were they ordered to proceed to Hawke's Bay.

A couple of years later, Napier's then priest, Father Reignier, tramped to Poverty Bay and came across those first vines, which were then bearing grapes. He made a cask of wine with the fruit and sent it by sea to Napier, earning himself a place in history as Gisborne's first winemaker. It must have been a reasonable tipple because when the brothers opened the cask in Napier, they found it full of sea water – the temptation to drink it having proved irresistible to the sailors!

The Ormond Vineyard, pictured soon after planting in 1970.

In the late 1890s and early 1900s Austrian Peter Guscka, a gardener for the Clark family at the Opou Station in Manutuke, began making wines with the European varieties and later went on to help Frank Chitty set up his small vineyard at Hexton prior to World War I. But it was German immigrant Friedrich Wohnsiedler who pioneered commercial winemaking in Gisborne. A former butcher, driven out of town by anti-German sentiments during World War I, Friedrich planted a small vineyard in the relative peace of the countryside at Waihirere using cuttings from Frank Chitty's vines. He produced mostly Port, Madeira and Sherry, the favoured drops of the day. After his death his son George continued to expand the business, diversifying into varieties such as Dr Hogg Muscat, Chasselas, Pinotage and Pinot Meunier. (In 1973 Wohnsiedler Wines was absorbed into the Montana fold.)

Friedrich Wohnsiedler pioneered commercial winemaking in Gisborne. The label on the left is from the 1960s, the one on the right is the present-day version.

The modern era of grapegrowing in Gisborne began in the late 1960s when Corbans and Montana started putting local farmers under contract to grow grapes on their behalf. The wine companies supplied the viticultural expertise, erected the region's first wineries and transported the wines to their bottling plants in West Auckland for finishing.

Phylloxera was identified here around that time, but the root-sucking aphid didn't cause major problems until the 1970s when it spread rapidly and soon held the region to ransom. Vines on clay soils succumbed the quickest. Growers were forced to consider replanting at a time when a number of them had only just yielded their first crops. With vines then costing $1.50 each, the industry suffered a severe blow.

Gisborne did bounce back: by 1982, it was the most planted region in the country and predominantly producing bulk wines. In fact, New Zealand as a whole was making so much wine, the country had a surplus. So the government funded a vine-pulling scheme in a bid to put the industry back on an economically viable footing. Some Gisborne growers saw it as a chance to abandon the wine business. Others, the more canny among them, instead used the vine-pull as an opportunity to replant with phylloxera-resistant rootstocks and dispense with hybrid varieties, such as heavy-cropping Seibels and Bacos that had fallen out of favour with the wine-drinking public.

Who takes the credit for identifying Chardonnay as the grape for Gisborne? A number of people were involved, but three key names spring to mind. Winegrower Kevin Schollum at Waihirere Winery trialled many different clonal selections of Chardonnay in the late 1960s. Bill Irwin of Matawhero Wines imported and trialled many Chardonnay (as well as Gewürztraminer) clones. And in 1973, winemaker Peter Hubscher, now managing director of Montana Wines, produced the first Montana Gisborne Chardonnay, a wine which quickly set the standard for New Zealand-produced Chardonnay.

Central Otago

Growing grapes in this, the world's most southerly and New Zealand's highest winegrowing region, requires a bigger leap of faith than an A. J. Hackett bungy jump off Queenstown's Kawarau Bridge. But there's no shortage of takers.

The constructed cave at Gibbston Valley Wines. The winery produced Central Otago's first commercial wines.

Conditions are sometimes said to be marginal for growing grapes – frosts a risk, the growing season short with heat summations teetering on the perilously low side – yet sprawling Central Otago is the country's fastest-growing wine region. Warmer, north-facing slopes with potential for viticulture are as much in demand now as land was during the gold-rush days 140 years ago – and for good reason.

Carefully chosen sites, planted in early-maturing varieties and managed for low yields consistently produce excellent fruit. Central Otago has an arid climate, with ice-cold winters, searingly hot summers, cool autumns and marked diurnal (day/night) temperature swings. Grapes can reach high physiological degrees of ripeness yet at the same time retain high levels of crisp acidity (the latter giving wines good ageing potential).

In this almost too-beautiful landscape Pinot Noir is the star and by 2005 will comprise three-quarters of the region's plantings. But Central Otago also has a fine reputation for crisp Pinot Gris, light but intensely flavoured Rieslings and well-structured Chardonnays, as well as a trickle of spicy Gewürztraminers and Sauvignon Blancs.

Its still-young wine industry owes much to the tourism industry, says Gibbston Valley Wines and Valli Wines winemaker Grant Taylor. Without the tourists who flocked to the alpine and lake resort of Queenstown and drank the region's early wines in the 1980s, local winemakers couldn't have afforded to keep producing and, over the years, improving their wines. Now Central Otago's wines are themselves as much a part of the tourism scene as whitewater rafting on the Shotover River.

A few of Central Otago's wineries have financed their expansion with investment from an influx of wealthy lifestylers to the region. Lifestylers have purchased blocks of land from wine producers. The producers in turn have contracted to plant the land in vines, manage those vines on the lifestylers' behalf and buy crops off them. The large-scale funding required for today's newer developments, however, tends to come from local producers and experienced foreign investors, some of whom have recently uprooted themselves from the United States to make wine here for the export market.

Chard Farm Vineyard clings to a narrow plateau above the Kawarau River.

Mt Difficulty Wines' Pipeclay Terrace vineyard in Bannockburn. The old sluicings (pictured rear) are an ever-present reminder of the district's gold-mining days.

Main winegrowing districts

The exciting thing about Central Otago is it's so new to winegrowing local viticulturists are only just beginning to unlock the differences between its sub-regions and the diverse terroirs within them, says Gibbston Valley Wines and Valli Wines winemaker Grant Taylor. Central Otago currently has four per cent of the national vineyard area, but is tipped to represent five per cent by 2005.

(1) **Gibbston** At about 350 to 420 metres altitude, Gibbston is Central Otago's coolest winegrowing region, so harvests here lag up to one month behind those of the warmest sites in the Cromwell Basin. Produces excellent Pinot Noir, crisp, lean, appley Rieslings and crisp Pinot Gris in the main.

(2) **Alexandra** Can become very hot on the north-facing, sunny sites which suit viticulture. Produces elegant, perfumed Pinot Noirs as well as some of Central Otago's best aromatic Gewürztraminers.

(3) **Wanaka** A small, high-altitude winegrowing area, home to Rippon Vineyard overlooking Lake Wanaka, one of Central Otago's earliest vineyards. Despite the area's 330-metre altitude, the climate can be a little more temperate around the lake because of the moderating influence of the water. Consequently, the frost risk is lower. Known for elegant Pinots with sweet fruit and good ageing ability, limey Rieslings and flinty Chardonnays.

Map key

This map is oriented to true North

- *Brown+grey: mountains*
- *Light brown: hills*
- *Bluish-green: plantation forest*
- *Dark green: native forest*
- *Brown/green: scrub*
- *Light green: lowland area*
- *Olive green: swamp area*
- *Putty: towns; white+grey: roads*
- *Grey (hatches): rail lines*
- *Light grey: river beds/shingle*
- *Dark grey (coastal): rocks*
- *Pale yellow: sand*
- *Pale blue: sea, lakes and rivers*

(4) Cromwell Basin (includes Lowburn, Bannockburn, Pisa, Northburn and Bendigo)

Central Otago's warmest sub-regions, known best for their powerful, concentrated Pinot Noirs; Rieslings with honeysuckle, lime and floral characters and sometimes higher alcohol; fresh Pinot Gris; and sparkling wines. New plantings of Syrah in the warmest area of all, Bendigo, are taking place. The district is home to more than 60 per cent of Central Otago's plantings, says Quartz Reef's Rudi Bauer.

The beautiful Rippon Vineyard on the edge of Lake Wanaka.

Central Otago – key varieties and styles

Pinot Noir Performs well throughout Central Otago's winegrowing districts. Styles range from perfumed, quite spicy wines with savoury notes and soft, silky tannins grown in cooler microclimates to more fruity, cherry, plum and 'grippier' tannins grown on warmer sites.

Pinot Gris Pinot Gris produces a range of styles in Central Otago, from crisp and spicy wines to richer styles with good concentration and oily texture.

Chardonnay Elegant wines which vary in style between oaked, malolactic styles to crisp, Chablis styles.

Riesling Ranges from leaner, higher-acid, green, appley flavours when grown in the cooler sub-region of Gibbston to more honeysuckle, lime, floral character wines when grown in warmer sub-regions.

Climate

Central Otago's climate is less maritime than all New Zealand's other winegrowing regions. It's almost continental-like, in fact – that is, the region experiences very hot, dry summers and ice-cold winters.

Long, cool, dry autumns mean the grapes can stay on vines for extended periods to build ripe, intense varietal flavours and intensity of colour. The best sites are slightly elevated where risk of frost is reduced. Autumn frosts can cause leaves to drop and the grapes to stop ripening. However, in the past decade only the autumn frosts of 1997 and 2003 have caused some difficulties.

Annual sunshine hours (mean)	1950* Queenstown 2225* Cromwell (2)
Annual rainfall (mean)	650 mm* Wanaka (Aero AWS) 997 mm* Queenstown 479 mm* Cromwell (2) 458 mm** Clyde
Growing degree days (mean)	867 Wanaka (Aero AWS) 822 Queenstown 983 Cromwell (2) 893 Clyde

*1993–2002 **1986–1995

Central Otago's arid climate is largely inhospitable to vine diseases. Only occasionally is powdery mildew seen and, on very rare occasions, an insignificant spot or two of botrytis. The vine louse, phylloxera, has recently been discovered here though.

Soil types

Gibbston: soils fairly fertile for Central Otago comprising mainly wind-blown loess over free-draining gravels.

Alexandra: varied – heavy clays on the flats and rocky outcrops of schist on hillier sites.

Wanaka: minerally glacial moraine and wind-blown loess topsoils over schist gravels.

Cromwell Basin: various low- to medium-fertility soils, ranging from heavier clay-based soils, free-draining silts and stonier schist-dominant soils.

Typical vintage

Begins in late March in Bendigo with Pinot Noir through to mid-May for Gibbston Riesling.

Trends

Central Otago's wine industry is set to continue to grow. But is the region setting itself up to rely too heavily on Pinot Noir, a few people are asking? Aside from its other key varieties, Central Otago could have a fine future with sparkling wine. The region's fruit retains the crisp, high acidity necessary to make premium méthode traditionnelle, as Quartz Reef in Cromwell is already proving with its elegant, harmonious wines.

The breathtaking scenery which has long lured tourists is now attracting a wave of permanent or semi-permanent wealthy lifestylers, many of whom come from overseas and bring with them money to invest in winegrowing. Those who have bought decent-sized parcels of land know they can market and sell their wines internationally and may have already set up distribution networks. Access to water could become a problem for the region's industry in the future.

History

When you catch a whiff of the wild thyme that fills the air in Central Otago, spare a thought for Frenchman Jean Desiré Feraud. Not only is he said to have introduced the herb to the region, he also planted Central Otago's first vines near Clyde in 1864 and won a prize for his Burgundy-style wine in Sydney in 1881. Viticulturist Romeo Bragato visited Central Otago in 1895 and declared the region suitable for grape-growing. But it was only when Rolfe Mills, the father of modern-day winemaking in Central Otago, and wife Lois, planted the Rippon Vineyard in Wanaka in 1976, that the region's wine industry made a true start. Alan Brady planted the first vines at Gibbston in 1981 and went on to produce Central Otago's first commercial wines.

The solar-powered fan is just one of the devices Central Otago winegrowers may use to protect their vines from frost damage.

Opihi Vineyard, in Pleasant Point, South Canterbury.

Canterbury

Canterbury Plains and Waipara Valley

Already a thriving winegrowing region producing some of the South Island's finest wines, the sprawling Canterbury province still has huge potential for growth.

The picturesque French Farm Vineyards at French Farm Bay on Banks Peninsula.

Canterbury divides into two main winegrowing districts: the older, more established flat Canterbury Plains surrounding Christchurch; and, to the north of the city a 40-minute drive away, the undulating Waipara Valley where most of the newer and larger vineyards lie. The region's burgeoning wine industry hasn't finished expanding either, say locals, pointing to the large tracts of arable land still available for conversion to viticulture.

Pinot Noir, Chardonnay, Riesling and, in Waipara, also Sauvignon Blanc, lead the list of wines grown in Canterbury. At best they are outstanding, thanks largely to the region's ability to grow naturally balanced, low-cropping vines which yield intensely flavoured, premium-quality fruit. The most heavily planted variety here is Pinot Noir, a grape which develops powerful aromas and flavours as well as sought-after soft, silky tannins as a result of the district's typically long, dry autumns. Likewise, Riesling responds well to Canterbury's climate and is set to become more prominent in the region.

Waipara Valley, located at the southern gateway to the Alpine Pacific Triangle trail between Christchurch, Hanmer and Kaikoura, is a small but extremely diverse winegrowing district, endowed with a wide range of exciting terroirs. Such is Montana Wines' faith in the valley's ability to produce premium wines, it recently planted 220 hectares in Pinot Noir, Riesling and Pinot Gris. 'It's a very promising, up-and-coming district,' says Montana's chief winemaker Jeff Clarke. 'The climate and the soils augur well for some very exciting wines in the future.'

Main winegrowing districts

Stretching from Waipara Valley in the north and along the Canterbury Plains to Pleasant Point, near Timaru, in the south, the Canterbury province occupies four per cent of the national vineyard area.

(1) **Waipara Valley** A warmer district than the Canterbury Plains, Waipara Valley-grown wines tend to show rich, ripe fruit flavours. In particularly warm vintages the valley can even yield good Merlot and Cabernet Sauvignon. It is home to most of the region's newer vineyard developments.

(2) **Canterbury Plains** Scattered with boutique vineyards between Amberley and Timaru, the plains generally produce lighter-bodied wine styles exhibiting great elegance and finesse. Grows mainly Pinot Noir and Chardonnay.

(3) **Banks Peninsula** The historic birthplace of Canterbury winegrowing, Banks Peninsula today produces a trickle of wines – mainly Pinot Noir, Chardonnay, Gewürztraminer and Riesling – from boutique wineries.

Canterbury – key varieties and styles

Pinot Noir Typically full-bodied, richly flavoured wines with berry fruit and black cherry characters and big, ripe tannins.

Chardonnay Canterbury produces a wide range of Chardonnay styles – including cool, crisp, vibrant fruity varietal wines and rich, full-bodied, complex examples.

Riesling Range from dry, elegant, tight-knit styles to richer styles with apricoty characters. Some local styles have a minerally tang reflecting the character of the soils in which they were grown. Canterbury's typically long, dry autumns yield some good late-harvest and botrytised wines, too.

Sauvignon Blanc Canterbury's Sauvignon Blancs share much in common with the riper styles of Marlborough Sauvignon Blanc – that is, they show riper characters such as passionfruit.

Montana's Camshorn vineyard, Waipara Valley, shortly after planting in October 2002.

Climate

Both the Waipara Valley and Canterbury Plains enjoy warm, dry summers and typically long, dry autumns. The biggest climatic risk for the region then? Late spring frosts.

Waipara Valley: The valley is warmer than the Canterbury Plains. During summer, temperatures of 35–39°C are not unheard of. The Teviotdale Hills shelter the valley from cool north-easterly winds. The closer vineyards are to the Teviotdale Hills, the warmer they are as a rule. Most of the valley's rain falls in winter.

Canterbury Plains: Cooler than Waipara on account of its exposure to cooling east-north-easterly and southerly winds. Windbreaks and poplar shelter belts are widely used.

Banks Peninsula: Some sites may be warmer than the plains, others are cooler.

Annual sunshine hours (mean)	2124* (Christchurch Aero)
Annual rainfall (mean)	601 mm* (Waipara West) 606 mm* (Christchurch Aero)
Growing degree days (mean)	1107 (Waipara West) 1005 (Christchurch Aero)

*1993–2002

The historic birthplace of Canterbury winegrowing, Banks Peninsula today produces a trickle of wines. Pictured here is the French Farm Vineyards.

Soil types

Waipara Valley: Has very variable soils, including: low-fertility stony soils (on flat lands in the central and west of the valley); limestone-derived clays on hillsides on the eastern side of the valley); and gravelly loams over alluvial subsoils (in the south). Incidentally, clay/chalky limestone soils make for good wines: the clay holds moisture and the limestone improves the vine's mineral uptake, while bigger particles of limestone help with drainage so the clays don't retain an excess of water. It is said their higher pH imparts an illusion of sweetness into wines.

Canterbury Plains: Highly variable soils, including stony, free-draining soils, which warm up quickly in spring, as well as moderately fertile soils (originating from flood plains) with good water-holding ability.

Banks Peninsula: Compact sub-soils over silt-loam topsoils. A few areas on the peninsula are situated on silt loams over clay sub-soils.

Typical vintage

Waipara – April: Pinot Noir and Chardonnay, Pinot Gris, Sauvignon Blanc, Gewürztraminer. Late April to early May: Riesling and Bordeaux red varieties.

Canterbury Plains – Mid-April: Pinot Noir, Chardonnay, Pinot Gris.

Trends

Locals anticipate substantial growth in the Waipara Valley, but it is likely that in the future access to irrigation water may limit the development of some sites. Many of the province's vines are planted on their own roots – phylloxera has not yet been identified here – although winegrowers expect to replant with grafted rootstocks in time. Already a number of rootstock trials are under way in the region.

History

Classical *Vitis vinifera* grapes arrived in Akaroa with French, mainly peasant, immigrants in 1840, a decade before the formal settlement of Canterbury by the British. But in between the colonial age and the establishment of Canterbury's first commercial vineyard, St Helena in 1978, Canterbury had no winemaking

Jason Doughty prepares to defend the Corbans' Omihi vineyard from bird attack.

tradition to speak of. Rather, its modern era began at Lincoln University in 1973, with the serendipitous meeting of Lincoln University fruit scientist Dr David Jackson and a young Prague-born winemaker named Danny Schuster (now of Daniel Schuster Wines in Waipara). Schuster was enlisted to research large-scale cider fermentation, but soon began assisting Dr Jackson with extensive viticulture and winemaking trials aimed at revealing which *Vitis vinifera* varieties would best suit Canterbury's cool-climate conditions. Back then, North Island viticulture experts maintained Canterbury was too cold to ripen the classical grapes. Yet Jackson's knowledge of growing fruit trees in moderate climates and Schuster's understanding of cool-climate winegrowing in Germany led the pair to believe otherwise. Between the late 1970s and early 1980s, they facilitated popular one- and two-day courses in viticulture and oenology. Many of the attendees went away to make their own wines. The pair's ongoing research not only advanced Canterbury winegrowing, it furthered the development of cool-climate viticulture in other winegrowing regions around the country. Today, their book, *The Production of Grapes and Wine in Cool Climates*, remains the first text newcomers to New Zealand winegrowing turn to, nearly 20 years after it was first published. Lincoln University, meanwhile, is now home to the Centre for Viticulture and Oenology. A leading training and research centre, it has around 150 students, variously engaged in undergraduate, postgraduate and research work. The department's influence is far-reaching: teaching and research staff work closely with the South Island industry, including the new Marlborough Centre of Excellence for winegrowing and winemaking. But its focus is not restricted to the south – it also maintains close contact with North Island producers.

Wairarapa

Martinborough, Masterton and environs

Like the nearby capital city of Wellington, located bang in the middle of New Zealand, Wairarapa's wine styles sit at a kind of halfway point, too. Not quite as lean as the South Island's, nor as rounded and tropical fruit flavoured as those from further north – rather, a delicious balance of the two.

Situated in the southernmost corner of the North Island, Wairarapa has everything it takes to make premium-quality wines: a sunny, generally dry climate, warm summer days, cool nights and typically low-vigour, free-draining soils. Little wonder the region grows naturally low-cropping vines which yield intensely flavoured grapes – Pinot Noirs combining both power and fruit elegance; Sauvignon Blancs with aromatic intensity and broad, rich flavours; and rich, fruit-flavoured Pinot Gris with good mouth-feels, to name but a few of Wairarapa's success stories.

Pinot is the biggest passion – verging on obsession. It is the variety which has brought Wairarapa its greatest acclaim and accounts for about half the region's vineyard plantings. Long-time Martinborough winemaker Larry McKenna, who recently developed his Escarpment Vineyard in Te Muna Road, south-east of the town, typifies local winegrowers' confidence in the variety – 70 per cent of his 24-hectare site is in Pinot Noir.

Wairarapa's producers are mostly small, boutique, owner-operator concerns producing less than 100 tonnes per year (the main exceptions being middle-sized Craggy Range of Hawke's Bay, which recently planted in the district, and Palliser Estate). Commercial-scale winegrowing began here in the late 1970s on Martinborough's river terraces' soils – land which today commands the sky-high prices that have forced winegrowers to look beyond the radius of the township for places to plant. Now most of the region's many newer vineyard developments are happening out to the south and east of Martinborough and to areas south and north of Masterton.

Wairarapa typically experiences radiation frosts – that is, cold, still air frosts – generally reaching about –2°C. Whirling windmills and helicopters flying overhead frost-affected vineyards circulate the still air, mixing it with warmer air from above the cold air, increasing air temperatures by about 2°C and thus preventing damage to vines. Wairarapa winegrowers are trialling some innovative approaches to frost-damage control, including a major experiment into the effectiveness of heating cables installed along the fruiting wires to protect vines from damage. Others are blowing hot air through their irrigation systems during frosts, while some have built or are building dams to supply water for overhead sprinkler systems. But you'll still see plenty of old-style portable diesel-fuelled 'frost-pots' about the district (right).

Craggy Range's new vineyards on the outskirts of Martinborough.

Wellington lies just over an hour's drive away from Martinborough, over the steep, winding Rimutaka Ranges. Wine-loving Wellingtonians claim Wairarapa's wine industry as their own and rank among its keenest supporters. 'Wellington's a fantastic market for us,' says Ata Rangi's Clive Paton who, with fellow winemaker and wife Phyll Pattie, has turned out Pinot Noirs which have collected the Bouchard-Finlayson trophy for Pinot Noir at the International Wine and Spirit Competition in London on three occasions.

With Wairarapa being so close to the political pulse of the country, it is not surprising it's been engaged in a little politicking of its own over the years. In 1986, a group of the region's then fledgling wine producers banded together to introduce the Martinborough Terrace Appellation of Origin System. Wines grown and produced in the designated area were entitled to wear the appellation seal on their bottles as a stamp of authenticity. But not everyone approved of the scheme, claiming the appellation's boundaries were arbitrary and that lookalike soils and climates were not confined to the Martinborough Terraces. Since then, use of the seal has largely been abandoned. But the issue itself hasn't gone away. One local winemaker suggested we form an opinion about it for this book. But we've decided to do what lovers of Wairarapa wines do everywhere – enjoy the wines and leave the politics to Wellington!

Main winegrowing districts

The Rimutaka and Tararua ranges help shelter Wairarapa's vines from north-westerly rains. The Wairarapa region occupies four per cent of the national vineyard area.

① **Martinborough township and environs** Home to Martinborough's earliest vineyards, planted mainly on stony silt loams over river terraces. Mainly produces excellent Pinot Noir, Sauvignon Blanc, Riesling, Chardonnay and Pinot Gris.

② **Te Muna** A very new sub-region, planted on the same river terraces as Martinborough, with exciting potential for future growth. Planted in mainly Pinot Noir, as well as a little Sauvignon Blanc, Pinot Gris, Chardonnay and Riesling.

③ **South Martinborough** Produces mainly Pinot Noir.

④ **Masterton** Newer vineyards have yet to crop, but much of the focus here is on Pinot Noir, Sauvignon Blanc and Riesling. Soils are mainly silt loams over stony river terraces.

⑤ **Gladstone and East Taratahi (or Dakins Road)** Home to some of the Wairarapa's original vineyards and now undergoing major expansion. The focus is mainly on Sauvignon Blanc, Riesling, Pinot Noir and Pinot Gris.

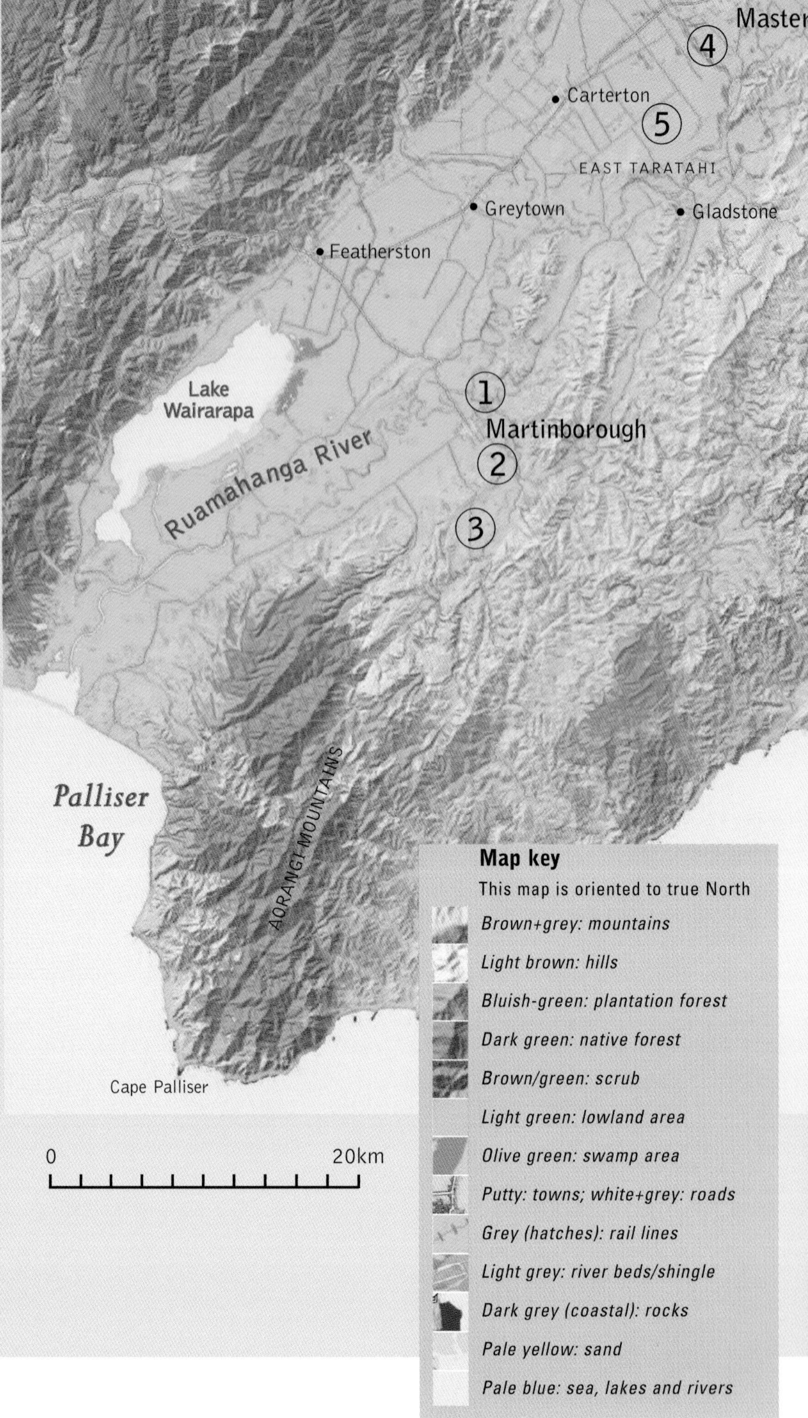

Climate

Enjoys a sunny climate and, in sheltered areas, warm daytime temperatures during the summer months. Cool nights help preserve the fruit's acidity and fresh, fruity characters. Wairarapa is relatively dry. Summer droughts can be a problem, so most vineyards install irrigation systems. Autumns usually remain dry and cool. Any rain that does fall comes from the south; consequently the rains are cool and botrytis infection doesn't follow as a rule. As in Hawke's Bay, spring frosts are a major risk for most Wairarapa winegrowers. Also, the dry, north-westerly winds that prevail during spring and summer can upset flowering and damage young shoots – but the region's low incidence of vine disease more than compensates for those risks, believe local growers. Masterton and its environs are a little cooler than the Martinborough area.

Annual sunshine hours (mean)	2065* Masterton (Te Ore Ore) 1978* Wairarapa (Martinborough)
Annual rainfall (mean)	875 mm* Masterton (Te Ore Ore) 728 mm* Wairarapa (Martinborough)
Growing degree days (mean)	1058 Masterton (Te Ore Ore) 1237 Wairarapa (Martinborough)

*1993–2002

Soil types

The Martinborough Terraces contain shallow loam topsoils overlaid by deep alluvial gravels laid down by the Huangarua River. Te Muna comprises lookalike Martinborough Terrace soils. In south Martinborough there are heavier clay soils with less alluvial gravels, although there are patches of river gravels now being exploited. Masterton has light loams and heavy gravels, whereas Gladstone and Dakins Road comprise free-draining river terraces.

Typical vintage

Vintages vary considerably depending on soils and degree of exposure to wind. First two weeks of April: Pinot Noir and Chardonnay. Mid-April: Sauvignon Blanc, Pinot Gris. Late April to early May: Cabernet Sauvignon.

Trends

There are still plenty of north-facing, significantly sized sites available in Wairarapa, but it's likely to remain the domain of mainly boutique owner-operators. Because of the region's proximity to Wellington and the strength of the Martinborough brand, any land suitable for viticulture sells at over $74,000 a hectare. Expect to see more vineyards on the region's gravelly soil areas, although in the future access to water could limit development at some sites. Growers' focus will stay on Pinot Noir, but other varieties will support the region's development: Pinot Gris, Sauvignon Blanc, Riesling and Chardonnay number the whites with the brightest futures.

History

William Beetham planted Wairarapa's first few vines in Masterton in 1883. Upon visiting Beetham's tiny vineyard in 1895, viticulturist Romeo Bragato reported to the government of the day that Wairarapa suited grapegrowing. But by the late 1970s, wrote historian Roberta McIntyre in *The Canoes of Kupe*, 'Martinborough appeared to be slowly sliding off the map'. In 1978 Alister Taylor began the region's first commercial winegrowing venture on a small area of river terraces and was soon followed by others.

Mebus Estate vineyard at Masterton.

Wairarapa – key varieties and styles

Pinot Noir Wines with a delicious balance of concentrated Pinot fruit in the red cherry, black cherry flavour spectrum and underlying power. Here Pinot seems to produce its best, most balanced wines in average Growing Degree Day vintages (between 1100 and 1300), says Ata Rangi's Clive Paton.

Sauvignon Blanc Not as herbal, nor as lean as most South Island styles, but not quite as tropical fruit flavoured as those grown further north. They show a breadth of flavour richness and yet retain aromatic intensity. Indeed, Wairarapa Sauvignon Blancs look very similar to riper Marlborough styles.

Chardonnay Often rich styles with aromas of peaches, pears and fig-like characters when grown in warmer seasons.

Pinot Gris Depending where and how the wine is made, Wairarapa can produce everything from light ethereal, floral styles to very rich, textural high-alcohol wines akin to Chardonnay. That said, the region is tending towards richer, broader mouth-feel styles of Pinot Gris.

Also of interest There is a handful of committed red Bordeaux-style producers in Wairarapa producing good wines on selected sites in warmer vintages. Syrah, planted on warmer sites, produces elegant yet powerful reds.

Nelson

Is Nelson the Promised Land? The lifestylers who flock here certainly believe so and who can argue with them? Nelson has everything – plentiful sunshine, golden beaches, rivers, mountains, three national parks on its doorstep – and some of the country's loveliest wines.

Owners of Neudorf Vineyards, Tim and Judy Finn say 'the brashness of youth' encouraged them to plant vines here in the Upper Moutere hills in 1979.

One of New Zealand's sunniest spots, Nelson's tiny but flourishing wine industry represents just a small slice of the national vineyard area. Two main factors explain why it hasn't grown into a large producer, despite the recent rush to plant boutique-style vineyards in the district. Firstly, Nelson's land prices have long been steep, making investment costly – particularly on the Waimea Plains where most of the region's vineyards huddle alongside fields of dairy cows, orchards and market gardens. (Indeed, only recently have Marlborough's escalating land prices overtaken those of Nelson.) Secondly, big parcels of land – of a scale that would pique the interest of New Zealand's larger producers – simply don't exist.

With the exception of the founding father of Nelson's modern winemaking era, Hermann Seifried, of Seifried Estate (the region's largest, albeit middle-sized, producer), Nelson's wine industry was founded upon the hard-working backs of enthusiastic, small-scale winemakers – lifestyle winemakers, who dreamed of crafting top-quality wines and somewhere along the way mastered the art beautifully.

Owners of Neudorf Vineyards, Tim and Judy Finn, were among the earliest modern pioneers when they dug their first vines into soils in the Upper Moutere hills in 1979. 'We planted anything that looked likely on paper to grow here,' says Tim. Then they began the lengthy job of evaluating which varieties suited the area best. 'Chardonnay did it for us, right from the early days.'

But it's fair to say the region as a whole doesn't yet have a single variety or wine style on which to hang its identity. Rather, it produces several wines very well – most notably Chardonnay, Sauvignon Blanc, Pinot Noir and Riesling. With good viticultural management, it can ripen Merlot, too, and in warmer years even have success with Cabernet Sauvignon, although the latter is on the way out as winegrowers channel their energies into varieties the region has consistent success with.

Fossil Ridge vineyards in the Richmond foothills in Nelson.

Main winegrowing districts

Ringed by mountains on three sides, the warm, sunny Nelson region escapes extremes of weather. Most vines grow on the Waimea Plains, but newer, boutique vineyards are springing up across the landscape – even in such faraway places as Golden Bay, once dismissed as too wet for viticulture. Nelson accounts for about three per cent of the national vineyard area.

① **Brightwater** Boasts stony, alluvial soils, credited with producing fruit-driven wines and, in particular, delicious Sauvignon Blanc. The bulk of the Nelson region's new plantings are located here, including a wide range of varieties, such as Chardonnay, Pinot Noir, Merlot and Riesling.

② **Waimea Plains** Tends to produce Chardonnay, Sauvignon Blanc, Pinot Noir and Riesling in fruit-driven styles.

③ **Upper Moutere hills** The generally heavier clay and gravel soils in these hills frequently produce complex, minerally, broad mouth-feel wines that don't push their fruit flavours forward. Known best for Chardonnay, Pinot Noir and Sauvignon Blanc. The district's clay and gravel soils also help impart Pinot Gris with textural, oily qualities, say locals.

④ **Richmond** The wineries near Richmond are situated on the Waimea Plains – see Waimea Plains above.

⑤ **Motueka** Very new to grapegrowing, but already producing interesting wines including passionfruit-flavoured Sauvignon Blanc.

⑥ **Golden Bay** Another new grapegrowing area for the Nelson region and situated on calciferous soils. With careful site, clone and rootstock selection, drier microclimates can produce very good grapes.

Kahurangi Estate vineyard in Nelson.

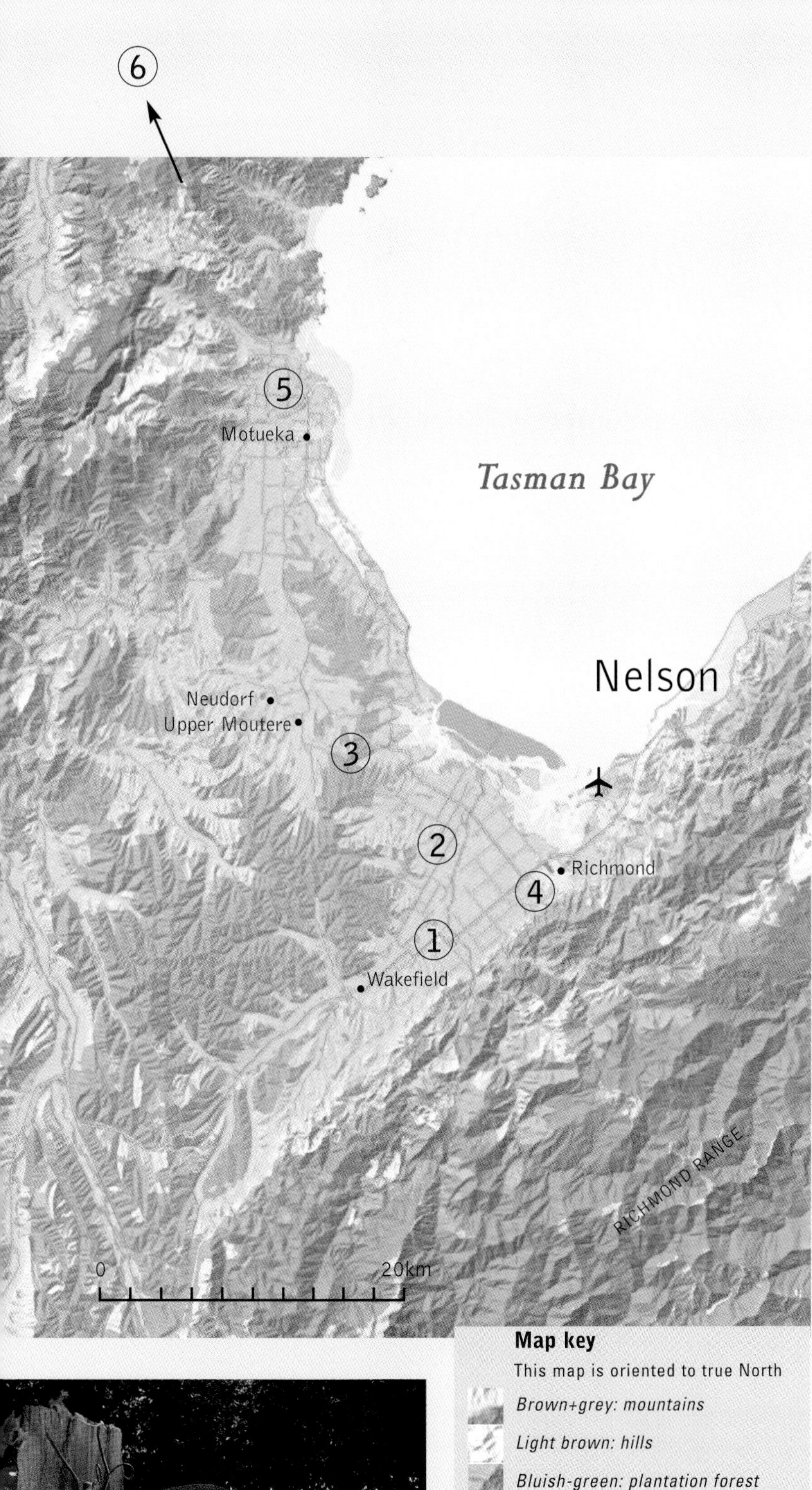

Map key

This map is oriented to true North

Hop-drying kilns are a common sight around the Nelson landscape. Where hops flourish, so too do vines, Hermann Seifried was told by his viticulture lecturer at Weinburg University in Germany many years ago.

Nelson – key varieties and styles

Chardonnay Nelson produces a wide range of styles: the Waimea Plains Chardonnays tend to be more floral, particularly the unoaked styles. Nelson Chardonnays generally have a fresh acidity, says Hermann Seifried, hence most undergo malolactic fermentation, resulting in rich, creamy, buttery-flavoured wines. Without the use of oak and malolactic fermentation, they can be quite crisp and fresh in style. Some say Chardonnays from the Upper Moutere hills often have quite a strong mineral backbone.

Sauvignon Blanc Generally, riper, fruit-flavoured styles of Sauvignon Blanc.

Pinot Noir May show a distinct plumminess and, if harvested from low-cropping vines, exhibit plenty of ripe tannins. The region's temperate climate agrees with Pinot Noir, but it's still too soon to say whether there's a definitive Nelson Pinot Noir style.

Riesling Range in style from delicious floral and ripe citrus characters to the more complex styles with greater mouth-feel. The latter may be less fruit driven, although you may notice some have citrus skin and pith characters.

Climate

The warm, sunny climate that draws expats and retirees to Nelson suits wine grapes down to the ground. Hermann Seifried hasn't seen a spring frost in the 30 years he's been making wine in Nelson. Most of Nelson's weather blows in from the north, hence the region doesn't suffer sudden changes in temperatures. The plains can become quite windy, windier than in the Upper Moutere hills district. But hail belts on the plains aren't as threatening to winegrowers as you may imagine – Nelson's typically very fine hail doesn't do serious damage to the grapes. Nelson's rain usually falls in winter, when downpours can be heavy and prolonged. Winegrowers on the plains usually install irrigation systems at their vineyards, but have no need to draw on them heavily.

Annual sunshine hours (mean)	2527* (Nelson AWS)
Annual rainfall (mean)	932 mm* (Nelson AWS)
Growing degree days (mean)	1088 (Nelson AWS)

*1993–2002

Soil types

Gravelly silt loams with reasonable water-holding ability dominate the Waimea Plains. Head towards Rabbit Island, however, and the soils comprise a greater proportion of silt. In the Upper Moutere hills district, low-pH yellow clay gravels hold sway (many of which are free-draining, forming up to a metre-deep clay loam over gravel sub-soils). Soils around the new Brightwater area vary significantly but are generally shingly.

Typical vintage

Late March to early April: Pinot Noir, young Chardonnay, Gewürztraminer.

First to second week of April: more mature Chardonnay, Sauvignon Blanc, Pinot Gris.

Late April to early May: Riesling, last of Sauvignon Blanc, Merlot, Syrah and Cabernet Sauvignon.

Trends

Nelson's wine scene is changing fast. Newer wineries employ trained winegrowers and winemakers, rather than rely on the traditional Nelson model of the owner-cum-beginner winemaker learning on the job. Hence the quality of Nelson's wines continues to climb. The recent flurry of plantings, especially on the Waimea Plains, now sees some of Nelson's Sauvignon Blanc 'exported' to wine producers in Marlborough who blend it with their local wines.

Overseas investors are eyeing Nelson with interest, says Tim Finn. Nevertheless, Nelson is likely to remain a winemaking haven for a band of small but enthusiastic boutique winemakers.

Seifried Estate has an experimental hectare planted in Austria's most popular red, Zweigelt, a variety which produces good, relatively complex red wines without a hint of greenness. Pinot Noir looks very promising: already Nelson has produced some excellent versions.

History

The planned settlement of the Nelson region began with the arrival of German immigrant winemakers in the early 1840s, lured by assurances about Nelson's winegrowing potential from the New Zealand Company. They soon abandoned the colony for South Australia, however, and tobacco, hops, tea, apples and berry fruits were to become Nelson's staple crops. Although over the next 130 years or so a few people did try their luck at growing grapes, it wasn't until Hermann Seifried arrived in the district that anyone had true success with the classical varieties.

When he planted two hectares of grapes in the Upper Moutere hills district in 1973, some warned he was taking a gamble. But Hermann was full of confidence – his viticulture lecturer at Weinburg University in Germany taught him that where hops and tobacco thrive, so too do wine grapes. He soon became a mentor to the small, beginner winegrowers who followed him to Nelson in the late 1970s. As a member of Lincoln University tasting panels (see page 169) who reviewed planting trials of classical varieties, he shared the findings first hand with local winegrowers still feeling their way. But perhaps the most significant thing he did for Nelson was to advise local growers to plant with phylloxera-resistant rootstocks – prudent advice which almost without exception they have followed.

Nelson is a paradise for birds. They start the summer season feasting on orchard fruits, then move into the vineyards determined to gorge on ripening grapes. Fending off their large populations is a major headache for local winegrowers. Out of desperation, some invest in electronic bird-scaring devices that scream out the terrified cries of birds under attack. Each of these very effective gadgets – which cost $10–12,000 – can be set to mimic the sounds of the breeds of birds plaguing vineyards at any one time. Winegrowers who use them still net their vines, but don't need to close up the nets so tightly.

Northland, Auckland and Waiheke

Lucky Aucklanders. Living in New Zealand's major cosmopolitan city – situated within easy reach of dozens of first-class wineries crafting sophisticated styles of wine – they're spoilt for choice.

With vineyards scattered between Kaitaia in the north, Papakura in the south and Waiheke Island out in the Hauraki Gulf, this expansive winegrowing district – not really a single region at all, rather a disparate collection of many – inhabits the sum total of three per cent of New Zealand's vineyard area. But small is often beautiful, of course, and no more so than in the case of upper North Island winegrowing.

The Auckland and Northland regions' main claims to fame are their rich, robust Bordeaux-style reds and ripe, rounded Chardonnays, wines which at their best number among the finest made anywhere in the country. And since their local winegrowers are an adventuresome bunch, you'll also find a medley of other fine wines grown here. Among them are styles not yet commonly produced in New Zealand, such

Goldwater Estate, on Waiheke Island, looking out to Putiki Bay. The country's biggest city, Auckland, consumes most of the domestic market's supply of Auckland-produced wine.

as exotic, spicy Viognier from Ascension, varietal Cabernet Francs forged by Kumeu's Harrier Rise and Italian-style Amarone (a traditional dry red wine made from raisined grapes left to dry on racks for several months) crafted by Enzo Bettio at Vin Alto in Clevedon.

Main winegrowing districts – Northland and Auckland

Auckland's vineyards largely lie in pockets of flat land on the drier east coast or in the shelter of the western Waitakere Ranges. Head north to small but rapidly expanding Matakana and most of the vineyards sit on warm, gentle north-facing slopes. Venture south to Clevedon and you'll encounter a few vineyards situated on steep hillsides – so steep, in fact, that tractors need army tank-like tracks, not wheels, to traverse their terrains.

(1) **Northland** The birthplace of New Zealand winegrowing, today it is home to several vineyards, scattered over three main areas: Kaitaia in the far north; around the Bay of Islands on the east coast; and near the city of Whangarei. Warm, ripe reds (Cabernet Sauvignon and Merlot) and ripe, full-bodied Chardonnays are among Northland's special highlights.

(2) **Matakana and Mahurangi** Located about an hour's drive north of Auckland, this premium wine-producing district crafts excellent, ripe, robust, Bordeaux reds, sophisticated Chardonnays and classy Pinot Gris to name but a few of its drawcards. Local growers partly credit the district's pinkish-red, iron-rich, granulated, free-draining soils for the flavour intensities they achieve in their grapes.

(3) **North-west Auckland (Kumeu/Huapai/ Waimauku)** Populated with wineries producing quality wines, such as ripe, rounded Chardonnays and harmonious Merlots and Cabernet Sauvignons. While producers such as Kumeu River and Harrier Rise craft their wines from locally grown fruit, others source grapes from further south. The region escapes some of the rain that falls on West Auckland.

(4) **West Auckland (Henderson Valley)** The traditional heartland of Auckland winemaking, a little over 30 years ago the Henderson-Oratia district vied with Hawke's Bay as the country's largest wine producer. Today, it remains home to some of the oldest, most well-respected names in New Zealand wine – Babich Wines and Collards to name two – even though their

Latu Mitwood, a team leader at Montana's bottling hall in Tamaki.

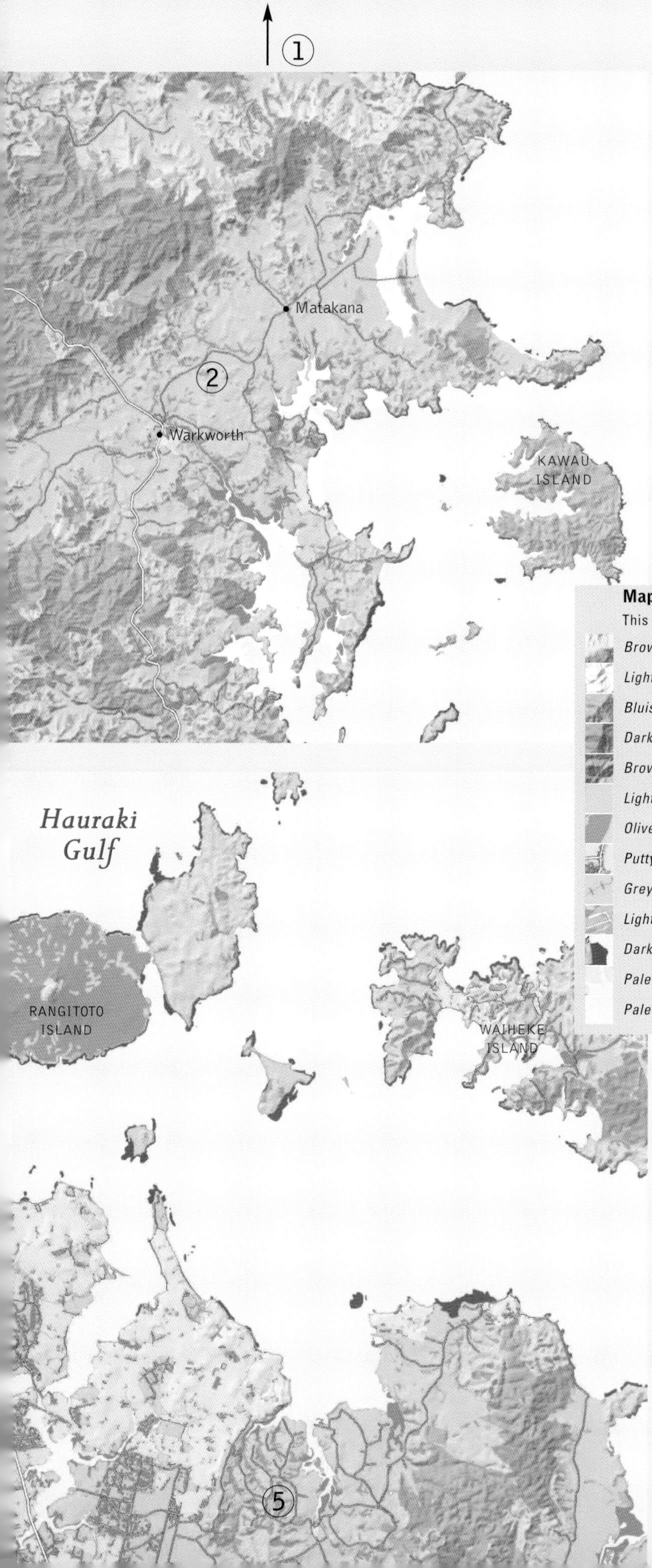

Babich Wines' 'showcase' vineyard adjacent to their winery in Henderson. Virtually all the company's grapes are now grown in Hawke's Bay and Marlborough.

Map key

This map is oriented to true North

- *Brown+grey: mountains*
- *Light brown: hills*
- *Bluish-green: plantation forest*
- *Dark green: native forest*
- *Brown/green: scrub*
- *Light green: lowland area*
- *Olive green: swamp area*
- *Putty: towns; white+grey: roads*
- *Grey (hatches): rail lines*
- *Light grey: river beds/shingle*
- *Dark grey (coastal): rocks*
- *Pale yellow: sand*
- *Pale blue: sea, lakes and rivers*

1
Matakana
2
Warkworth
KAWAU ISLAND
Hauraki Gulf
RANGITOTO ISLAND
WAIHEKE ISLAND
5

vineyards now reside hundreds of kilometres away in places such as Hawke's Bay and Marlborough. New Zealand's traditional Sherry and Port producers still base themselves in West Auckland, too.

4 Auckland city, South Auckland and Clevedon

Auckland houses two of New Zealand's largest wine producers – Montana and Villa Maria – each of whom centralise the bottling, distribution, sales and marketing sides of their businesses in the city, as well as some aspects of their winemaking. Villa Maria also operates a 20-hectare vineyard on the Ihumatao Peninsula, near Auckland's airport. Further south in Clevedon small pockets of specialist vineyards managed for low crops produce, for the most part, premium reds such as Merlot, Cabernet Sauvignon, Malbec and Syrah, as well as a smattering of luscious sweet wines (from dried Chardonnay and Pinot Gris) and ripe fruit-flavoured whites. Most of Clevedon's vineyards are situated on north-facing hillsides, where the majority of the fruit is hand picked. Spot a collection of Italian varieties planted here – at Vin Alto, Montepulciano is now the dominant variety.

Northland and Auckland – key varieties and styles

Chardonnay Ripe, rounded, tropical fruit-flavoured wines.

Merlot Spicy, earthy wines with soft, ripe, plum-like characters.

Cabernet Sauvignon Rich and concentrated fruit flavours.

Cabernet Franc Usually blended with the other Bordeaux reds (although Harrier Rise makes a varietal Cabernet Franc with savoury, earthy characters and fine tannins).

Pinot Gris The upper North Island produces two main styles – wines with ripe stone-fruit (more Alsatian-style) characters at one end of the spectrum and at the other end dry, austere, quince-flavoured (North Italian) styles.

Pinotage Among the country's best: rich, soft, oily-textured wines with typically smoky, meaty characters.

Syrah Ripe-flavoured, elegant European style Syrahs (as opposed to big, gutsy New World styles).

Climate

Like their counterparts in every other region of the country, the local winegrowers in the Northland and Auckland regions have their own sets of climatic challenges to deal with. In these warm, humid climates, the summers are sticky and consequently the risk of fungal disease is high. Yet growers can mitigate the effects of humidity by planting on sites exposed to gentle, drying winds and by training vines to grow open, airy canopies. Northland shares a similarly humid climate to Auckland, but also boasts the country's highest annual mean temperature.

Annual sunshine hours (mean)		
	2086*	Northland (Kaitaia Observatory)
	1999**	South Auckland (Mangere)
Annual rainfall (mean)		
	1350 mm*	Northland (Kaitaia Observatory)
	1334 mm*	Whangarei (Aero AWS)
	1342 mm*	West Auckland (Henderson River Pk)
Growing degree days (mean)		
	1619	Northland (Kaitaia Observatory)
	1637	Whangarei (Aero AWS)
	1597	West Auckland (Henderson River Pk)
	1583	South Auckland (Mangere)

*1993–2002 **1988–1997

Soil types

Auckland: Mainly shallow clays over hard, silty-clay sub-soils or sandy loams. The hillside vineyards of Matakana and Clevedon districts share similar free-draining soil structures.

Northland: Soils vary throughout the region from shallow clay soils over sandy-clay loam sub-soils to free-draining volcanic structures.

Typical vintage

Second week of March: Pinot Noir; late March: Chardonnay; third week of April: Cabernet Sauvignon.

Trends

New Zealand Winegrowers forecasts a steady 15–16 per cent growth rate for Auckland and Northland over the next couple of years. Locals expect that growth to be driven by small producers seeking to combine the regions' enviable lifestyle opportunities with winemaking.

History

Northland is the birthplace of New Zealand wine. The Reverend Samuel Marsden planted New Zealand's first grapevines at the Kerikeri Mission in 1819. In the 1830s British Resident James Busby made the country's first wines at Waitangi. Later that century two Englishmen, coppersmith Charles Levet and his son William, achieved another first by becoming the earliest winemakers to earn their living solely from winemaking. They planted their vines against manuka stakes in the Kaipara Harbour district and built their winery in the 1860s. By the 1880s the Levets were rowing barrels of wine eight miles down a nearby tidal creek to Port Arthur for shipping to Onehunga where they were then sold at Israel Wendel's Wine Bodega, in Karangahape Road, Auckland. Winemaking provided the Levets with a livelihood for more than 40 years, but it wasn't an easy life for them or their fellow winemakers struggling to do likewise. The British immigrants who made up a large slice of the population had, for the most part, no tradition of drinking wine and so the market was small. Meanwhile, the temperance movement's influence brought about increasingly restrictive liquor

Wadier Corban and his father, A. A. Corban, crushing one of their earliest vintages.

The Corbans family homestead and the Corbans mobile wine shop.

legislation which only hampered the wine industry's course.

From around the 1900s, Auckland's wine industry, along with Hawke's Bay's, was one of the two most important winegrowing districts in the country. Immigrant winemakers from Mediterranean regions dominated the late 19th century and first half of the 20th century's wine scene. Many had departed Dalmatia to dig for kauri gum in the fields of Northland, their dream to save enough money to bring their families out to New Zealand and then buy land on which to carve out the orchards and vineyards that would support them. Clusters of immigrants eventually settled in West Auckland: Josip Babich of Babich Wines and Stephan Yelas of Pleasant Valley Vineyards, both in Henderson, for instance. But the winemaking enterprise which was to lead the New Zealand scene for decades to come was born out of a tiny four-acre vineyard planted by Assid Abraham (A. A.) Corban at Henderson in 1902 and named Mt Lebanon. A. A., a Lebanese immigrant who arrived here in 1891, had peddled jewellery in the goldfields and later operated haberdashery shops to raise the capital to bring his family to this country and buy his little plot of land. From such modest beginnings, Corbans later grew to become the first nationally distributed New Zealand wine brand. What's more, the company pioneered a number of then modern winemaking techniques in New Zealand, such as temperature-controlled fermentation in stainless steel tanks and the Charmat process for sparkling wines. It dominated the industry until the early 1960s and was eventually absorbed into the Montana fold in 2000, but the Corbans wine brand lives on today.

Immigrants with winemaking aspirations continued to flow into West Auckland during the first half of the 20th century, among them Yugoslav Ivan Yukich who planted his vineyard 'Montana' in the hills above Titirangi in 1934 and whose sons Frank and Maté expanded the enterprise under the company Montana Wines; George Mazuran who started producing Ports and Sherries at Mazuran Vineyards in Henderson in 1938, and which still specialises in fortified wines today; the Brajkovich family, who in the 1940s planted vines in Kumeu, then sold their wines under the label San Marino Vineyards and continue to produce fine wines today under the Kumeu River Wines label; and Nikola Nobilo who founded a vineyard at Huapai during World War II in 1943 when an influx of thirsty American servicemen proved just the financial tonic the wine industry needed; now it's the large Nobilo Wine Group, purchased by BRL Hardy in 2000 (which itself merged with Constellation Wine Group in 2003).

The region's winegrowers produced predominantly fortified wines: substitute Ports and Sherries and various concoctions of so-called wine cocktails and liqueurs largely made from North American-European hybrid grapes. But by the 1960s table wine consumption was on the rise and Auckland's winemakers were busy supplying the market with wines known by their Old World names: 'Hock' (dry white wine), Moselle (semi-sweet wine), Sauternes (sweet wine), Burgundy (soft reds) and Claret (firm reds). Come the 1970s, larger producers looking to expand further were eyeing regions south for large tracts of land that would suit viticulture. Corbans and Montana pioneered contract grapegrowing in Gisborne, and Montana made a heroic leap of faith into Marlborough in 1973. Today, a number of New Zealand's largest wine companies base themselves in Auckland, but grow grapes and make wine in other parts of the country.

Main winegrowing districts – Waiheke Island

Colourful Waiheke Island, with its blue waters, lush green native bush and vibrant art and café scene produces some of New Zealand's most impressive red wines.

Local winegrowers claim it is the only place in the country that over the past quarter century has ripened Cabernet Sauvignon every year. But to anyone dreaming of growing grapes here, the advice from those already doing so with great success is 'don't give up your day job'. Yields are low, the island's hilly terrain costly to cultivate. And yet, these same Waiheke winegrowers say with wide, satisfied grins on their faces, the results are worth all the hard work. 'Waiheke is one of the few places in the world that can produce very fine, silky, complex Bordeaux-style red wines based on Cabernet Sauvignon, Merlot and Cabernet Franc,' says Kim Goldwater, of Goldwater Estate, the founding father of Waiheke Island winegrowing. In fact, adds Kim, if there's one unifying thread which ties all the island's wine styles together, it's their fine structure.

1. Far Eastern end of the island Especially renowned for intensely flavoured whites and good fuller-bodied Chardonnays. Slightly cooler than the central areas of the island.

2. Western end of the island (including central west and Onetangi Valley) Acclaimed in the main for its ripe, concentrated, well-structured reds and rich, full-bodied, generous Chardonnays.

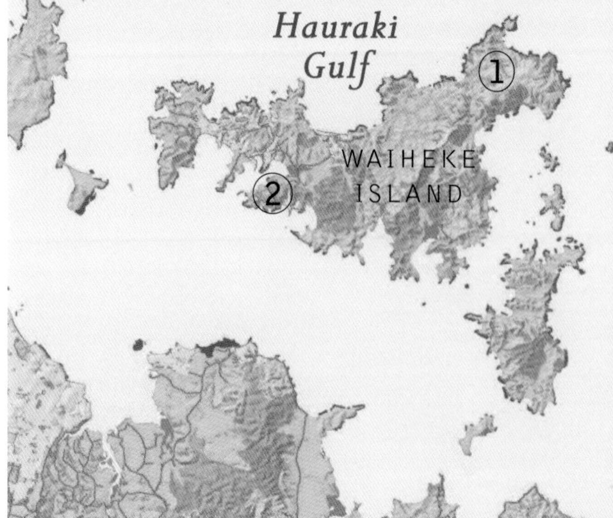

Climate

Waiheke's climate is similar to Bordeaux, except that in spring the island warms up earlier and more gradually than Bordeaux does, according to Kim Goldwater. Locals have long boasted the island enjoys a warmer, drier maritime climate than mainland Auckland. While weather statistics don't appear to support the claims, they may hold true for individual microclimates. The nights remain agreeably warm in summer so that effectively the grapes work a 'double shift', that is, the grapes continue to ripen through the night. Sea breezes help keep fungal diseases at bay.

Annual rainfall (mean)	1342 mm* (Awaawaroa Valley)
Growing degree days (mean, calculated on four years)	1575 (Awaawaroa Valley)

*1993–2002

The Stony Batter Estate vineyard on Waiheke Island.

Soil types

Largely comprise old, extremely weathered sedimentary rock, littered with pea-sized manganese nodules which not only promote good drainage but also impart the wines with good colour, minerally characters and elegance.

Waiheke Island – key varieties and styles

Cabernet Sauvignon Intensely concentrated, well-structured wines.

Merlot Wines with very ripe flavours, fine tannins, good weight and well-integrated acidity.

Chardonnay Rich, broad, full-bodied styles of Chardonnay.

Waiheke also grows a little Cabernet Franc, Malbec, Syrah and Sauvignon Blanc displaying the typical Waiheke characteristics – ripe, rounded, well-structured wines.

Typical vintage

Begins with Chardonnay at end of February and ends first week of April with Cabernet Sauvignon.

Trends

Land on Waiheke is expensive, but vineyard growth is expected to continue for as long as space permits and the island's lifestyle attracts wealthy investors. Experimental plantings of Italian varieties Sangiovese and Barolo are under way. Italian viticulturists believe Waiheke is too cool for either variety, but it's possible the island's relatively long growing season may compensate for its cooler climate.

History

In 1978 Kim and Jeanette Goldwater, of Goldwater Estate, were the first to plant *Vitis vinifera* vines on Waiheke and did so against all advice from viticultural experts of the day. They were followed by Stephen White of Stonyridge in 1982 and Doug and Ann Hamilton of Peninsula Estate in 1984. The Dunleavys of Te Motu arrived in 1988. Most of Waiheke's other vineyards have only been in existence since 1995.

Waikato and Bay of Plenty

The lush, fertile farming landscapes are home to several wineries producing excellent wines, a trickle of them from locally grown grapes, the balance sourced from further south.

Soft, rounded, mouth-filling wines with ripe fruit flavours sums up the characteristic of wines grown in vineyards scattered across the Waikato and the Bay of Plenty. These regions have enjoyed great success with locally grown, tropical fruit-flavoured Chardonnays and Sauvignon Blancs as well as full-bodied Cabernet Sauvignons and also, in Waikato, sweet, botrytised dessert wines – the last benefiting from the relatively humid climate.

The districts' larger-scale producers tend to source most, if not all, of their fruit from other regions. Tauranga's highly acclaimed Mills Reef, for instance, doesn't grow a single vine in the Bay of Plenty, but instead grows the majority of its fruit in Hawke's Bay. Why locate their winery, restaurant and cellar door miles away in Bay of Plenty then? Because it makes commercial sense, says co-owner, Tim Preston: Tauranga is a major tourism region, halfway between their vineyards in Hawke's Bay and their main domestic market in Auckland.

Climate

While Waikato has relatively high humidity and annual rainfall, by the time the autumnal rains arrive, the region's winegrowers have usually already harvested their predominantly early-ripening crops. Bay of Plenty is sunny, warm and mild. Districts such as Galatea near Murupara in south-eastern Bay of Plenty experience large diurnal temperature variations: local grower Bob Covell says it is not uncommon for them to experience hot 23°c days followed by cold 1°c nights, conditions well suited to Pinot Noir and Chardonnay.

Top left: The Waikare vineyard, near Te Kauwhata, planted by winegrower Ross Goodin in mainly Cabernet Sauvignon, Sauvignon Blanc and some Merlot. Left: Firstland Vineyards, in the Mangatawhiri Valley, grows most of its grapes in regions further south. Almost all of its wines are destined for the export market.

Main winegrowing districts

Waikato and Bay of Plenty's vineyards are thinly spread and together account for one per cent of the national vineyard area. Several of the country's important wineries base themselves in the districts and source most or all of their grapes elsewhere.

Annual sunshine hours (mean)	2024* Waikato (Ruakura) 2390* BOP (Tauranga Aero AWS)
Annual rainfall (mean)	1198* Waikato (Ruakura) 1178* BOP (Tauranga Aero AWS)
Growing degree days (mean)	1255 Waikato (Ruakura) 1432 BOP (Tauranga Aero AWS)

*1987–1996

Soil types

Waikato: Mainly fertile clay loams, which generally require good viticultural management to control vine vigour and keep vine canopies open and airy. Also outcrops of river stones where rivers have flowed.

Bay of Plenty: Volcanic loams are common.

Typical vintage

Mid-March: Pinot Noir; third week of March: Chardonnays; end of April: late-harvest and botrytised wines.

Trends

Pinot Gris has growth potential for Waikato and Bay of Plenty. So, too, does Malbec, believes local grower Ross Goodin ONZM, one of the founding members of the New Zealand Grape Growers Council.

History

The New Zealand Viticulture Research Station, built at Te Kauwhata in 1903, was where government viticulturist Romeo Bragato experimented with the classical varieties. In the 1980s, viticulturist Dr Richard Smart was one of those who conducted a raft of varietal trial work at the station, now the site of Rongopai Wines.

Waikato and Bay of Plenty – key varieties and styles

Chardonnay At its best, gold-medal standard with soft acidity (without a large portion of the wine requiring malolactic fermentation) and tropical fruit flavours.

Cabernet Sauvignon Full-bodied wines with ripe flavours.

Sauvignon Blanc Tropical fruit-flavoured, full-bodied styles.

Sweet botrytised dessert wines One of the region's specialities. Rongopai Wines produces two styles: a late-harvest, slightly botrytised wine and a fully botrytised wine, made from Riesling and Chardonnay.

Pinot Noir Not an easy variety to grow, nevertheless, Pinot Noir has unrealised potential for the district, believes winemaker, Mark Compton. The regions' styles tend to show dark berry fruit flavours and you may occasionally notice aromas of violets.

Sémillon Can produce powerful, yet elegant wines.

Marlborough propagation unit manager Arthur Collyns.

Gisborne viticulturist Warwick Bruce.

Hawke's Bay winemaker Tony Prichard.

Marlborough prur wrapper Stan Thc

Careers in wine

The propagation unit manager

During 2002, Montana's propagation unit in Blenheim was responsible for grafting 1.7 million vines. Of those, about 1.2 million developed into established plants and were distributed to various vineyards around the country for planting. The propagation unit's manager, Arthur Collyns, says anyone going into a role like his today needs a degree in horticulture, an aptitude for meticulous attention to detail and a flair for information management. 'If anyone were to inadvertently mix up the budwood clones, no one would know until the vines were producing fruit.'

The viticulturist

Viticulturists are the architects of the vineyards, the people whose insights and skills – capricious weather aside – determine the quality of the grapes grown and, to a large extent, the quality of our wines. Viticulturist Gary Woods puts it in a nutshell when he says of his role: 'I'm a flavour-maker.'

New Zealand viticulturists usually work on a bigger scale than their counterparts in France, growing a wider number of grape varieties on generally larger tracts of land than the vigneron. New Zealand winegrowers tend to share knowledge with one another on an open basis. Our wine industry is still young, hence the more our viticulturists collaborate with one another, the quicker New Zealand's collective winegrowing knowledge and experience develops. New Zealand viticulturists usually have either a degree in viticulture or a degree in horticulture followed by postgraduate work in winegrowing.

The winemaker

It is the winemaker's job to set the style of the wine and steer it towards that end goal. 'With every decision you take as a winemaker, you keep the style of wine you're aiming to make in mind,' says winemaker Tony Prichard. Winemakers have a huge range of options at their disposal as explained in the Winemaking chapter. Although some of the choices they may make individually have only a minor effect on the developing wine, add their combined effects together and they can have an enormous impact on the finished product. Tony likens the role of winemaker to that of his spare-time hobby of cabinetmaker. 'When I'm making a piece of furniture, I fix on the style of furniture I want to make first. If you use cheap, readily available wood, then no matter how good your skills as a cabinetmaker, at best you can only produce an average piece. On the other hand, if you take top-quality timber and shape it into a

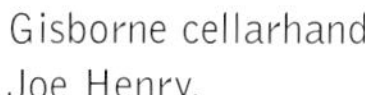

Gisborne cellarhand
Joe Henry.

Gisborne winery laboratory supervisor
Rehette Stoltz.

Auckland wine specialist
Philip Bothwell.

style of furniture that doesn't suit the timber, then the piece will be lacking.' The same is true of winemaking: the style of wine must suit the fruit. Winemaking, believes Tony, is roughly 80 per cent science and 20 per cent art. 'For the most part, you're making technical decisions, once again always staying focused on the end style you're aiming to create.' The majority of people embarking on a career in winemaking today have a degree in winemaking or biotechnology.

The pruner

While the basic principles of pruning can be taught quite quickly, the pruner probably needs to prune thousands of vines before they can be said to have mastered the art in terms of ability and speed. New Zealand's best pruners demonstrate their skills by competing in the national Silver Secateurs competition after qualifying as the top pruners in their respective regions.

The cellarhand

Like other cellarhands up and down the country, Gisborne cellarhand Joe Henry carries out many of the day-to-day jobs around the winery, such as racking and filtering, explained in the Winemaking chapter. What does Joe enjoy most about his work? 'The fact that there's always something new to learn,' he says, even after 14 years' experience. Ongoing training is part and parcel of the job, with the work of the cellarhand now the subject of unit standards under the New Zealand Qualifications Authority.

The laboratory technician

Winery laboratory technicians analyse developing wines daily throughout the winemaking process to make sure their progress is on track. Says laboratory supervisor Rehette Stoltz: 'We start out with the "raw juice", work with it all year and see it through to the finished product. In a way, the wine is like a baby and you have a hand in its development.' Most winery laboratory workers have a science degree or at least considerable laboratory experience.

The wine specialist

Philip Bothwell counts himself lucky. He has made a career out of his passion – enthusing others about wine. As a wine specialist for Montana Wines, it is his job to share his sound knowledge of premium wines with many of the country's leading wine retailers and restaurateurs. 'Ninety per cent of what I do is about bringing the wine to life for people in the wine trade. If someone is going to spend $100 on a bottle of wine, they want to know what makes it special,' says Philip.

Viticulture: a balancing act

How good a wine tastes depends largely on the calibre of grapes used to make it. Winemakers can't produce great wines out of anything less than great grapes, no matter how many clever winemaking techniques they wield.

Growing the best fruit

If all the best wines are made, first and foremost, in the vineyard, then what does it take to produce the requisite top-quality fruit?

Ask winegrowers and they'll talk about the overriding importance of growing 'balanced vines' – vines where the ratios of canes, shoots, leaves and fruit on a plant strike a happy equilibrium, giving the grapes an odds-on chance of ripening to their best advantage.

To the uninitiated, that may sound as simple as growing a cracking crop of garden runner beans, but nothing could be further from the truth. New Zealand winegrowing, or viticulture, encompasses a highly complex body of practical and scientific knowledge, one that has taken some giant strides forward during the last 20 years and deserves a large chunk of the credit for the advancement of this country's wines.

Looking ahead over the next 20 years, both winegrowers and winemakers agree that significant gains in the quality of New Zealand wines will likely spring from making further research headway in the vineyard, rather than in the winery.

In essence, viticulture is all about one thing: getting the grapes to reach full ripeness. In hotter climates than ours, fruit ripeness (as measured by sugar accumulation) happens without too much persuasion from winegrowers. But in New Zealand's cool climate, winegrowers (or viticulturists) have to work much harder at encouraging the fruit to ripen.

Bear in mind that at harvest, wine grapes are extraordinarily ripe – about one-third sweeter, in fact, than table grapes and almost twice as sweet as a juicy ripe Fuji apple. It's the tiny increases in ripeness that come towards the end of the season that are hardest to win from grapes, but which make all the difference to the quality of the wine at the end of the day. Viticulturists do their utmost to help a raft of separate ripening (or maturation) processes occur – among them flavour, colour and sugar development, acid reduction and tannin maturation. Ideally, each individual aspect of ripeness reaches its peak, or as close to perfection as it's likely to reach, at the point when the viticulturist decides to harvest. Viticulture is something of a balancing act and viticulturists are its jugglers.

The challenge to produce ripe, top-quality fruit has seen New Zealand viticulture evolve markedly in the last two decades. In the 1980s, viticulturists turned much of their focus onto the vine canopy (the area within and immediately around the shoots, leaves, fruits and general framework of the vine). New canopy-management techniques, promoted by those such as Dr Richard Smart, trained vines to grow on trellising systems which opened up their canopies, increased the grapes' exposure to sunlight, decreased the incidence of fungal diseases and improved yields.

In the 1990s, as viticulturists started paying more attention to the relationship between vine balance, yield and wine quality, many winegrowers gained renewed respect for some of the older conventions of viticulture. Having learned through experience that lower yields can be an important aspect of producing superior-quality grapes, some traditions made a come-back. Pruning for vine balance, where each vine is cut back to its ideal growth potential, rather than laying down too many buds, is now standard practice, for instance.

The move to less fertile, low-vigour sites, which began with the founding of Montana's Marlborough vineyards in the 1970s and gained ground with the establishment of vineyards on the stony, infertile Gimblett Gravels area of Hawke's Bay in the 1980s, continued to gather momentum during the 1990s. Today it's the key driver influencing site selection. Soils with lower fertility can produce naturally balanced vines – and hence superior-quality fruit – without the need for intensive vine canopy-management techniques.

In the new millennium, two things are happening. Firstly, as our winegrowers continue to develop much greater levels of understanding about individual vineyards and blocks within vineyards, they're focusing attention on adapting viticulture management styles to suit the characteristics of each site with the aim of optimising their potential. Secondly, winegrowers are managing sites in more environmentally sustainable ways. For, despite all the advancements of modern winegrowing, there has been one constant: the natural environment has always been – and will always be – the viticulturist's biggest asset. Looking after the long-term needs of our soils, streams, aquifers, microbes and living organisms is imperative for the future health of our wine industry.

The best wines boast complex layers of flavours...

flavours which, for the large part, are grown in the vineyard, not crafted in the winery. By choosing a range of different sites, planting systems, rootstocks and varietal clones, today's viticulturists can grow a diverse spectrum of flavours for winemakers to weave their magic with.

Wines grown in single vineyards express an individual terroir.

But terroir expression isn't the be-all and end-all of winemaking. Only a portion of New Zealand's wines set out to make big, bold terroir statements. Others, including some of our country's finest, are blends which originate from several vineyards – fusion wines if you like – where the whole is greater than the sum of the parts.

The best grapes come from struggling vines: true or false?

False. Stressed vines, whose vine vigour – or vegetative growth – drops perilously low, struggle to ripen their fruit and barely manage to yield even second-rate grapes. Well-balanced vines grow the best grapes.

Tapping into terroir

The separate elemental influences that make up a vineyard's terroir can literally include everything under the sun: the soils, climate, rainfall, sunlight, drainage, aspect and topography – indeed, any environmental factor you care to mention. It's the viticulturist's job to tap into the terroir and amplify its expression in the grapes.

Climate

In the world of viticulture, climate is a subject in its own right, one that viticulturists must study with the same intensity as astronomers study the stars.

Big-picture regional climate (or macroclimate) statistics tell winegrowers next to nothing about what's going on in their individual vineyards. It is the mesoclimate inside the vineyard and/or the broader areas and the microclimate in or immediately around the vine canopy which influence grapes' development.

Wines made from grapes grown in excessively warm climates or hot vintages tend to be overly soft (or flabby) due to their low acidity. Conversely, wines made from grapes with poor measures of physiological ripeness, grown in overly cool vintages, typically have higher degrees of acidity and unpleasant 'green' flavours (since at temperatures below 10°C the rate of photosynthesis decreases to almost zero and no sugar accumulation occurs). Other physiological ripening processes are also hindered by low temperatures.

Fewer fluctuations between 24-hour day- and night-time temperatures (diurnal variations) throughout the season favour the development of aromas, flavours and colours in the fruit, it's said. But you only have to look at the intensity of flavours in Sauvignon Blanc from Marlborough to see this is no hard and fast rule. (See Marlborough climate, page 136.)

Vineyards closer to New Zealand's coastline and exposed to the moderating influences of sea breezes generally experience cooler days and warmer nights, that is, less diurnal variation. Hence, frosts are fewer and less severe. Being subject to lower daytime temperatures and, consequently, lower rates of photosynthesis the vine's growing cycles can stretch out by several weeks. Bud burst tends to happen in early spring but the grapes may not ripen until several weeks behind their counterparts on warmer inland sites.

Sunshine hours

The best vintages stay sunny and warm throughout the growing season. In early summer, sunshine and warmth aid good fruit set (or self-pollination) and encourage new shoot growth. Warm, sunny conditions throughout early summer also promote fruitfulness in the developing buds. High levels of sunshine during autumn allow sugars to rapidly accumulate in the fruit and build good colour in their skins. Viticulturists train vines to grow in ways that promote exposure to sunlight.

Rainfall distribution

Climates with generally settled summers and autumns suit grapes best. Warm rains can cause fungal diseases, as well as promote the growth of a jumbled mass of vine vegetation (which shades developing clusters). Rain around veraison (the beginning of ripening) and harvest time dilutes the grapes' flavours and sugars. From veraison onwards, vines need enough moisture to stay stress-free, but not so much rain as to cause the grapes' thinning skins to split. Heavy autumnal rains pose a serious threat, particularly to thin-skinned varieties. Training vines to grow open, airy canopies minimises the effects of prolonged wet spells.

Aspect and topography

North-facing slopes boast a string of positive attributes, including good drainage and optimum sunlight interception. If sufficiently elevated, they allow cold, frost-causing air to drain away. In contrast, south-facing slopes are likely to be cooler given their reduced sunlight interception and exposure to cool southerly air flows. But slopes may suffer from erosion and access issues which present management difficulties. Low-lying gullies or basins are more frost prone.

Altitude

The higher the altitude of a vineyard, the lower its temperature. In a cool-climate country like New Zealand, that fact alone limits where new vineyard developments occur. Higher altitude sites experience later bud burst as well as later ripening and may be prone to harsh winds. But, on the positive side, they may experience improved drainage of cold air away from the vines.

Frost risk

Jack Frost may as well be Jack the Ripper as far as vines are concerned. Frosts can wipe out a vineyard's entire spring bud burst, destroying most of the season's crop potential. Autumn frosts can kill vine leaves before the grapes fully ripen. North-facing slopes are generally less prone to frosts. Bare soils and soils whose cover crops are mown short retain more daytime heat which they radiate at night, thus reducing the severity of frost damage. When frosts do strike, windmills, helicopters and heat-emitting frost buckets are some of the devices winegrowers use to warm air temperatures, while turning on water sprinklers protects the vines from freeze damage.

Wind stress

Gentle breezes are friends of the vine. They help dry the microclimate and deter fungal diseases. Breezes also open up the inner canopy to shafts of sunlight. But harsh winds can blow vines' flowers off at flowering (thus slashing crop potential), snap weaker canes, break growing tips and damage leaves. Cold southerly winds close leaf pores and hinder photosynthesis. Putting in windbreaks reduces wind risks.

Hail

Hailstorms at any time of the season can shred leaves and bunches, and break canes, and may create ideal conditions for botrytis bunch rot.

Top left: Young shoots and bunches can be killed by spring frosts which turn the leaves and bunches chocolate-brown to black within hours. Left: On account of New Zealand's fiercely strong sunlight (or solar radiation), sun-exposed grapes can become 5–8°C hotter than the surrounding atmospheric temperature. Leaf plucking during periods of high temperatures can cause sunburn (cell damage) to the grapes' skins.

Felton Road Wines in Bannockburn, Central Otago, is situated in a north-facing gentle valley. The natural gullies guide cold, frosty air through the vineyard away from the vines.

Warm soil temperatures play a key role in ripening the grapes. Stony soils absorb heat from the sun during the day, then radiate their stored warmth onto the vines at night, giving the grapes about two more hours of valuable ripening time over a 24-hour period. Soil temperatures below the ground also play an important part in controlling vine growth.

Soils

Compared to most fruit crops, grapevines ask for very little from the earth. Drought-tolerant plants, they grow successfully in a diverse range of soils, many of which – on the surface anyway – don't even resemble soil. Look at the photograph on the left and at first glance you could be forgiven for thinking it's a rocky shoreline, not the highly acclaimed Stoneleigh vineyard in Marlborough.

- Vines planted in fertile ground can grow like topsy (unless the viticulturist intervenes) producing masses of canes and leaves at the expense of developing and ripening their fruit.

- Soils of low to moderate fertility produce naturally balanced vines. In these soils, vines put less energy into producing a luxuriant mass of canes and leaves and more effort into ripening the grapes.

- New Zealand has an enormous variety of soils because, geologically speaking, it's a young country. Hence our soils are still in the throes of being weathered by climate and vegetation.

- Our soils include everything from tiny clay particles to rough-hewn stones. Many comprise coarse materials – gravels laid down by rivers, for example – ideal for winegrowing due to their vine-devigorating, low to moderate fertility and moisture-regulating, free-draining structure.

- New Zealand's soils are well-balanced from a pH perspective – neither excessively acidic or alkaline – and thus allow good nutrient uptake by the vine.

- It's not uncommon to find four or five different types of soils within one small vineyard, a situation winegrowers in geologically old countries, such as our neighbour, Australia, would less likely encounter.

- Some soils perform better than others in certain years. Hence, the winegrower with a range of soils has a distinct advantage over another working with a more homogeneous set.

The soils pictured above on the banks of the Awatere Valley in Marlborough comprise silt loam topsoil over free-draining, stony riverbed deposits and deeper subsoils of clay. It strikes an interesting balance between fertile silts, devigorating gravels and stones and heavy, moisture-retaining clays.

Winegrowers may plant cover crops in their vineyards to improve soil structure and, on fertile sites, control vine vigour. Fescue (pictured at Graham Johnson's Waipaoa Vineyard in Gisborne) is a popular devigorating cover crop grown in New Zealand.

Kym Rayner of Torlesse Wines has high hopes for Pinot Noir grown in these soils atop the hills of Waipara. Intriguingly, the soils' profile (right) looks as if it belongs at the bottom of a river terrace, not on a hilltop.

• Soils and climates always work in tandem with one another. For example, clay soils in hot, dry, drought-prone conditions can grow exceptionally good wines because their fine particles hold water and nutrients, releasing them to the vine in a slow, steady, drip-feed fashion. This protects plants from sudden, stressful changes to moisture or nutrient status. But in prolonged wet conditions those same clay soils can pose challenges – producing dense canopies, larger, weaker-flavoured berries and tight, disease-prone bunches. Indeed, if the vine remains waterlogged for more than a month it will probably die.

• Soil diversity can become a headache for viticulturists when there's too much variability within a single site, meaning they can't apply the same vine-management techniques throughout.

• Cover crops, irrigation, mulch, compost and fertiliser can modify how the soil influences the vine's development.

French vignerons (or winegrowers) believe in their souls that characteristics in soils show through directly in their wines. The flinty soils of Chablis – said to be responsible for the aromas of gunflint in that region's wines – is a case in point, they argue. New Zealand winegrowers have no doubt soils contribute to the development of aromas and flavours. But whether that's because of a direct relationship between the nutrition vines receive from soils or whether it's due to the way the soils affect vine growth is yet to be established. 'I believe there's an element of both involved, ' maintains Montana's national vineyard manager, Tony Hoksbergen. Not that any conclusive evidence yet backs up claims that vines draw minerals from the soils in such a way that one can taste them in the wine. We haven't yet the technology to test the sorts of beliefs New Zealand's first winemaker, James Busby, reported from France back in 1825: 'a sandy soil will, in general, produce a delicate wine, the calcareous soil a spirituous wine, the decomposed granite a brisk wine.' Time will tell if there's something in it.

Birth of a vineyard

New vineyards are usually planted in winter or spring so that the fledgling vines can make the most of the warm growing season ahead. There are many ways to set up and plant a vineyard – the following steps outline the most common techniques used when developing a larger New Zealand vineyard.

The 10 key steps

1. Clearing the land Most new vineyards are planted on former sheep and cattle territory, cleared of its farming vestiges. The more enlightened winegrowers leave any native trees and shrubs intact.

2. Marking out the vineyard Surveyors mark out the vineyard on the ground using pegs delineating the beginning and end of each row to be planted. The soil may need some lime to bring it to neutral pH. Applying fertiliser (pictured below) at this stage gives the young vines a good head start, too.

3. Ripping the soils Bulldozers equipped with lasers to guide them in straight lines down the marked-out rows use a long metal tooth to 'rip' or crack open narrow trenches up to one metre deep into the soil's surface. 'Ripping' opens up compacted soil so young vines' root systems can establish themselves quickly.

4. Cultivation Discing and cultivating equipment, towed by tractors, turns the soil over, breaking it into fine particles. It may be rolled into a flat surface, but retaining the natural contours preserves the integrity of the soil's structure, fertility and organic matter.

5. Marking the plot out If the rows have been mapped out in the usual north/south orientation, the next job is to score evenly spaced, laser-guided lines across the soil's surface in an east/west direction, dissecting the row lines and creating a grid across the site. The points where grid lines intersect mark where the plants and posts are to go.

6. Planting the vines Laser-guided, tractor-towed planters follow the planting lines and make planting furrows in the ground. The planter operator drops the vine into the soil at the intersection of the grid lines and the planter machine closes the furrows and compacts the soil. Cover crops are often planted at this point, too.

7. Irrigation (left) If the site needs an irrigation system (see page 229), it may either be installed now, or alternatively, prior to planting.

Vineyard workers at Montana's Camshorn vineyard in Waipara.

8. Bringing in the posts Vineyard workers lay the posts out at the junctures on the grid. Post-driving equipment rams the posts into the ground. Lastly, the 'strainers' (larger, sturdier posts at the ends of each row) and their stays are put into place.

9. Wiring up the posts Spinning jennies mounted on tractors unravel coils of wire down the rows. Next, the wires are either stapled or nailed to the posts. Some wires, called fruiting wires, are fixed into a permanent position with staples. Others, called foliage wires or floating wires, supported by nails, can be height adjusted as foliage grows. Modern vineyards use about 30 kilometres of wire per hectare planted.

10. Protecting the young vines Grow-guards – plastic, breathable green jackets – shield vines from harsh elements (see opposite). In the coolest wine-growing regions, viticulturists may protect the vines with plastic tubes that extend up to the fixed fruiting wires. These create a hot-house-style environment in which the young vines develop more quickly. On the more fertile sites, new vines can yield their first small crop about 18 months after planting and their first full crop the following year.

Planting a vineyard is a labour-intensive job. A team of more than 50 people prepared and planted this 130-hectare vineyard at Camshorn in Waipara.

Chicory planted between the vines as a cover crop.

Selecting and designing a vineyard

As New Zealand's search for new wine styles and new terroir influences continues and as land on valley floors becomes increasingly scarce, many of our more recent vineyard developments are situated on hillsides.

Selecting a site

When looking for 'new' pastures, viticulturists where possible:

- Keep in mind the styles of wine they are aiming to grow.
- Carry out investigative work using electronic recorders positioned throughout the site to monitor microclimates over many months and analyse the soils' drainage, moisture-holding capacity, aeration, chemical make-up (such as fertility, pH levels and toxicities), nutrient-storing organic matter and so on.
- Gather the history about the sites' former uses.
- Assess the ease with which vineyard machinery can operate around the site.
- Ascertain how close the site is to an all-important skilled labour force and services.
- Make decisions about varieties, clones, rootstocks, spacings between the vines and rows, trellis-training systems, irrigation and so forth based on accumulated data.

Selecting rootstocks

Local research is still examining which rootstocks suit certain soils, conditions and clones best, but today's viticulturist chooses mainly devigorating rootstocks such as Riparia Gloire, 3309 Couderc, 101-14 Mgt and Schwarzmann. On low-fertility sites, So4 and 5C Teleki are often used.

Choosing clones

Viticulturists choose clones after assessing their ability to perform well at a particular site and/or their individual flavour characteristics.

- A vine clone is not genetically engineered. It's a plant born from a cutting taken off a single parent vine deemed to be good breeding material because it grows in an atypical fashion compared with other members of its varietal family.
- Planting a range of clones can give the winemaker extra blending options: for example, Chardonnay clone UCD 6's lemony flavours blend well with Chardonnay clone Bernard 95's pineapple flavours.
- New Zealand winegrowers tend to import new clonal material, mostly from California and France. A few home-grown clones have been selected here, however, such as Chardonnay Rua 1, which yields medium-sized bunches and moderate to large crops.
- Some varieties are much more prone to mutation than others, especially Pinot Noir. In Burgundy Pinot Noir is said to have more than 1000 clones.
- In France, it takes five years to observe, study and evaluate newly identified clones before only the most promising win official certification.

Deciding on row orientation

Most New Zealand vineyards are laid out in a north-south direction so the sun shines equally on both sides of the vines. When rows run east-west, the fruit on the northern side is well exposed to sunlight, but as summer progresses and the sun drifts further north, fruit on the southern side remains shaded and develops different, often less-ripe, flavour characteristics.

The distinctive Kumeu River Chardonnay vines, trained into the divided lyre system trellis, follow the undulating landscape.

Fixing vine and row spacing

In very old European vineyards, the distance between vines and rows of vines is often no more than a metre. But by the time most modern New Zealand vineyards were planted, machines had long replaced horse-power and rows had to be spaced far enough apart to leave room for tractors to manoeuvre. The majority were planted three metres between rows and 1.8 metres between vines. With the advent of customised vineyard machinery, the standard has shrunk to 2.4 to 2.7 metres between rows and 1.5 to 2.0 metres between vines. Now the trend is towards even tighter plantings, in a bid to grow even better wines. Over the next 10 years we'll see even more experimentation into vine densities.

Choosing cover crops

Cover crops – selected species of plants grown between the vines – are optional. They're mainly used to improve soil structure (aeration and water infiltration) as well as increase organic matter, but they may also augment a soil's biodiversity, help prevent erosion and, very importantly, may bring vine vigour under control. Cover crops sap soils of some of their moisture and nutrients, creating a competitive environment for vines in which they grow less-luxuriant canopies and, ultimately, better-quality grapes. The viticulture team at Church Road, Napier, helped pioneer the use of chicory, now widespread throughout New Zealand. A thirsty, deep-rooting plant, chicory deprives the vine of water and depletes the soil of some of its nitrogen, resulting in better-balanced vine growth on certain sites. Hawke's Bay reds grown on fertile soils, for example, do particularly well with chicory cover crops, displaying improved colour, tannin and acid balance. Fescue is another popular cover crop.

October 2002

January 2003

Propagating vines

Viticulturist Romeo Bragato first identified the sap-sucking vine louse, phylloxera, in New Zealand in 1895. He later showed local winegrowers how to graft the classical varieties onto the roots of phylloxera-resistant North American species of vines, but few followed his advice and the curse of phylloxera swept through the winegrowing regions of the day. Today, the majority of new New Zealand vineyards are planted with grafted vines on phylloxera-resistant rootstocks. And many of the older, phylloxera-affected vineyards have been pulled out and replanted.

Vineyard nursery workers cut rootstock material from selected species of 'mother vines' (above) which they have trained to grow long, horizontal canes.

Opposite: Millions of newly grafted vines are planted out (inset) in vineyard nurseries around the country each spring. By summer these same plants have grown significantly. Here vineyard workers check up on their charges in Montana's Spring Creek nursery in Marlborough.

Newly grafted Viognier vines, ready for planting in outdoor nurseries. New Zealand viticulturists are constantly trialling new rootstocks and clones in their ongoing quest to grow even better quality fruit.

Grafting vines

1 + 2: The lighter-coloured budwood (or scion) of the chosen classical variety is cut into a uniform size. Each scion bears a single bud. The darker-coloured rootstock wood of a North American-European hybrid is selected mainly on the basis of its ability to grow a root system that suits the site.

3 + 4: The nursery worker measures the thickness of the budwood and rootstock before grading and sorting them for size to the nearest half-millimetre diameter. A deep 'V' shape is cut into one end of a rootstock and the tip of a matching-sized budwood is cut to fit inside it.

5 + 6: The budwood and rootstock are taped together and dipped in hot wax to help the budwood retain moisture. In most cases, the cambium layer, found between the wood (xylem) and the green bark (phloem), produces healing tissue that covers the site of the graft union. This callus tissue grows together at the graft site and produces new cambium and, in time, new bark over the graft.

7, 8 + 9: The newly grafted plants are incubated in hot-houses for about six weeks, during which time they develop roots. (See picture 9, taken inside Montana's Fairhall propagation unit in Marlborough.) Once they're sturdy enough, the fledgling vines are normally planted in an outdoor nursery for one season. Only those with well-formed graft unions and well-developed root systems are later selected for planting in the vineyards.

New Zealand vines grow from cuttings to ensure they are true to type, although they are self-pollinating plants.

Vine and canopy management: nurturing the vines

Nature meets viticulture at the vine canopy, the area in and around the framework of the vine. It's to this tiny realm that viticulturists bring much of their skill, expertise and research resources.

In fact, revolutionary advances in New Zealand canopy management over the past 20 years can take credit for quantum leaps in the quality of our wine grapes – although even the most expert techniques cannot make up for a poorly sited vineyard.

Unlike many hot winegrowing regions in continental Europe, which grow low, bushy vines, cool-climate New Zealand vines are trained to grow tall on vertical trellis systems so that canes, leaves and developing fruit catch plenty of sunlight. Then they're trimmed during the growing season to maintain their canopies' exposure to sunlight and fresh, circulating air.

The vineyard worker is training a two-year-old vine's new spring growth, using a mechanical tape dispenser that loosely ties the shoots to the supporting wires.

As any backyard orchardist can tell you, the best-flavoured, richest-coloured fruit sits close to sun-exposed leaves and ripens sooner. Shaded fruit struggles to ripen, tastes more tart, is weaker in flavour and less vivid in colour than fruit grown on the sunny sides of trees.

Grapevines respond to sunlight in the same way. A well-exposed vine canopy bears leaves with higher photosynthetic capacity which feed the developing grapes with the sugars (or carbohydrates). Hence, well-exposed bunches are more likely to reach full flavour, colour, aroma and tannin development. But shady vines, with dense, dark, over-vigorous canopies, hide the fruit from the sun and hinder ripening.

On the other hand, sparse vines whose vigour is too low (often caused by not getting enough water, oxygen or nutrients) have no trouble catching the light, but lack the wherewithal to put it to good use. With too few leaves to carry out sufficient photosynthesis, the fruit doesn't ripen well at all.

So, once again, nurturing the vine to produce top-quality fruit comes back to balance. Too much of anything, even sunshine, doesn't necessarily serve the vine well. Winegrowers must take care not to overexpose the canopy to harsh sunlight or previously shaded leaves may suffer sunburn. Overexpose grapes (particularly white varieties and especially Chardonnay) and they will show increased levels of phenolic compounds which can cause bitterness in wine. Dappled light may suit some varieties best at certain sites. Indeed, growing a portion of the fruit in partial shade works well for Sauvignon Blanc – the shaded fruit's less ripe, more herbaceous flavours present winemakers with some interesting extra options at the blending stage of winemaking.

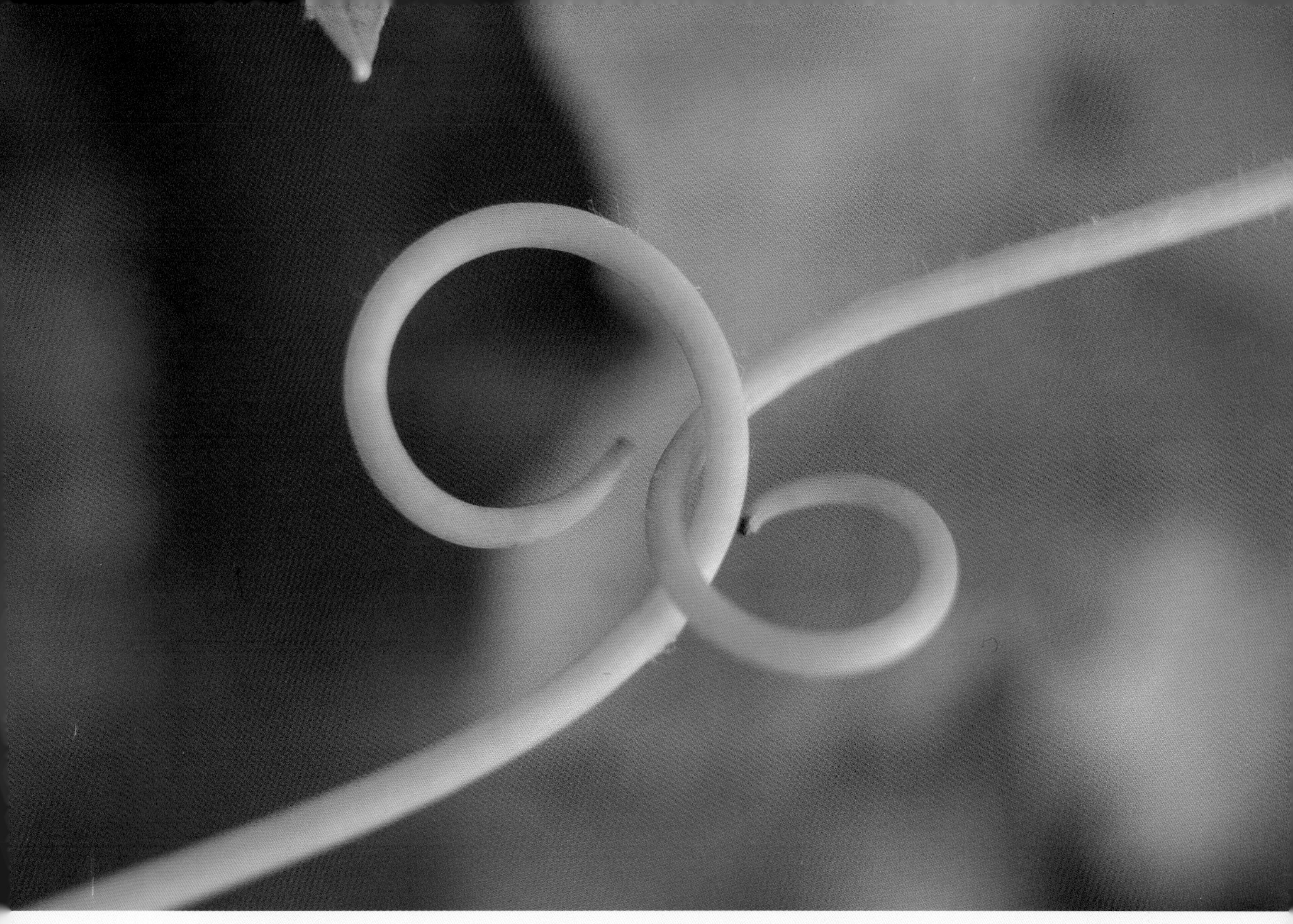

Parts of the vine

Canes The thickest, main branches of the vine, born of the previous season's shoots which lost their leaves in autumn and turned woody, golden brown.

Cordon Permanent part of the vine (derived from canes which are more than one season old) which supports the fruiting spurs.

Spurs A cane cut short, one or two buds above where its growth began. The following winter, woody shoots which developed from the season's growth may either be pruned back to new spurs or may become the canes from which the pruner selects.

Shoots Spring and summer growth on canes or spurs that in autumn develop into hard, woody canes – and whose fate lies in the hands of the pruner in winter.

Buds Found where the leaf meets the shoot. The following season they grow their own shoots.

Laterals Side-shoots that generally don't mature into promising canes and are pruned during winter. They're generally non-fruiting or given to producing a late fruiting, called second-set, which is cut away, since its development lags behind the main crop.

Leaves Each variety has its own characteristic leaf shape and leaf vein structure (see Grape varieties chapter). Early in the growing season, viticulturists may identify the different varieties by looking at the shape of their leaves. The science of describing and identifying vines species is called ampelography.

Tendrils Delicate 10–12 cm long curly 'arms' which grow from shoots and cling onto the trellis wires (pictured above). They do not carry leaves or fruit.

Trellising, canopy training and pruning systems

Vertical trellis training systems, which train the shoots upwards and sometimes downwards in a vertical fashion, are the norm in our cool climate. Neat and tidy trellis-trained vines are well exposed to the sun, no trouble to trim, less prone to disease and pest infestation, and easier to machine harvest. Today's viticulturist has a selection of methods to choose from – which systems they use depends on the varieties they're growing and the idiosyncrasies of their vineyard sites. Each system is pruned in winter to lay the groundwork for the bud burst and vine growth in spring and summer. Here are some of the more common pruning and training systems in use in New Zealand.

Wire lifting: as the vines grow in spring, vineyard workers lift the 'floating wires' up to the next peg, encouraging the vine to grow upwards.

Cane pruning / Vertical shoot positioning (VSP)

Cane pruning is the most commonly used pruning system in New Zealand.

Winter (before pruning)

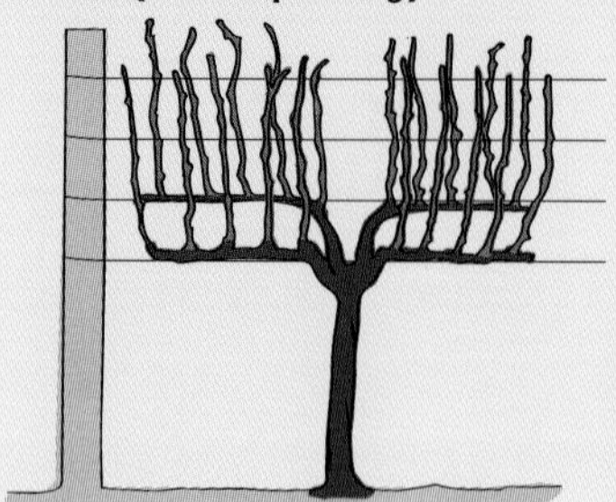

The vine prior to pruning. The pruner selects the best canes to retain for next season's crop (see page 225).

one-season-old canes

old wood

Winter (after pruning)

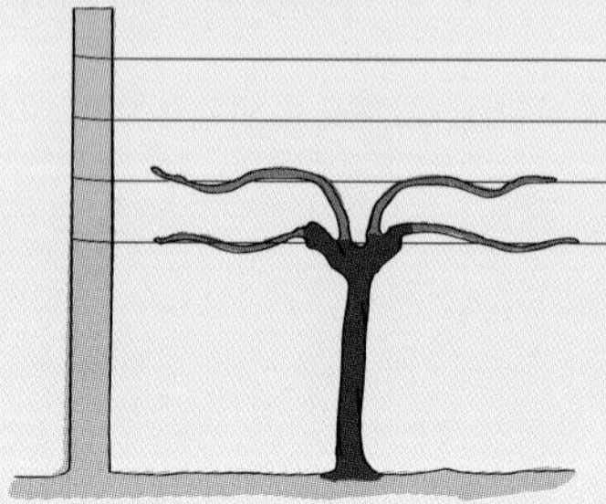

Two or more one-season-old shoots (called canes) are selected and retained for wrapping onto the trellis wires. This example has four canes (drawn here in orange).

Spring (bud burst)

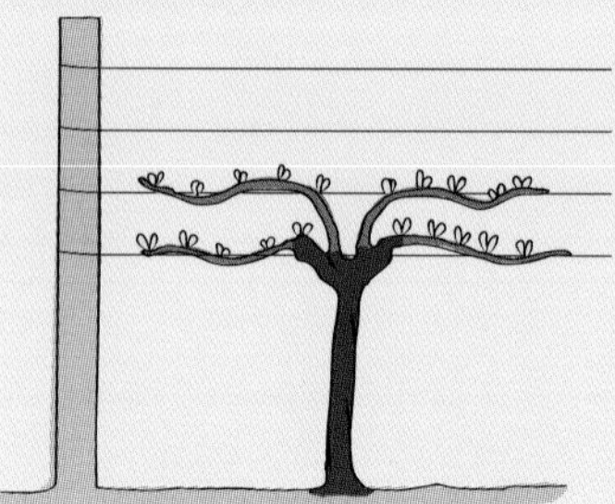

New season's shoots emerge from the canes retained by the pruner. It is from these shoots that the new season's crop will develop.

Summer (mature canopy)

With the vertical shoot positioned (VSP) canopy training system the new season's shoots are trained upwards between moveable foliage wires. The most widely used trellis in New Zealand because of its ease of management and ability to produce viable yields of good quality, it suits all varieties.

Cane-pruned / Scott Henry training in summer (mature canopy)

Typically pruned to four canes where the top-tier shoots are trained upwards and the lower-tier cane shoots downwards, effectively splitting the canopy in two, exposing the fruit and leaves to more sunlight, and thus increasing the rate of photosynthesis. Gives higher potential yields. Has been particularly successful with vigorous Sauvignon Blanc vines in Marlborough.

Spur pruning / Vertical shoot positioning (VSP)

An increasingly popular permanent cordon system which retains low numbers of buds, situated in the main on two-bud spurs. Promotes even bud burst and thus helps grapes ripen uniformly. Suitable for high-quality, low-yield crops.

Winter (before pruning)

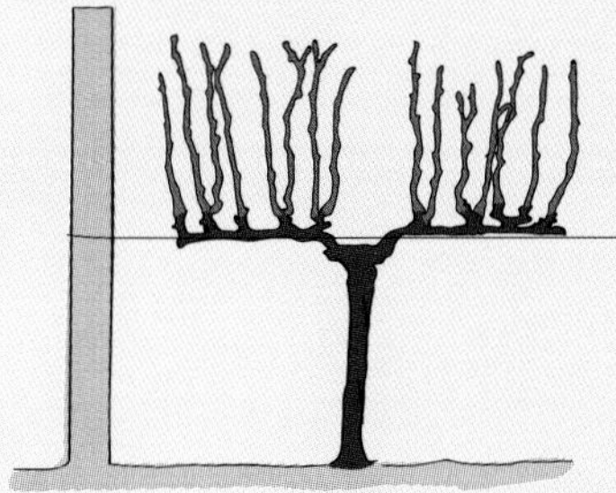

Winter (after pruning)

The pruner removes most of the previous season's growth, but retains spurs, usually two buds in length, which arise from the permanent cordon.

Spring (bud burst)

New season's shoots emerge from spurs.

Summer (mature canopy)

As with cane-pruned systems, most spur-pruned vines are trained upwards between moveable foliage wires (VSP).

Sylvos pruning

A permanent cordon system which retains both spurs and canes at pruning time. The spurs point upwards while the canes are directed downwards vertically and attached to a low wire. The shoots grow upwards and downwards, opening the canopy to increased light and airflow. It is a system which can support a high number of buds. The greater bud numbers lead to larger numbers of bunches (with smaller berries) which may require thinning. Particularly suits large volume, commercial-quality grapes.

Winter (before pruning)

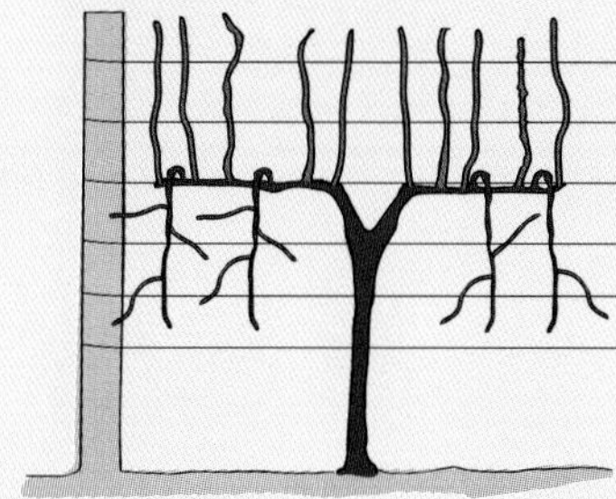

Previous growing season's shoots (canes) which arise from cordon spurs are selected by the pruner. All downward-pointing canes and shoots are removed.

Winter (after pruning)

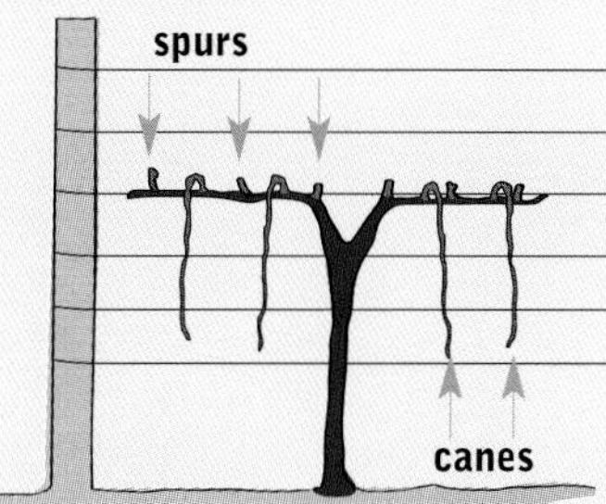

The pruner selects last season's shoots arising from spurs. These are retained as canes which are attached downwards. New spurs are also selected which point upwards from the cordon.

Spring (bud burst)

New season's shoots emerge from canes and spurs.

Summer (mature canopy)

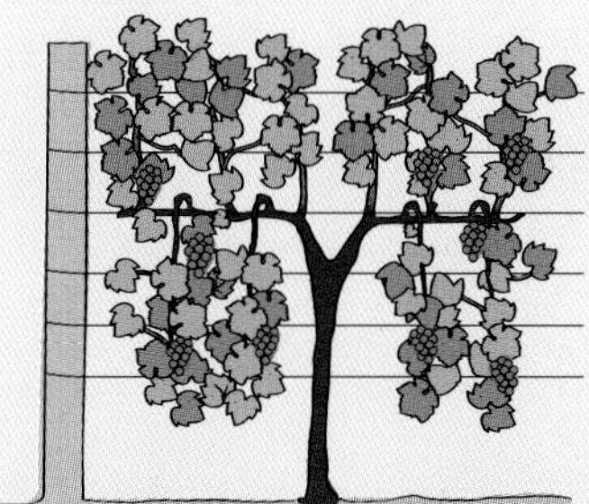

Shoots from spurs are trained vertically upwards between moveable foliage wires.

The annual cycle of the vine: from buds to grapes

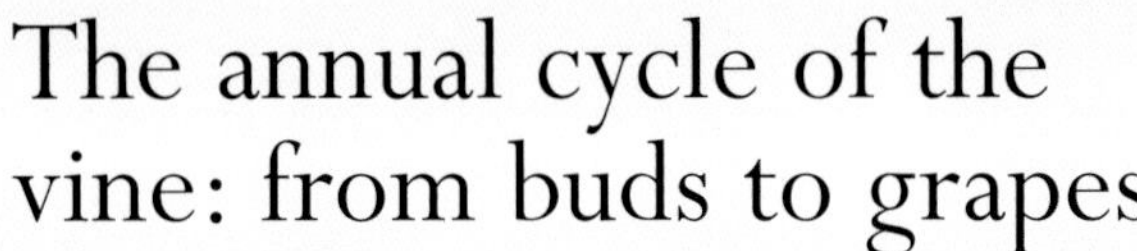

Every year, the vine embarks upon a new growth cycle that begins with bud burst in spring and ends after the last leaves have fallen in autumn. Each grape variety, like each child in a family, develops at its own pace.

Some, like Chardonnay, start growing sooner and mature early. Others, like Cabernet Sauvignon, dawdle towards ripeness, arriving there barely in time to catch the last warmth of the retreating autumn sun.

It is not only the current growing season's crop that develops throughout this growing cycle. Look at a vine leaf and you will see an embryonic bud at the base point where it joins the shoot (the leaf axil). All being well, next season this bump, or node, will produce a shoot with a cluster of flowers that will self-pollinate and develop into grapes. So each season the vine not only matures its current crop, it also puts in place the basic framework for the following season's crop.

1 Buds burst The vine's root system undergoes a little growth spurt in early spring to prepare itself for the approaching season. Vines use their reserves of carbohydrates to kick-start the growth cycle. Buds begin to swell and tiny, woolly rosettes with just-visible leaf tips emerge. Bud burst happens earlier in New Zealand's warmer districts, usually commencing in the Northland/Auckland region first.

Threats: Late frosts can wipe out a vineyard's bud burst. Buds can re-bud, but the second time around they are significantly less fruitful, and third time around totally unfruitful. Mealy bugs, blister mites and the fungal disease powdery mildew may appear.

2 Shoots grow Within 10 days tender young leaves and minute clusters of flowers appear on the lengthening shoots. These grow rapidly – up to three centimetres a day – throughout spring and summer. The tiny flower clusters, which now look like miniature bunches of green grapes, develop into larger, individual florets.

Threats: Both leaves and flower clusters remain vulnerable to late spring frost damage and harsh winds. In wet springs developing leaves may be prone to downy mildew, a fungal disease quite common in Gisborne and Hawke's Bay. Black spot and deadarm diseases may also make an unwelcome appearance.

3 Caps fall The cap covering the floret detaches and falls off, exposing the pollen-bearing anther and ovary that, if luck will have it, develops into a grape.

Threats: The tiny berries may become infected with botrytis, although evidence of the disease may not show up for many weeks.

The annual growth cycle of the vine

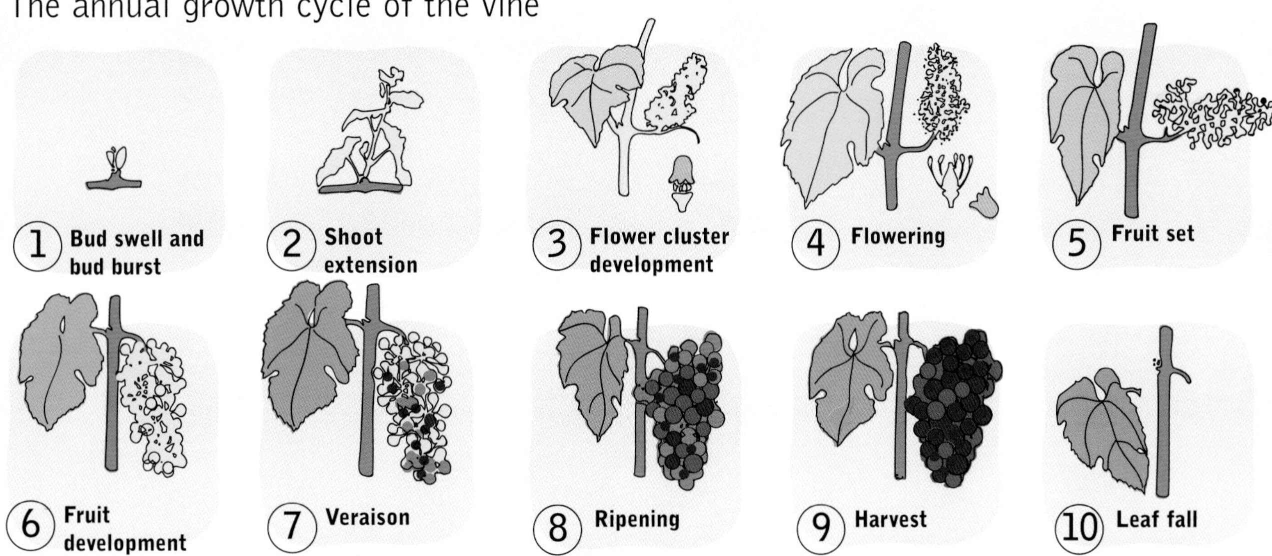

4 + 5 Clusters flower and the fruit 'sets' About 10–13 weeks after bud burst, flowering begins and with it the fertilisation that forms tiny, seed-bearing grapes. The flowers – small, green and without petals – self-pollinate and the fruit is said to be 'set' when fertilisation has happened: the flowers' anthers have dropped off and the now pinhead-sized, hard, green berries resemble miniature bunches of grapes. Flowering and fruit set can last any-thing from five to more than 14 days, depending on the weather. The warmer and drier the weather, the quicker the fruit set.

Threats: Cool temperatures leading up to and during flowering can hinder the fertilising pollen tube from developing. Rain can wash away pollen. Strong winds can cause flowers and the new fruit set to fail. Some varieties are more susceptible to poor weather conditions during flowering.

6 Berries develop The hard, pinhead-sized green berries go into a sudden growth spurt immediately after fruit set, gaining rapidly in size. Once they reach about half to two-thirds the size of their fully ripened girth, their growth temporarily plateaus out.

Threats: Diseases, pests and fungi.

7 Veraison commences Veraison, the grape's equivalent of puberty, marks the beginning of the ripening process. The grapes' cells expand. Sugars begin accumulating and acid levels drop sharply. The fruit starts to soften and its colour begins to turn. Red varieties assume their deep, rich colours; whites their characteristic yellow-green hues. At the same time, green and springy canes start to become brown and woody.

Threats: The grapes' thinning skins and higher sugar levels put them at risk of botrytis and other fungi during wet weather or damp, slow-drying conditions. Birds gather in the vineyards, scouring for juicy, fruity morsels.

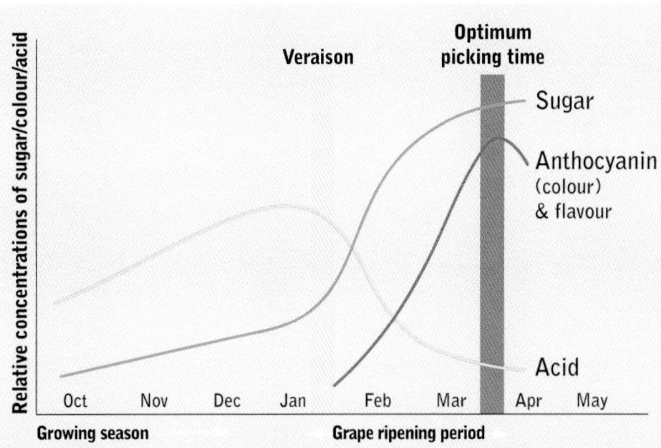

8 The fruit ripens The grapes become sweeter still, while their acid levels continue to fall. As they ripen, they accumulate more colours, aromas and flavours.

Threats: Birds, pests and diseases. Dreaded autumnal rains can cause the grapes to swell, diluting their flavours and, at worst, splitting their skins so that they rot on the vines.

9 + 10 Harvest and leaf fall After the grapes are harvested, the vines' leaves eventually fall.

The annual vineyard cycle

The winegrower's New Year begins in the cold, barren winter landscape and ends with a rush to harvest autumn's mellow fruits. Each season is subject to fixed routines, adapted to suit prevailing conditions.

Winter

June to late August

The vineyard sleeps.

Bare vines rest motionless

against the soldierly posts

who stand guard over them.

Jobs around the vineyard

- Pruning to set the size of next season's crop.
- Mulching of prunings (if not removed for compost).
- Repairing wires and replacing damaged posts.
- Fertilising to correct nutritional imbalances in the soil, if necessary.
- Inside the vineyard nursery: workers collect and sort budwood and rootstock for grafting in the spring, lift young dormant vines and prepare them for despatch to the vineyards.

Pruning lays down the potential of next season's crop. Vines only grow clusters on new shoots springing from one-year-old canes or spurs (themselves last year's shoots). When cane pruning, the pruner hand-cuts away parts of the vine that won't be needed next growing season and trains the chosen canes – those that look like the best cropping candidates – onto trellis wires. The skill lies in identifying the best new canes to keep intact. Canes with prominent, potentially fruitful buds and short internodes (the distance between buds), suggesting they resided on the outside of the previous season's canopy are the best bets. To meet bud targets set by the supervising viticulturist, the pruner must recognise every vine's individual potential and preserve the right number of buds on each. Leave too few buds and, with a few ill-considered snips, the pruner effectively slashes the potential size of the coming season's crop. Retain too many buds and the vine's crop-load may be heavier than it can successfully ripen. With spur pruning, the pruner leaves the permanent cordon on the wire and cuts its new canes back to short, evenly spaced, (usually) two-bud-long spurs that face upwards, leaving the vine looking like a hedgehog. In the growing season to come, shoots that grow on the stumpy spurs produce the next crop.

Spring

September to early December

Spring's warmth stirs the stark vineyard from its winter slumber. Soon the landscape teems with lush new life.

Jobs around the vineyard

- Shoot thinning (usually carried out by hand) to avoid problems associated with overcrowded shoots, such as excessive shading, which lead to poor fruit set and unripe bunches.
- Mowing of cover crops.
- Planting one-year-old nursery vines in the vineyard.
- Training the prolific new growth between the trellis' floating wires.
- Spraying for fungal diseases at bud burst and flowering stages (in conventional vineyards).
- Testing irrigation systems.

Sap bleeds from the new pruning cuts and the tiny buds begin to swell, giving rise to the first delicate, woolly shoots of the season. As temperatures climb and spring rains arrive, the new shoots grow in such profusion that vineyard workers soon need to lift the foliage support wires higher and tuck the still-fragile shoots into them, culling any flotsam and jetsam – the lower buds and shoots which arise from the trunk – as they go. As spring turns to summer they'll probably need to trim back the new growth so it doesn't grow too high and shade the next row. Mowing cover crops preserves soil moisture, lowers humidity around the vine and helps reduce the severity of any frost damage.

Summer

Late December to February

The summer vineyard

draped in sun-baked earth,

threaded with long, green ribbons of vines

and bejewelled with precious ripening fruit,

strikes a sensuous form.

Jobs around the vineyard

- Trimming the vine canopy, either by hand or mechanically, to allow sunlight to catch on the developing grapes.
- Careful leaf plucking (where necessary) to expose fruit to the sun. Often carried out extensively on slow-to-ripen Cabernet Sauvignon vines, but less comprehensively on Sauvignon Blanc vines, which may benefit from a little dappled light in order to help preserve some of the grapes' herbaceousness.
- Thinning the fruit, where necessary, to keep crop-loads and quality goals on target.
- Irrigating in dry, hot conditions.
- Watching for and responding to signs of pests and diseases as well as battling the birds.

The healthy vine grows into a strapping plant under the warmth of the summer sun, drawing nutrients and water from its growing environment. Vineyard workers continue to lift and tuck its growing foliage between the wires, trimming the vine at the sides and top if necessary to keep it in balance, while viticulturists closely monitor the progress of the developing grapes. If flowering and fruit set have been particularly prolific, some bunches may need thinning – usually just before veraison – to make sure the vine can fully ripen the rest. Crop-heavy vines produce inferior-quality grapes, remember. Working out how much crop to cull takes some very careful planning – no one wants to drop perfectly good fruit on the ground.

Irrigation

The French ban irrigation in most of their winegrowing regions, arguing its use is inconsistent with growing quality grapes. Then again, they're lucky enough to grow most of their fruit on soils with excellent moisture-holding capabilities. By contrast, many New Zealand vineyards wouldn't survive without irrigation to supplement water shortages during long, dry spells that can put vines under extreme stress, especially at the flowering and veraison stages. Certainly, in an ideally watered world, vines with deep, well-established root systems would be better off finding water for themselves, since they're equipped to draw the degrees of moisture they require from the soils. But, in reality, water isn't always there when they need it.

Studies show that careful application of modern irrigation doesn't detract from the quality of the fruit. Most systems use computer-controlled drip-feeders, with two or more drippers per vine (see above) trickling forth about 6–12 litres per day in sometimes water-short regions such as Marlborough. Irrigation has to be very carefully controlled though: over-water a vine and it produces the very thing all canopy management techniques aim to avoid – a dense canopy of leaves and canes.

Used tactically, irrigation can work small miracles. By restricting the water available to the vine at key, strategic periods, the viticulturist can improve fruit quality. Limiting water at the post-fruit set period slows down the vine's vegetative growth and restricts the size of the berries. During the post-veraison period, limiting water accelerates ripening. The result? Intensely flavoured, slightly smaller grapes with the advantage of a higher ratio of flavour- and colour-enhancing skins to juice. On the other hand, by increasing the amount of water available to vines, they produce bigger grapes and bigger bunches.

So how do viticulturists know if vines are thirsty or would be better off with a little less to drink? Sophisticated, high-tech irrigation monitoring systems – usually in the form of neutron probes or capacitance probes – test for soil moisture around the vine's roots. And now new experimental work is measuring water uptake in the vine, as opposed to water availability in the soil. Not that the best technology in the world can foreseeably replace the experienced eye of the viticulturist.

Autumn

March to May

The mellow sun sits a little lower in the sky, shorter days signal the imminent end of autumn's golden lustre and the vine's canes bend under the weight of their fulsome fruit.

Jobs around the vineyard

- Following and analysing the progress of the ripening fruit.
- Keeping birds at bay – a bigger challenge as the grapes mature.
- Monitoring the vines for diseases and pests.
- Harvest (or vintage) – the culmination of the entire season's work – when everything swings into top gear.
- Post-harvest vineyard maintenance work.
- Irrigating vines after vintage to help them retain their carbohydrate-producing leaves for as long as possible – energy the vine stores for next season.

During autumn, as the grapes ripen, they undergo major changes. Their sugars, colours and flavours all increase markedly, while acid levels fall. The goal is to harvest the fruit as soon as each individual aspect of ripeness arrives at its peak.

The key measure of ripeness – although certainly not the only measure – is the crop's average Brix (or sugar levels). To explain: some of the vineyard's grapes may only achieve a barely ripe 20°Brix, others a very ripe 25°/26°Brix. But the crop's overall average may stand at, say, a perfectly acceptable 23°Brix. If the viticulturist has taken management steps throughout the season to help the fruit ripen evenly, the variation between Brix levels across the crop probably won't be major and, as a rule, the wine will be better as a result. (All-ripe fruit is the key to good red wines and most whites. Sauvignon Blanc can, however, be an exception to the rule: harvesting some less-ripe, rather more herbaceous-flavoured fruit and blending it with riper fruit may add an interesting fresher, grassier edge to a wine.) Of course, other important physiological aspects of ripeness come into the harvesting equation, too – among them acidity, pH, flavour development and the degree of disease pressure on the fruit.

Hand-picking whole bunches of late-harvest Pinot Gris at Opihi, South Canterbury.

View through the beating bars of a mechanical harvester.

Viticulturists and winemakers work closely together in autumn, touring the vineyards every day or two as vintage draws near, tasting and testing sample grapes from each block. Together they decide when and how to harvest. Sometimes their decisions involve compromises. Maybe the fruit isn't quite ready, but factors outside everyone's control – such as impending bad weather – mean it is wise to pick sooner, rather than later.

Whether they decide to hand or machine harvest depends on the styles and the quality of the wines they are aiming to make. Machine harvesting is by far the cheaper, quicker option. In fact, it is 10 times less expensive to machine harvest than hand harvest because it's less labour intensive. Mechanical harvesters can cover one hectare and pick more than 10 tonnes inside an hour. The machines straddle the rows, using beater rods to vibrate and knock the grapes onto a moving conveyor belt which, in turn, tips the fruit into bins or gondolas, ready for loading onto the trucks that transport them to the winery.

Hand harvesting is usually reserved for top-quality fruit destined for premium wines and is practised on a wide range of varieties. Unlike machine harvesters which tend to break up the bunches and rupture the grape skins, hand-pickers can harvest whole bunches intact. Herein lies hand-picking's chief advantage over machine harvesting. By preserving the bunches, unwelcome phenolics in grape skins, such as bitter-tasting substances and unwanted colour, cannot leak into the juice before crushing. (Once hand-harvested fruit reaches the winery, the whole bunches usually bypass the crusher and go directly to the press, whereupon the juice is gently separated from the skins.)

Hand harvesting has another key advantage over machine harvesting. Pickers can select only the ripest,

Hand-pickers hard at work in the Whitmore-Benson vineyard, Gisborne, during vintage 2003.

healthiest bunches and leave behind the less-ripe bunches for picking at a later date (see Sauternes-style winemaking, page 282, for example).

There's a picking order, of course. Vintage often commences with crisp (about 19°Brix) Chardonnay and Pinot Noir fruit for méthode traditionnelle and ends with slow-to-ripen Cabernet Sauvignon and late-harvest or botrytised fruit for sweet dessert wines.

Harvesting can take place seven days a week, 24 hours a day, if necessary. Wineries stay open around the clock, weighing in grapes and testing them for quality before starting winemaking. At some wineries, it's tradition for the entire staff to wait outside to greet and pass judgement on the first truckload of grapes to arrive on their doorstep. But by the end of a New Zealand vintage – which may last perhaps 60 days for wineries handling many varieties – most admit to being too weary to engage in any post-harvest celebrations, as is the custom in Old World countries.

Mechanical harvesters at Kaituna Estate vineyard working around the clock to bring in the grapes in tiptop condition.

Montana vineyard worker Michelle Campbell drove and operated this New Holland SB 58 BRAUD harvester, at Kaituna Estate vineyard in Marlborough during vintage 2003.

Harvest 2003 in Gisborne. Harvest usually happens 100 to 120 days after flowering, but some years can take place anywhere between 90 to 145 days later.

In Marlborough, Lawson's Dry Hills Wines' Labrador, Tomi knows a ripe, ready-to-harvest grape when she sniffs one. When Tomi's owner, Ross Lawson, picks and tests bunches prior to harvest and throws them to the ground, the dog only ever eats the fruit with 22°Brix (sugar levels) or more.

Vineyard vandals

We know for a fact that vine diseases have existed for thousands of years, because the ancient Romans wrote about them. But we can blame many of the diseases and pests that afflict today's cultivated vines on the introduction of North American species of vines.

Planted as curiosities throughout the Old and New Worlds in the 19th century, these immigrant vines carried pests and diseases to which the classical *Vitis vinifera* varieties had no immunity. Some of them pose serious threats to the quality of New Zealand wine and today much of the research focus in viticulture is aimed at coming up with natural, environmentally friendly ways to control their harmful effects.

① Phylloxera

A tiny sap-sucking louse which feeds off vines' roots. Colonies of these alien aphids stowed away on the backs of North American vines voyaging to the New World on sailing ships and spread like a plague throughout Europe and the New World. Now dispersed throughout the North Island and parts of the South Island. Controlled by grafting classical scions onto North American-European hybrid rootstocks (see page 214).

② *Botrytis cinerea* (bunch rot or noble rot)

A grey mould which thrives in warm, humid climates such as those of Auckland/Northland, Gisborne and Hawke's Bay. It does its most obvious damage to grapes – settling on their skins and piercing tiny holes in them from which moisture escapes so they may eventually shrivel up to resemble raisins. Under very wet conditions botrytis affects leaves, too.

At flowering and cap fall, botrytis is particularly unwelcome. As the caps die, botrytis invades dead tissue, where it may remain hidden within developing bunches until revealing itself later in wet weather. If it appears at veraison, botrytis often brings with it a flush of other sorts of fungi and yeasts which compound the damage.

Botrytis infection spells disaster for growers of all red wines. It lightens their colour and causes the wines to brown prematurely. Nor does botrytis do dry white wines any favours: again it causes oxidative browning and, in severe cases, musty odours and flavours. Riesling is especially susceptible, in part due to its tight bunches and soft skins. Yet botryis can come as a blessing when growing grapes for sweet dessert wines (see page 282).

③ Powdery mildew or oidium

A fungus which attacks vine leaves (rendering them less able to photosynthesise) as well as flower clusters, bunches and shoots. From bud burst onwards, this ash-grey to white, powdery, web-like fungus can spread, usually in shady canopies, during dry, mild weather, stunting diseased shoots and distorting the shape of young leaves, making them fall early. Infected berries fail to mature properly and sometimes split. Powdered sulphur sprays or other fungicides help prevent it.

④ Downy mildew

A fungus which spreads its spores in warm, moist weather. Its white downy growth can smother flowers and young clusters. As the infected grapes mature they eventually turn brown and fall. More mature berries are resistant to infection, although leaves are not.

Shows up as yellowish, oily-looking spots on leaves that dry out to reddish-brown spots. White downy growth appears on the undersides of leaves. Severely affected leaves fall prematurely and young berries wither. Copper-based sprays or other fungicides may control it.

⑤ Vine viruses

Viruses pose major threats to grape vines, particularly in the North Island. Leafroll virus is New Zealand's most prevalent and debilitating grapevine virus – causing lower sugar levels, higher acids, lesser flavours and poor colour in grapes. Red varieties succumb to it more severely than white varieties. The virus causes pronounced downwards rolling of the leaves and autumn colours between green leaf veins, for which there is no cure. It spreads on infected budwood and, to a lesser extent, rootstocks cut for propagation. In the North Island, mealy bugs also carry leafroll from plant to plant.

⑥ Mealy bugs

Soft-bodied insects, fringed with white filaments and covered with white powdery wax. Widespread throughout the North Island, over winter they lurk under vine bark and cracks in trellis posts as well as among weeds on the vineyard floor. At bud burst they re-emerge and weave their way through developing vine canopies, sucking sap from vine tissue and depositing a sticky honeydew-like substance over which a sooty mould develops. They spread the leafroll virus.

⑦ Bunchstem necrosis (also known as shanking)

A disorder which usually expresses itself after veraison. Bunch tissue collapses and also causes parts of the bunch beyond the affected area to wilt, effectively preventing any further ripening. It can be serious in some seasons. Ongoing research is seeking to understand its causes.

⑧ Mites

The most wide-spread mite in New Zealand is the sap-sucking blister (erinose) mite, which lives on the undersides of leaves. Although it causes blister-like galls or growths, it doesn't do significant damage to mature vines unless left unchecked. Sulphur sprays control it. Other types of mites seldom need controlling in New Zealand.

Vine disorders

The most common disorders are the result of nutrient deficiencies, whose symptoms often don't show until levels in the plant tissue have dropped perilously low. Prevention is always better than cure, hence regular tissue analysis identifies nutritional deficiencies before they do irreparable damage.

Foreign diseases (not in New Zealand)

New Zealand remains free of some of the pests and diseases plaguing overseas winegrowers such as black rot, a fungus that blackens bunches in America and Europe, and Pierce's disease, a crippling bacterium (spread by an insect called the glassy-winged sharp-shooter) that kills grapevines.

⑨ Leafroller caterpillar

A caterpillar which crawls inside bunches and chews away at the developing fruit, subsequently causing botrytis infection. To monitor the caterpillar's prevalence, vineyard workers trap and and count the numbers of leafroller moths (see above left).

⑩ Brazen birds

Birds, especially starlings, blackbirds and sparrows, are very partial to sweet, ripening grapes. And little silvereyes, mostly on the lookout for tasty insects, peck holes in fruit. Besides robbing the winegrower of grapes, birds spread disease between vines. Scare tactics to shoo them away include everything from gas-fired bellowing 'bangers', imposing scarecrows, kites styled to look like fearsome hawks and waving balloons sporting glaring, reflective owl-like eyes. Veiling the vines in netting helps thwart birds' pecking habits. Providing a regular supply of meaty morsels to territorial-minded harriers encourages them to police the vineyard and frighten smaller birds away, while the rare native New Zealand falcon is an especially effective predator. Shotgun-toting vineyard workers, roaring up and down the rows like cavalry on motorbikes, are the last line of defence.

⑩

Growing grapes the environmentally friendly way

The concept of 'triple bottom-line accountability' – where environmental health and social responsibility issues rank equal to financial considerations – is increasingly evident in New Zealand's wine industry.

'New Zealand wine – riches of a clean, green land': it's the New Zealand wine industry's catchphrase, but rest assured it's no empty advertising slogan. Today, more than half the nation's vineyards live by a strict, independently audited code of practice called Sustainable Winegrowing New Zealand (SWNZ), an ever-evolving scheme dedicated to providing eco-friendly solutions to managing vineyards. It's an ethos that looks out for the long-term needs of our winegrowing regions' natural resources, built around a highly practical system of educational manuals, assessment scorecards, and training and information-sharing forums which guide wine-growers down the sustainable management track. It rivals the best eco-friendly schemes in the world.

SWNZ (formerly known as Integrated Winegrape Production or IWP) was born in the mid-1990s out of concern within the industry that a number of then common viticultural practices were neither environmentally sustainable nor necessarily serving the best interests of vineyard workers, surrounding communities and the burgeoning number of spray-wary, environmentally conscious wine consumers.

At that time, New Zealand's standard viticultural practices weren't always consistent with the country's oft-touted clean, green image. Routine fortnightly calendar spraying (regardless of whether any insects or diseases had launched assaults), blanket use of pre-weed emergence herbicides and less than carefully monitored irrigation programmes were widespread. Legislation governing issues such as spray use and pesticide residue levels ignored a number of wider issues troubling the conservation-minded within winegrowing circles: that of the sustainable management of our natural resources, namely our soils, streams, aquifers, microbes and living organisms.

It was left to the industry to act. A working party set up in 1995 by the then Wine Institute of New Zealand, Grape Growers Council and industry representatives modified a Swiss sustainable viticulture management programme to suit New Zealand conditions, put the resulting pilot programme through three years of trials at various growers' vineyards and rolled out the fine-tuned scheme just in time for the 2000 vintage.

Sustainable grapegrowing is all about minimal intervention – interfering as little as possible with the workings of nature.

Since then, SWNZ has helped provide focus, direction and resolve to member winegrowers keen to develop sustainable practices. The scheme sees vineyard workers monitor vineyards weekly for harmful insects and disease hot-spots, spraying only if a pest or disease reaches a certain threshold or infection period. Wild flowers, buckwheat and alyssum lure beneficial insects – such as ladybirds, lacewings and tiny species of wasps – into vineyards to prey on insect pests that vandalise the vines. Herbicide usage is down dramatically in many vineyards – without compromising weed control. So too is water usage. Oats, sown annually, improve soil structure and organic matter. Legumes such as lupins help supplement soils with nitrogen. Returning mulch (from prunings) to the soil replenishes it with organic matter (which holds nutrients and improves soil structure in terms of aeration, water infiltration and drainage). Winery marc (leftover grape solids) goes into vineyard compost. All of which spell good news for the environment.

Cutting back the number of spray applications is always good for the vineyard. Fewer numbers of spray-carrying tractors trudging up and down the rows equates to fewer opportunities for the soil to compact, less chance of agrochemical-resistance developing, reduced risk of agrochemical residues in wine – and makes vineyards healthier places in which to work and live near. In a global market which increasingly demands wine producers uphold unblemished environmental records, those things are imperative for our industry's future.

Organic winegrowing

Wines grown and made without the use of agro-chemicals and stamped with certified organic trademarks now appear on our shelves in greater numbers than ever before.

Visit a New Zealand organic vineyard and the winegrower will most likely pick you what's called a herbal ley from underneath the vines. It may look like a banal bunch of garden weeds – commonplace flowering plants like dandelions, buttercups, clover, houndstooth and plain-Jane plantain – but only if you know nothing about growing organic wine.

These weeds are, in fact, the organic producer's (and nature's) chosen cover crops. Besides contributing to the soil's micro flora, they attract friendly predatory and parasitic insects into the vineyard to devour vine-attacking pests such as mealy bugs and caterpillars. Organic growers maintain that by catering for friendly insects they have no need to spray vines with insecticides – although they acknowledge rather more tolerance to pests' presence than most conventional growers.

If pests or diseases do risk running amok, however, certified organic growers – who by definition cannot use chemical herbicides, insecticides or systemic fungicides – are not without the means to come to the vines' rescue. They can spray with permitted vegetable oils and clays known to impede the movement of pests. And they can apply sulphur and tiny amounts of copper and/or light-reflecting silicates to ward off fungal diseases. It's an approach designed to put the vines 'at ease' thereby lessening the requirement for 'dis-ease' protection, organic growers say.

Inside the organic winery things are done a little differently as well. Wild yeast ferments are preferred, although not insisted upon. Cellarhands limit the use of sanitisers and cleaning agents (such as caustic soda),

Left: The presence of friendly insects in the vineyards can reduce the need for chemical sprays.

The Millton Vineyard's compost heap.

preferring to use hot water to clean equipment. That's because the winery's waste ends up in the organic compost heap – the keystone of any organic winegrowing enterprise – where any harsh cleaning agent residues would harm the compost's biology.

Current organic wine production in New Zealand is tiny, but expanding fast. 'It's a sunrise industry,' says James Millton, co-owner of The Millton Vineyard in Gisborne, which has been not only organic, but also biodynamic (see below), for 18 years. 'Organics gets easier and easier,' to follow as one sticks with its principles over time, he maintains. But many, perhaps most, New Zealand producers fear organics is too risky, believing it is labour intensive and lower yielding. Organic producers argue the contrary, pointing to commercial successes among their fellow producers both in New Zealand and overseas.

New Zealand organic wine producers now have their own organisation – Certified Organic Winegrowers of New Zealand (COWNZ) – whose current main objective is to bring the country's organic winegrowing standards in line with international standards.

Biodynamic winegrowing

Philosopher and educator Rudolph Steiner started the biodynamic farming movement back in the 1920s, a philosophy which combines organic principles with an understanding of the planets' influence on all living things in the cosmos.

The name biodynamic comes from the Greek word 'bio', meaning life and 'dynamic', meaning energy. Proponents of biodynamics hold that understanding the forces at work in life starts with an understanding of the rhythms at work in the universe – the seven-day cycles influencing the rotation of the moon, the movement of the tides and the flow of sap inside plants. Winegrowers use a biodynamic calendar to guide them on the best times to plant and harvest. Five main principles govern their everyday work around the vineyard: crop rotation; the integration of micro fauna into the vineyard; recycling; conservation of all natural resources; and the use of homeopathic preparations and sprays brewed from the vineyard's plant material to enhance the soil and facilitate balanced vine growth.

Three internationally recognised certification standards for organic and biodynamic products apply in New Zealand:

- Bio-Gro for organic products certified by Bio-Gro New Zealand
- CERTENZ for organic products audited by AgriQuality
- Demeter for the more specialised biodynamic products.

Winemaking: an art and a science

Decisions, decisions, decisions. Winemakers have myriad options to choose from at every juncture in the winemaking process.
01T 0047

The starting point

Which decisions winemakers take depend on the varieties and styles of wine they want to create, be it a fresh, crisp $15 bottle of Riesling or a $50 version, crafted in a complex, sweet, dessert-wine style.

Decisions made this year may not necessarily work for next year's grapes either. Winemakers learn to juggle the many techniques and devices at their disposal to suit the circumstances of each individual vintage. There's no place for rote recipes in winemaking – it's both an art and a science.

Yet the basic process which turns grape juice into wine is indeed the stuff of elementary science. Yeasts convert the sugars found in the juice of sweet, ripe grapes into alcohol and carbon dioxide during a heat-producing fermentation. It is what the ancients discovered, no doubt serendipitously, thousands of years ago.

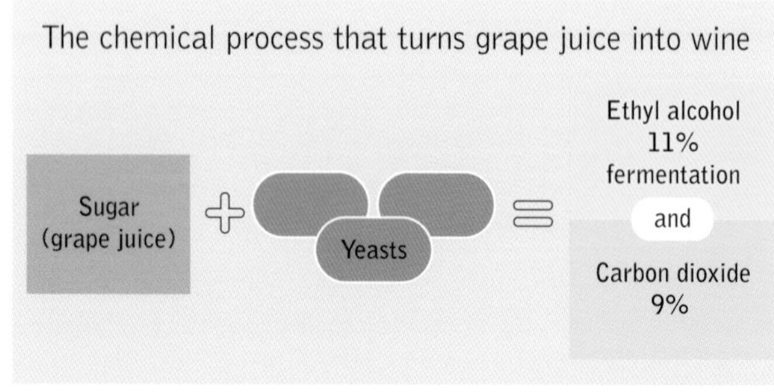

In nature, of course, no winemaker stage-manages the process. It happens of its own accord – and entirely on its own terms. If you were to pile some ripe grapes into a container and set them aside for a week or two during warm weather, chances are the naturally occurring yeasts that dust the grapes' skins would start to ferment the sugary juice. A couple of weeks later that little pool of liquid in the bottom of the container would, technically at any rate, constitute wine, although it would probably have more in common with vinegar than any self-respecting tipple.

The problem with nature's own impromptu take on winemaking is it offers no guarantees. All too often

Only grapes contain sufficient natural sugar to produce the level of alcohol – at least 10% by volume – required to make a stable wine. All other fruits and vegetables cannot make wine without the addition of extra sugar – and even then, never achieve the subtlety of bouquet or nuances of flavour of wines made with grape juice.

the wine would succumb to harmful bacteria, fungi, oxidation or yeasts that die off early before properly finishing their work.

What winemakers seek to do then – and this particularly applies to progressive winemakers – is use their skills to exert some control over the process, preserving the fruit flavours nature has bestowed, eliminating the risks nature might otherwise impose and, where stylistically appropriate, leave his or her mark on a wine.

Advances in wine science and decision-making tools now give winemakers an opportunity to exert an unprecedented level of control over every aspect of winemaking – breakthroughs that 20 years ago would have appeared mere pipedreams. Take the latest Fourier Transform Infrared Technology (see page 256) which generates profiles of developing wines' key components inside 30 seconds.

Winemaking assumes so many different forms. This chapter outlines a number of the ways wine is made in New Zealand including the classic red-wine styles, white wines, sparkling wines in the traditional bottle-fermented manner, sweet dessert-wine styles and the fortified wines, Sherry and Port.

Archaeological evidence suggests people have cultivated the vine since the Stone Age.

Next step – Sustainable Wineries

With sustainable winegrowing practices now playing an increasingly important role in the vineyard, the pressure is on New Zealand's wineries to follow suit. The Sustainable Winegrowing New Zealand for Wineries programme operates along the same principles as the vineyard programme (see page 242). An independently audited scheme, it encourages wineries to find sustainable solutions for the disposal of winery and production waste – and allows wineries to benchmark themselves against other like-minded producers.

Our 'flying winemakers'

The earliest New Zealand winemakers, who came to this country as immigrants from the Old World, brought their centuries-old winemaking techniques with them. Today, many of our local winemakers journey in the opposite direction, back to Europe, to work the northern hemisphere vintage soon after finishing the southern hemisphere harvest. Dubbed 'flying winemakers', they effectively double the experience they gain in a single year and, to boot, often end up sharing their innovative approach to winemaking with their Old World counterparts.

A number of New Zealand wine producers have forged ongoing partnerships with Old World producers, too. When, for instance, back in 1988, Montana wanted to improve its méthode traditionnelle winemaking, it formed a working alliance with Champagne Deutz that saw senior winemakers from the Champagne house travel to New Zealand to share their expertise on everything from viticulture to winemaking.

Today, the distinction between Old World and New World approaches to winemaking has become blurred. Leading producers everywhere now use the best of traditional winemaking methods alongside more technologically advanced techniques. Thus winemaking continues to evolve, as it has done for millennia.

Some things never change, of course. Just as the earliest winemakers had to understand the effects on the grapes of the elements – soils, sun, rain and wind – today's winemakers still need to know as much about winegrowing as they do the art and science of winemaking if they are to craft the best possible wines.

Red winemaking

Where do red wines get their rich colours, many of their robust flavours and characteristic mouth-feel? From their skins, not from their juice. Winemakers ferment red grapes with the skins on, so the nascent wines soak up everything the skins can confer in the way of colours, flavours, berry fruit aromas and weight-giving, mouth-puckering tannins.

Herein lies the major difference between making red and white wine. With white wine, the winemaker wants to preserve the wine's fresh, delicate characters and so quickly separates the juice from the brawnier-flavoured skins or, at most, permits the two a strictly limited, well-supervised few hours' contact after crushing.

Red winemaking calls for the opposite approach. Before sending the fruit anywhere near a press, the winemaker lets the juice and skins sit with one another in a fermentation vat for two or three weeks to make sure the skins' attributes rub off on the developing wine.

Red wine's richer flavours, colours and tannins spring from a group of grape substances called polyphenols (also found in white wines at much lower concentrations). Their magnificent colours derive from a sub-group of polyphenols, called anthocyanins, present in grape skins. And those pivotal, mouth-warming tannins comprise another sub-group of polyphenols, found mostly in skins and pips.

Making top-quality red wine demands a lot more involvement on the part of the winemaker than white wine does, as you will discover in this chapter.

Wine flavour components of the grape

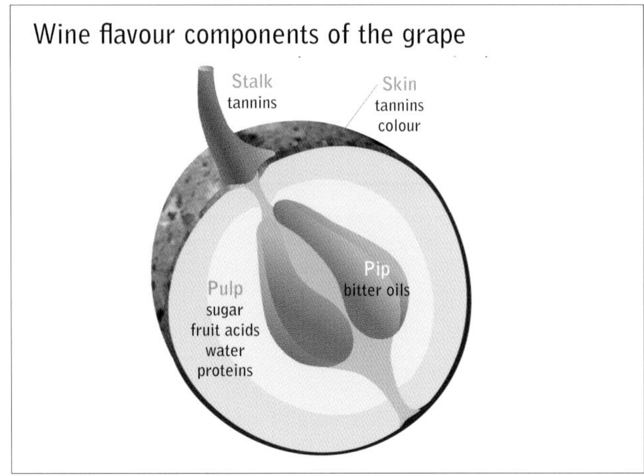

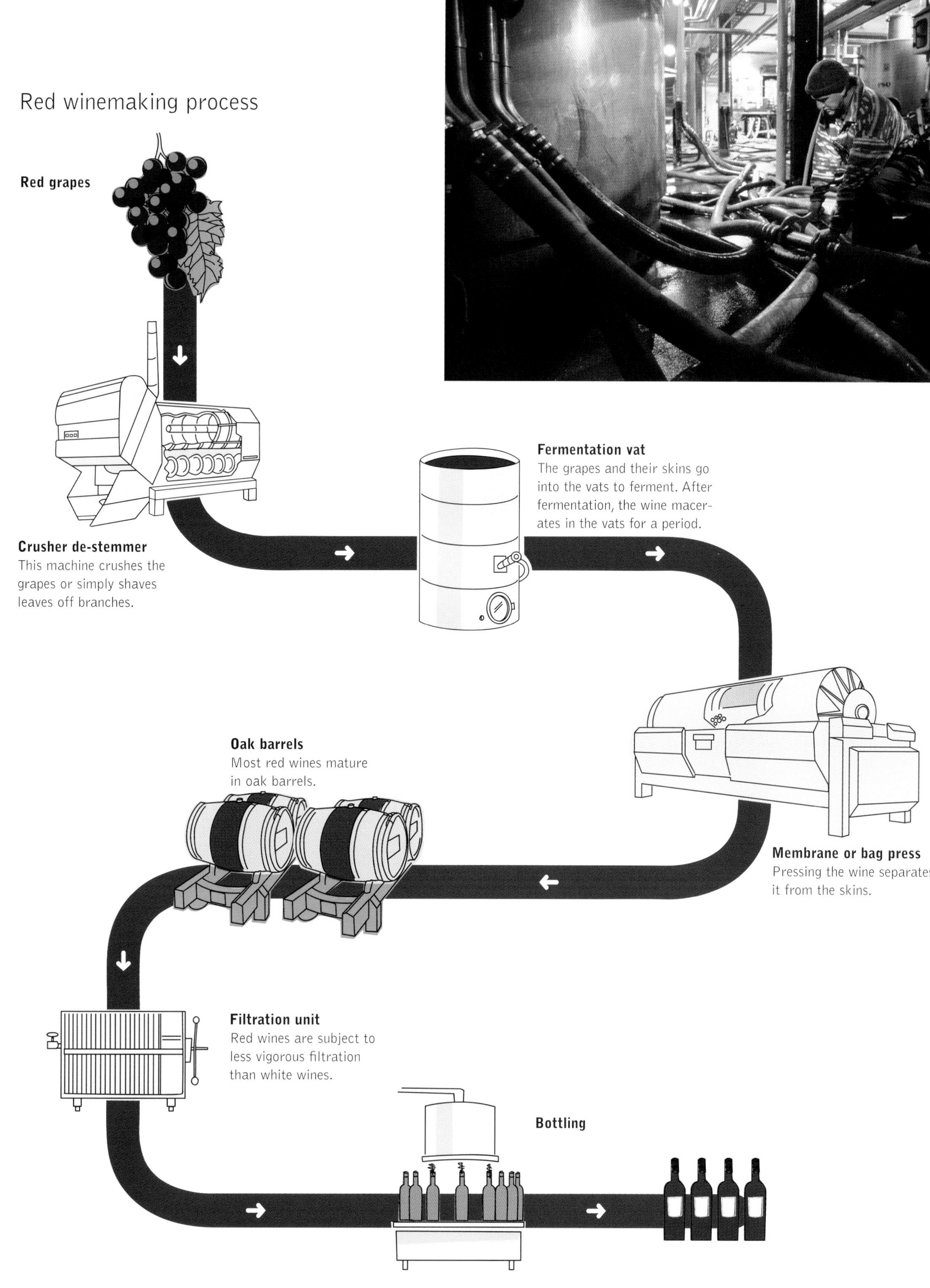
Red winemaking process
Red grapes
Crusher de-stemmer
This machine crushes the grapes or simply shaves leaves off branches.
Fermentation vat
The grapes and their skins go into the vats to ferment. After fermentation, the wine macerates in the vats for a period.
Membrane or bag press
Pressing the wine separates it from the skins.
Oak barrels
Most red wines mature in oak barrels.
Filtration unit
Red wines are subject to less vigorous filtration than white wines.
Bottling

Crushing

Parcels of fruit of the same variety harvested from individual terroirs are usually kept separate from one another, not only during fermentation, but also throughout the winemaking process. That way, winemakers have plenty of blending options later on.

• Mechanical crusher de-stemmers either crush the grapes and remove the stems, or simply shave stems off bunches, keeping the whole berries intact. The latter approach suits Pinot Noir.

• The optional addition of sulphur dioxide to fruit (either directly after harvest or in the crusher) guards against oxidation, microbial infection and holds off fermentation until the winemaker is ready to proceed.

Pre-ferment handling

In Bordeaux-style winemaking, the must (pulp) or whole fruit is pumped away from the crusher de-stemmer to tanks and usually left for two to three hours. The winemaker then adds (or inoculates it with) a carefully chosen strain of cultured yeast bred in the laboratory. Winemakers usually select a single, pure strain of yeast culture for each tank (see yeasts, page 271).

Another option: cold soaking

Keeping the must or whole fruit chilled to around 10°C for about three to five days (under a protective blanket of carbon dioxide) imparts the juice with more colour and bright, fruity flavours. It is an ideal treatment for Pinot Noir, where the objective is to elicit lifted fruit flavours. And it's one way to create a fruitier batch of wine to blend with more robust, tannic batches later.

Hot stuff: fermentation and maceration

Most New Zealand red wines ferment in sealed, stainless steel tanks, but an increasing number do so in traditional European-style open-top vats. The ferments become hot, peaking at temperatures of around 28–32°C.

• After crushing the must into the vat, the skins and pips float to the top to form a dense, crusty cap, bearing the must's most prized possessions: the polyphenols which bestow colours, flavours and tannins on the wine.

Squeeze the juice from a black grape and you will see it is colourless, like the juice from a white grape. Winemakers can just as easily make white wine out of red grapes, providing they swiftly separate the juice from skins.

Above: The 'cap' contains the polyphenols which bestow colours, flavours and tannins on red wine.
Opposite: The refrigerated open-top fermenters at the Brancott Winery, Blenheim.

Pumping over

Pumping red wine over the top of the cap performs several vital functions.

As the wine percolates through the cap's surface, it draws colours (from the skins) and tannins (from both the skins and the pips). The 'pumping over' action also gently aerates the wine with micro-quantities of oxygen. Yeasts depend on oxygen to multiply and stay healthy. And newly extracted colours, which can lose their intensity easily, require oxygen in order that anthocyanins can combine with tannins to form a colour-stabilising anthocyanin-tannin complex. Likewise, tannins also need minute quantities of oxygen to help them 'complex'. The single phenolic molecules that form the basis of tannins join together with help from oxygen to form chains and three-dimensional shapes or 'complex'. The length of these chains and the shape of the molecules determine the astringency, or aggressiveness, of the tannins' sensation on the palate. Winemakers may also take advantage of 'pumping over' to warm the wine if it's too cold or cool it if it's too hot.

Fermentation options

Fermenting in oak cuves Fermenting wines in traditional open- or closed-top oak cuves (or vats) imparts very subtle savoury oak characters into the wine, but a cuve's chief advantage is its ability to retain heat after fermentation. Wood makes a good insulator: as the wine cools down during post-fermentation maceration, the five-centimetre-thick oak cuve stores heat longer than a steel tank can. That extra period of warmth helps the tannins evolve and the colours further stabilise. Cuves create a more favourable environment for the cap: their slightly tapered shape traps the cap so it stays in contact with the surface of the wine during fermentation. And after fermentation (when pressure subsides) the cap drops into the body of the wine. Therefore, extraction of colours, flavours and tannins is more thorough.

Racking off into barrels Near the end of fermentation, a few winemakers may rack a small portion of the wine into oak barrels. At the blending stage these wines are combined with other batches of ferments. It's a stylistic technique that imparts wine with subtle, smoky, mocha coffee aromas.

The submerged cap technique A less frequently used technique, whereby a wooden-slatted device holds the cap submerged below the wine's surface throughout fermentation. This is probably the most gentle way to extract from the skins. Since the cap remains soaked in wine throughout fermentation, imparting colours, flavours and tannins into the wine, there's no need to pump over.

Carbonic maceration An alternative fermentation process used for lighter, fruity styles such as Pinot Noir where whole bunches of fruit ferment spontaneously, blanketed under a protective layer of carbon dioxide. The weight of the upper grapes crushes the fruit on the bottom, releasing 'free-run' juice without the need for mechanical pressure. Enzyme activity triggers fermentation inside the grapes sitting on top. It produces softer, fruitier and lighter-structured wines.

Temperature control

Red wine ferments typically reach temperatures of 30–32°C. Heat (and alcohol) help draw anthocyanins and tannins from the skins. If temperatures are allowed to exceed 32°C, however, the fermentation can become what winemakers call 'stuck', and the yeasts die. Every Brix degree in the fruit generates approximately one degree Celsius of heat during the fermentation.

Stainless steel vats fitted with refrigerated cooling bands around their exteriors are easier to control temperature-wise than open-top vats. Wines fermented in vats without refrigeration units are pumped to chillers (external heat exchangers), then flushed back over the cap.

Winemakers use any one or more of the four techniques described on this page to 'pump over' their wines:

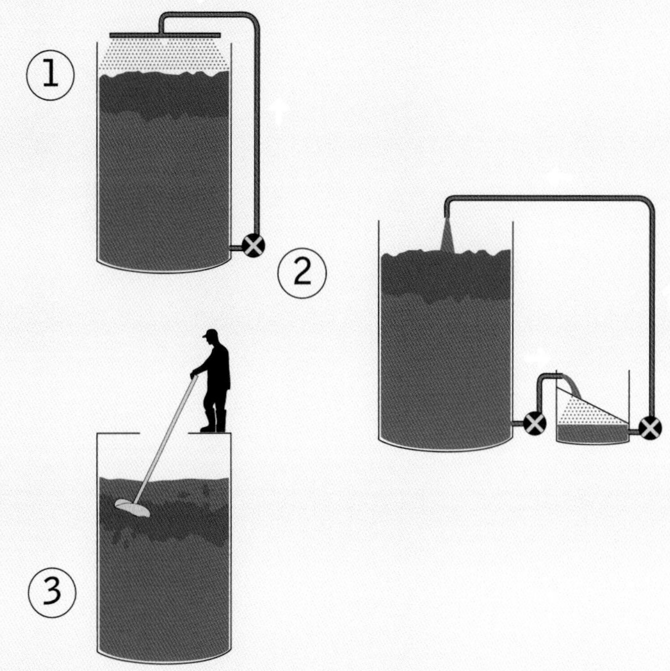

1. Pumping the wine from the bottom of the vat and spraying it over the cap.

2. Pumping the wine into a smaller tank, called a 'splash rack', aerates the wine before it's sprayed back over the cap.

3. Plunging the cap into the wine by means of a plunging device is a very gentle means of aerating the wine and bringing it into contact with the skins.

4. Delestage or performing a 'rack and return' involves: (4a) draining all the wine into another tank, thus leaving the cap behind (4b) in the original vessel and then pumping the wine back into that vessel – either spraying it over the cap (4c) or, alternatively, pumping the wine into the bottom of the vat and refloating the cap. Once the wine has been drained away, the cap collapses to the bottom of the vat. Cracks in the cap's hard, crusty surface break up, wine trapped within it is released and the cap effectively reforms. As the wine is pumped back over the cap, it soaks through the cap's entire surface area, instead of merely leaking (or 'tracking' in winemaker parlance) through cracks as it does during the 'pumping over' method (in diagram 1).

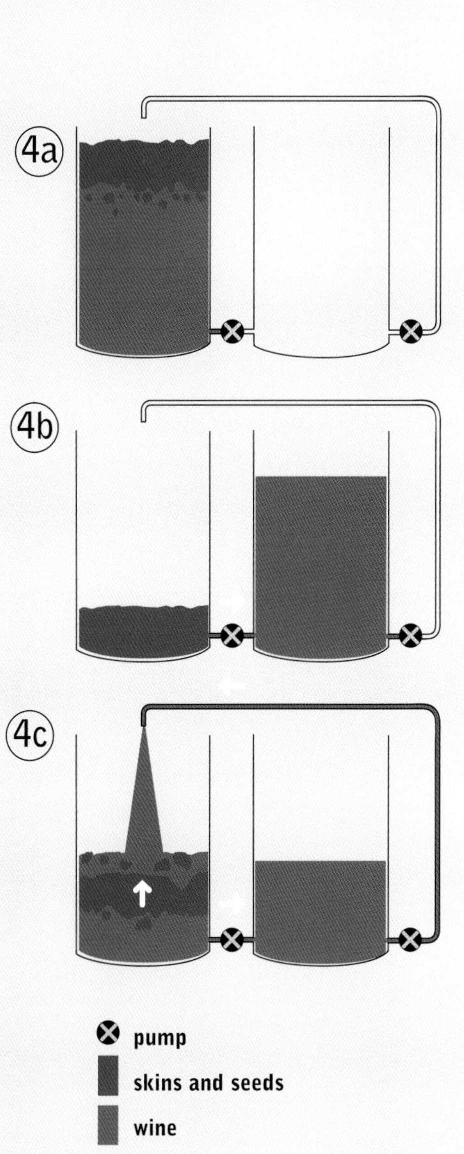

Cellarman Alex Douglas operates a hydraulic plunger device to submerge the cap on a batch of Pinot Noir fermenting in an open-top vat at the Brancott Winery.

Making Pinot Noir

Being less tannic than most other reds, Pinot Noir receives different treatment than the Bordeaux varieties.

Generally, it's hand-picked in whole bunches and, once it arrives in the winery, winemakers very often simply de-stem the clusters and tip them directly into traditional open-top fermentation vats. Here, the fruit may be cold-macerated at temperatures of 5–10°C for around five days, during which time colours, flavours and tannins are gently extracted from the skins. Towards the end of this period, as indigenous yeasts begin to spontaneously ferment and warm the juice, the winemaker may inoculate it with a cultured yeast. (See also carbonic maceration on page 254.)

Fermentation then takes a further four to five days during which time the wine usually reaches at least a very warm 32°C. Cellarhands periodically plunge the cap into the juice, either using a hydraulic plunger (see page 255) or alternatively by hand – two suitably gentle means of aerating the wine and bringing it into contact with the skins and pips. Once fermentation and maceration are complete, the wine is typically drained into barrels. At this point the winemaker may decide to initiate the secondary malolactic fermentation (see page 259) or, alternatively, delay it until spring. After the malolactic fermentation, the barrels are topped up with wine and sealed, then left to rest with their light lees (yeast sediment) for approximately 12 months.

If a fuller-bodied style is the goal, cellarhands stir the lees to give the wine a broader mouth-feel.

Pinot Noir may receive little or no fining and filtration, depending on the individual winemaker's philosophy.

Carbon dioxide blankets

During fermentation, the fermenting wine spontaneously produces a protective layer of carbon dioxide which protects it from vinegar-forming acetobacter bacteria that cause spoilage. But once fermentation finishes, carbon dioxide production ceases also. If air then comes into contact with the wine it encourages bacterial growth. Hence, to keep bacteria at bay during the post-maceration phase, the winemaker usually seals the fermentation vat and pumps a blanket of carbon dioxide inside it to fill the space between the cap and the vat's ceiling.

Tasting and testing

Winemakers taste the ferments at least daily to monitor their development and make decisions about, for instance, how many 'pump overs' to give the wines or whether to cool the ferments. Even those wineries which have access to high-tech laboratory testing equipment still rely to a greater extent on tasting rather than technological testing. With red wine what winemakers are looking at most closely, day in and day out, is tannin development.

One of the latest developments in winery laboratory equipment...

is Fourier Transform Infrared Technology (FTIR). These high-tech machines take a wine sample, direct a raft of different wavelengths of light across it and come up with a profile measuring around 18 different components (including colour, ethanol, pH, tartaric, malic and other acids as well as tannins), then mathematically compare the sample to other wines – and all inside 30 seconds. But testing doesn't replace tasting. People can taste aspects of a wine that even the best technology cannot.

The wooden cuve's chief advantage is its ability to retain heat after fermentation finishes, thus allowing the tannins to further evolve and the wine's colours to stabilise.

Post-fermentation maceration

Fermentation finishes after about five or six days. The wine then stays put in the vats for up to three weeks to further 'complex' (or change the physical structure of) the tannins. The duration of post-fermentation maceration plays a big part in the wine's style.

To produce a robust, full-bodied red wine, winemakers leave the wine macerating with its skins for anything up to three weeks. Active wetting of skins generally occurs less frequently and for shorter periods.

Post-fermentation maceration changes the wine's coarse, harsh tannins into softer, more subtle forms via natural chemical transfigurations. Firstly, the tannins continue to 'complex' (via the same chemical mechanisms that occur during the 'pumping over' procedure). Secondly, complex, sugar-like molecules, called polysaccharides (extracted from yeasts and skins) wrap themselves around coarse tannins, softening them and enhancing the mouth-feel of the wine.

Maceration also helps fix colours. Anthocyanins – small, notoriously unstable molecules – bind with tannins to become more stable and protect the wine from colour loss. As a result wines may develop deeper colours at this point. The longer the wine remains on its skins the greater the loss of primary berry fruit flavours. These are usually replaced with complex, earthy nuances – variously described as leather, tar, 'forest floor' and tobacco. But if winemakers leave the wine on skins for too long the wine may develop unpleasant vegetal characters. Long maceration best suits very high-quality, extremely ripe grapes with big tannins, destined to make long-living wines.

Pressing

Free-run wine is drained away from the skins into settling tanks, while the skins left in the bottom of the vat are dug out and sent to the press to extract the last of the wine. Press wine is usually quite astringent, has less colour than free-run wine and (contrary to myth) often has fewer tannins. It's usually kept separate from the free-run and later either partially or totally recombined with the final blend.

When there's nothing further to gain from prolonging skin contact, the free-run juice – around 650 to 700 litres per tonne of fruit – is drained to tanks to settle for about 24 hours before being racked to barrels or tanks. Pressing the slushy skins extracts about another 100 litres per tonne: press wine has distinctive 'pressy' characters, the product of forcing extractives out of skins and pips, as well as more yeasty flavours.

Basket presses are still relatively common in smaller wineries. They're simple, low-cost and they allow the press operator a greater level of hands-on control over the quality of the juice they extract.

Acid reduction

New Zealand's cool climate generally produces grapes with higher levels of acidity than those grown in hot, dry countries such as Australia. The further south our grapes grow, the greater their acidity. An attractive acid balance for reds is around five to six grams per litre of acid (measured as tartaric acid), compared with about six to seven grams per litre for whites. Too much acidity in a wine renders it tart and unpalatable.

Grape acids mainly comprise tartaric acid and malic acid, present in about equal proportions. As discussed in the Viticulture chapter, winegrowers do their utmost throughout the growing season to ensure that the fruit ripens to its best advantage and that levels of acids – important measures of ripeness – achieve the desired balance (see diagram page 221). Nevertheless, many freshly made white wines and virtually all New Zealand red wines are overly acidic when first made. Winemakers have two main techniques at their disposal to lower wines' acidity: 'chalking' to reduce both tartaric and malic acids; and malolactic fermentation to convert malic acid into softer lactic acid (see story at right).

Adding calcium carbonate chalk to the wine, or 'chalking', causes tartaric and malic acids to form long, needle-like calcium malotartrate crystals which precipitate out of the wine, thus lowering the wine's acidity. It is a de-acidification technique that is less commonly used in New Zealand nowadays since, as a result of good viticulture management, our grapes are generally riper at harvest than in the past.

Malolactic fermentation

Malolactic fermentation converts the harsh, tart malic acid present in all newly made wines into softer, more congenial lactic acid. Since lactic acid is about half the strength of malic acid, it effectively lowers acidity in wine.

Many people know that the buttery flavours and silky textures of some of our most popular Chardonnays arise from a secondary (bacterial) fermentation called malolactic fermentation. But fewer realise that virtually all New Zealand red wines undergo what in winemaker's parlance is called complete 'malo' to soften their otherwise potentially harsh acidity.

Malolactic-fermented wines boast a silkier, smoother mouth-feel on account of a substance produced during the fermentation called diacetyl. It's the same substance that imparts white wines with that tell-tale buttery flavour, although it doesn't generally alter the flavour of red wines.

All grapes carry malolactic bacteria, hence 'malo' fermentation can happen spontaneously. But where winemakers want to exert complete control over the process they inoculate either the must or the newly fermented wine with cultured strains of the bacteria. Winemaker-initiated malolactic fermentations are more predictable in terms of their speed and their effects on flavours and aromas. Spontaneous malolactic fermentations, by contrast, are riskier since they may occur after bottling, when they may cloud wine or create carbon dioxide bubbles.

Almost all red wines undergo a complete, winemaker-initiated malolactic fermentation. Not so with white wines. Depending on the style of wine being made, winemakers may put either a portion of a final white blend or the entire wine through 'malo'. Many New Zealand Chardonnays and an increasing, but as yet very small, number of Sauvignon Blancs, as well as the occasional Chenin Blanc, Pinot Gris and Sémillon, receive at least partial 'malo' treatment. But the treatment is almost never used on the aromatic varieties, such as Riesling. (Therefore adding sulphur dioxide to wines prevents spontaneous 'malo'.) Different strains of malolactic bacteria can affect wines in separate ways. Winemakers are experimenting with strains seeking to, for example, increase the wine's tactile qualities, without lifting the buttery (diacetyl) characters.

Maturing and finishing the wine

You wouldn't want to drink most freshly made red wines. They taste raw, harsh, acidic and astringent.

Still lacking balance and structure, the alcohol, acid, fruit and oak haven't yet integrated with one another.

High-quality red wines mature in oak barrels before bottling to soften their tannins and impart the wines with oaky flavours and aromas.

Almost every newly made red wine selling at more than $10 a bottle is racked (or drained) from settling tanks into oak barrels where it may age for around nine to 18 months. During that period it may be racked every few months. Racking not only gently aerates the wine but also helps clarify it, since sediment settles in the barrel's bilge (see page 263). Generally, between 25 and 60 per cent of the final blend matures in new oak, with the balance usually ageing in one- or two-year-old oak, but the formulae vary widely depending on the style of wine being made.

Unlike white wines, most reds don't require cold stabilisation. Tartaric acid crystals form on the inside of the barrels and precipitate out of the wine.

Fining

Egg white is the red winemaker's preferred fining agent. Its primary job is to polish any remaining coarse tannins after the wine has aged in oak. Most red wines are clear when drained from the barrels, so the winemaker doesn't generally fine them for clarity. (See fining wine, page 273.)

Gibbston Valley Wines ages its Pinot Noirs and Chardonnays in a 76 metre-long cave which was blasted into the schist hillside behind the winery in 1995 by the same team who constructed the Clyde dam. The cave's consistent year-round 14–15°C temperature is ideal for ageing wines and imitates the conditions in the underground caves of French winemakers.

Blending

This is where art takes over from science. Nine times out of ten the winemaker takes wines which have originated from separate ferment batches and blends them together to create a finished wine whose whole is greater than the sum of its parts. It's the winemaker's opportunity for artistic expression – the goal to compose a wine with layers of aromas and flavours and, at the same time, balance its structural elements (such as acidity and tannins) in the most attractive way possible. But blending actually begins, in winemakers' minds, even before harvest. As they stand among the vines in the vineyards and start formulating their ideas about the styles of wines they want to create, they're already earmarking separate parcels of fruit for their future roles.

Once the fruit arrives in the winery and the wine-making process commences, every time winemakers taste the developing wines they find themselves either reinforcing or challenging their earlier ideas about how they'll eventually blend the separate batches. But the day of reckoning doesn't come until after the wines have finishing maturing. That's when winemakers line up all the separate components and put together a first, tentative blend – one they hope best matches their aspirations. Invariably, these trial blends require some fine-tuning. Maybe they need to increase one batch component at the expense of another in a bid to attain the hoped-for flavour spectrum. Or, even at this late stage, perhaps they decide to create something different from the wine they originally had in mind. Only once they're absolutely confident with the blend do they go ahead with blending the wine.

Filtering

Red wines are rarely the subject of vigorous filtration – one reason why you occasionally find sediment in reds, but very rarely see it in whites (which, by comparison, generally receive more thorough filtration). Heavy-handed filtering of red wines often risks stripping them of varietal flavours and colours, hence winemakers are very cautious in their approach to filtering.

Montana Gisborne cellarhand Joe Wharehinga demonstrates how to toast a barrel. Having first lit a fire inside a small stainless steel pot containing oak chips, Joe places the pot inside the barrel. He then keeps a watchful eye over the fire for the 20 minutes or so it takes to toast the barrel to his satisfaction.

Oak barrels: the inside story

Used well, oak works wonders on a wine. Used badly, it makes a wine smell like a carpenter's yard – all sawn wood and not much else.

To get it right, the winemaker must arrange a successful marriage between the newly made wine and an appropriate oak partner.

The key to using oak to its best effect is to select a type of barrel that harmonises and enhances the wine's attributes – no simple task given the vast number of styles of oak to choose from. Even the same oak, handled by the same cooper in the same ways can produce two barrels of varying quality and flavour.

grained species that gives up its tannins freely – such as French pedunculate oak (or common oak, *Quercus robur*) from the forests of Limousin.

The cooper or barrel-maker's treatment of the barrel influences its style, too: how he selects trees for felling, cuts the wood into staves (by machine or by hand), seasons the wood (either by stacking it in the cooper's yard and leaving it to air-dry naturally for two to three years or by kiln-drying), and then

With its centuries-old design, the barrel is one of the winemaker's greatest allies. When stored horizontally, sediment pools in the barrel's bilge (or bulge) and can be dispensed with after drawing off the wine.

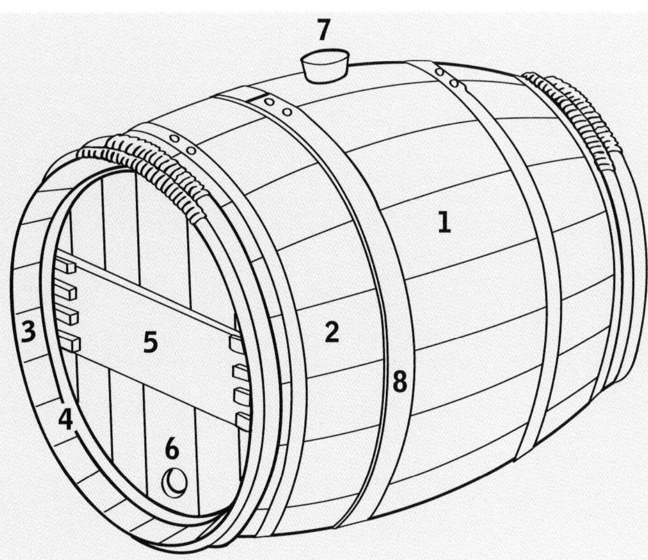

1. Bilge
2. Staves
3. Croze iron
4. Chime
5. Bar
6. Evacuation hole
7. Bung
8. Iron hoops

Every oak barrel, like every wine, reflects the natural environment in which it grew as well as the hands that crafted it. The more slow growing the tree, the tighter its grain. Wine takes longer to integrate with tight-grained oak, but once everything does come together, the oak influence is fine and subtle. That's why the tight-grained oak from the sessile oak tree (*Quercus petraea*) – such as those found in the Nevers, Allier and Tronçais forests of France – especially suit subtle-flavoured, lighter-bodied New Zealand Pinot Noir and Sauvignon Blanc. Their tannins, the mildest of all, release themselves slowly into the wine.

Oak that grew quickly bears a coarser, looser grain and more powerful tannins. When winemakers want wines to integrate quickly with oak, they choose a wide-

later manufactures it into a barrel, all have a significant bearing. So does the barrel's size: smaller barrels have a bigger surface area to volume ratio, hence they have more oak characters to impart and are able to gently soften or 'complex' wine quicker – two reasons why New Zealand winemakers prefer smaller 225-litre 'barrique' barrels.

To make a barrel, coopers bend oak staves into shape using heat, either immersing them in boiling water and/or toasting them over an open fire to soften the wood and render it pliant. The degree of toasting or browning accounts for the degree of toasty, smoky aromas and flavours in wines. Heavily toasted barrels impart softer oak tannins, but at the same time may mask some of the wine's fruit flavours. Wines matured

The wood–wine maturation process

Inside an oak barrel a number of complex changes occur to the maturing wine, thanks to the effects of micro-quantities of oxygen which enter through the wood's pores. These tiny amounts of oxygen allow single molecule phenols to combine with one another and form chains or three-dimensional shapes which stabilise the wine's colour and soften its tannins. For example, single colourising anthocyanin molecules (A in the diagram above) can lose their colour easily. But by reacting (or polymerising) with tannins (T in the diagram above) they become much more stable and the wine's colour fixes. Likewise, single and small-chain tannin molecules tend to be quite coarse and astringent. As the polyphenol chain length increases they become even more harsh. Further reactions increase chain length to the point where their molecular shape changes and they become softer and more supple, giving the wine a smooth texture. Even further reactions can cause anthocyanins and tannins to precipitate out of the wine where they form sediment or 'lees' in the bottom of the barrel.

Oak barrels also share their woody flavours, aromas and oak tannins (collectively called oak extractables) with the wine as it matures. Oak tannins (ellagitannins) react in similar ways to the tannins in wine.

Each of these separate reactions continue for as long as the chemistry of the wine, the physical storage conditions and availability of oxygen allow.

Three environmental factors present in the cooperage govern the rates at which water and/or alcohol and/or carbon dioxide migrate from the wine inside the barrel to the atmosphere on the outside – namely humidity, temperature and air flow.

In a dry cooperage atmosphere some of the wine's water slips through the wood's pores, tiny gaps between staves and the barrel bunghole whereupon it evaporates into the air. Thus, the wine loses a little water and, as result, its alcohol concentration climbs proportionally.

By contrast, very little water evaporates from wine stored in a humid or damp cooperage. Rather, a tiny portion of its alcohol content escapes through the barrel's walls and, correspondingly, the wine's alcohol level drops slightly. As for carbon dioxide, the gas passes from the wine to the atmosphere during storage.

With repeated use, the oak's pores become blocked with tiny particles that impede the passage of air into the wine and, furthermore, hinder the movement of water, alcohol and carbon dioxide travelling in the opposite direction. Tartaric acid deposits out of the wine as potassium bitartrate crystals. These reduce the porosity of the barrel and consequently impair the wine's ability to absorb wood flavours from the oak. Rinsing the barrels after use with hot water helps wash the crystals away, but it's never possible to restore the used barrel to the status of a new one.

in lightly toasted barrels have more fruit aromas and flavours, but their oak tannins may be a little more aggressive.

Used barrels have weaker effects on wine than new barrels. Every time a barrel matures a wine it leaches oakiness and has progressively less woody characters to share with the next wine. This isn't necessarily a bad thing. No good comes of teaming a delicately flavoured wine with a brand-new barrel, strutting all its full-blown, potentially overbearing oaky stuff. Nor does maturing a rich, concentrated wine in a tired, over-worked barrel approaching the end of its career do full justice to the wine. Winemakers must decide how much new and/or old wood to use, depending on the wine's style. Most – and certainly the best – aim for deft, rather than heavy-handed, oak influences.

It's inside an oak barrel that many of our wines grow up. Virtually all superior red wines mature in oak, as do most New Zealand Chardonnays and a few of our Sauvignon Blancs.

Barrels come in different shapes and sizes but New Zealand winemakers aren't beholden to Old World traditions when choosing which ones to use. That's why you may find a Bordeaux-shape barrel maturing a Burgundian-style Pinot Noir – or vice versa if that's what best suits the wine.

	Bordeaux barrel	**Burgundy barrel**
Length	95 cm	87.5 cm
Circumference at the bulge	218 cm	228 cm
Volume	225 litres	228 litres

Barrel oak comes from many countries. France has 14 million hectares of mainly private and, to a lesser extent, government-owned oak forests; Germany, Portugal, North America and now Eastern European countries, such as Russia and Hungary, also supply oak to the world's wine industry.

New Zealand winemakers import ready-made and ready-toasted barrels, mostly from France and North America. French oak imbues wines with spicy, cedary nuances. Sweeter, coconut- and vanilla-like oak charac-

teristics, on the other hand, reveal a wine's former live-in relationship with an American oak partner.

Barrels have a working life of four to seven years, not long considering a new American oak barrel costs about \$600–\$800 and a French one around \$1300–\$1500. Shaving about four millimetres off the inside of a barrel to expose new wood extends its career by about two years, but doesn't get around the fact that older barrels' pores become blocked with tiny particles which prevent oxygen from passing through their walls. Hence, New Zealand winemakers tend to retire barrels without going to the trouble of shaving them.

The characters of the oak should never dominate the wine. Says French oenologist Jacques Puisais: 'Only the memory of the wood need speak and then it should be a whisper.'

White winemaking

When making most New Zealand white wines, use of sophisticated winemaking techniques is usually kept to the bare minimum, the winemaker's primary aim being to preserve the wines' fresh, fruity flavours and aromas – not subdue them with characters introduced during the winemaking process. Chardonnay, however, lends itself to a number of approaches more commonly aligned with red winemaking.

To press or to crush first?

To make a light, elegant, delicate wine, hand-harvested grapes are crushed directly into a press (see pressing, page 268). But when making a fuller-bodied wine, the fruit is crushed in a crusher de-stemmer and pumped to separation tanks.

Crushing and maceration

The crusher, armed with pairs of adjustable rollers which don't quite touch, lightly bursts the grapes' skins to yield about 550–600 litres of free-run juice – the extra virgin juice, if you like – per tonne of grapes. Most crushers also have a de-stemmer which removes stems and plant material.

The 'must' (juice, skins and seeds) is then drained into chilled separation (or holding) tanks where it's left to settle. Those winemakers intending to make fuller-bodied whites allow the must to sit in separation tanks for up to 24 hours. During this 'maceration' stage, flavours, aromatics and colours pass from the pulp into the juice (and give the finished wine extra body).

Winemakers may reserve the maceration technique for selected batches and later blend these with those that haven't had 'skin contact' to create more complex finished wines.

Once the winemaker sees fit, the free-run juice is drained away from the skins through sieve-like mesh screens in the base of the separation tanks.

Common additions

- **Sulphur dioxide** (SO_2) at 1–100 parts per million and/or ascorbic acid (vitamin C) prevent diseased fruit from oxidising, stop vinegar-forming acetobacter bacteria breeding and inhibit potentially undesirable wild yeasts from spontaneously fermenting. They may be added at either the harvest, crushing, tank or press stages.
- **Enzymes** Pectinase enzyme, added at the crusher, press or drainage tank, breaks down pectins, separating the free-run juice from the pulp and helps release flavours and colours from the skins. It also helps clarify the juice.

White winemaking process

White grapes
Hand-picked bunches of grapes destined to make delicately flavoured wines.

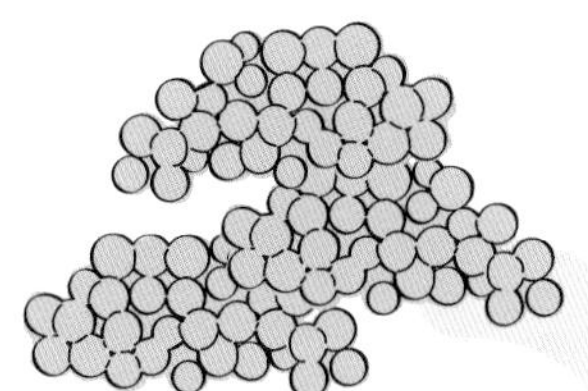

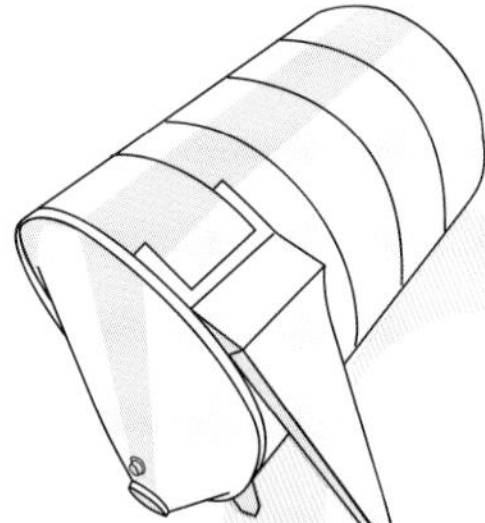

Separation tank
To make fuller-flavoured whites the crushed 'must' macerates for several hours.

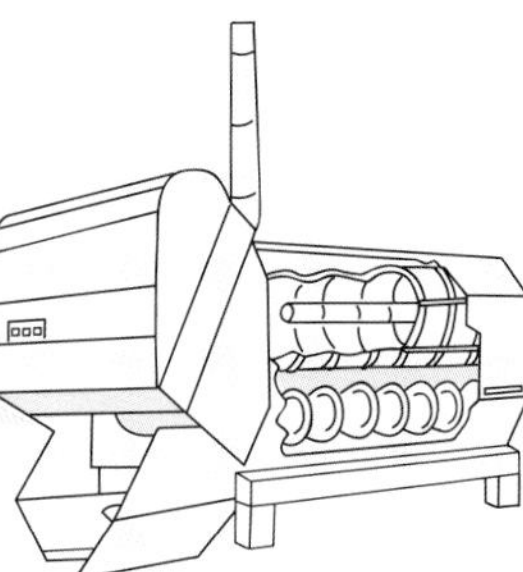

Crusher de-stemmer
Grapes are crushed and the stalks separated.

White grapes
Large batches of grapes, mechanically harvested.

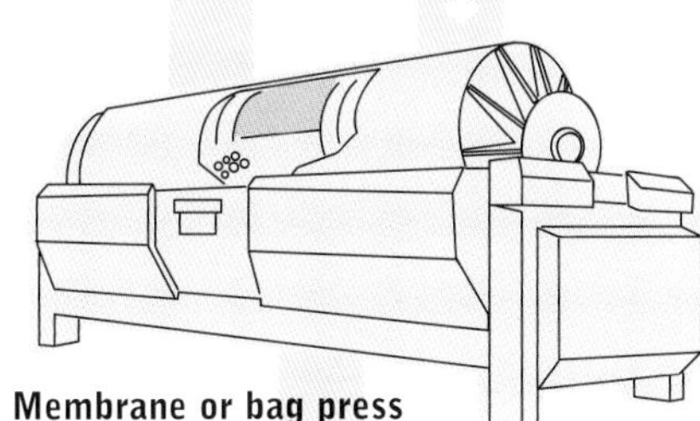

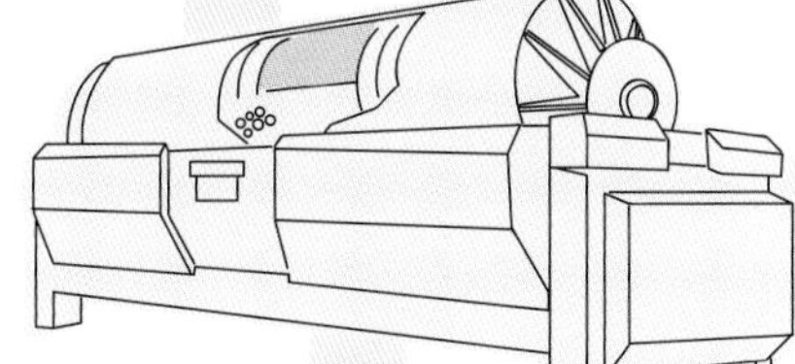

Membrane or bag press
An air bag squeezes juice out of crushed fruit.

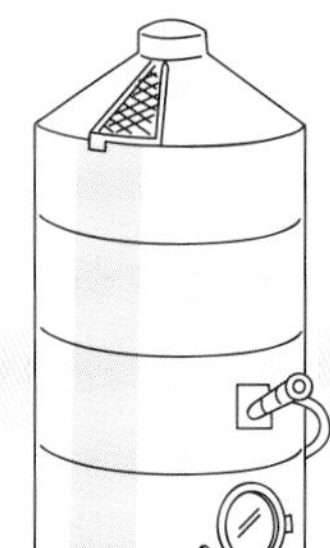

Fermentation vat

Barrel fermentation

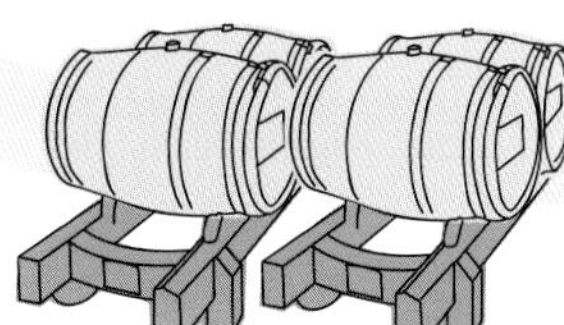

Storage and blending unit

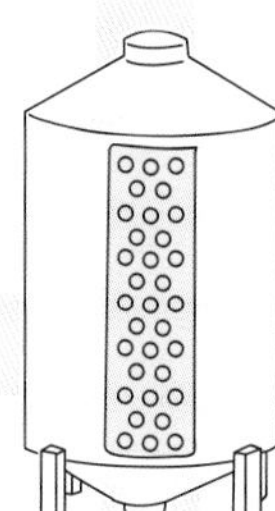

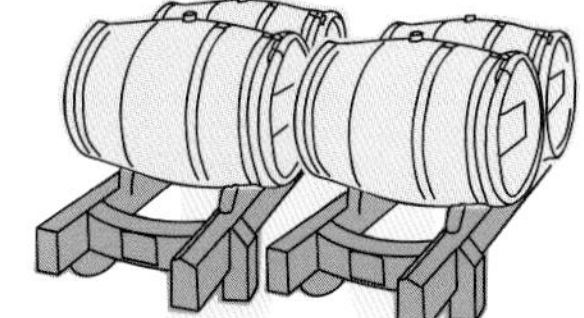

Oak barrels
Some white wines may be aged in oak barrels.

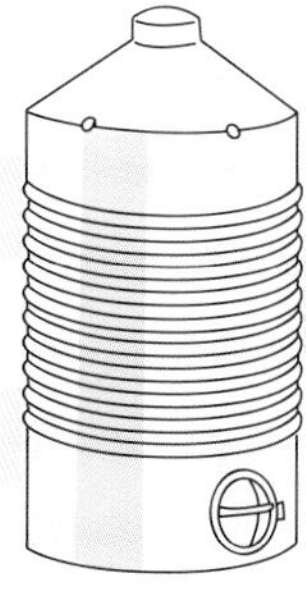

Refrigeration tank
Wine is chilled to precipitate tartrates, which might otherwise cause white crystalline deposits in bottled wine.

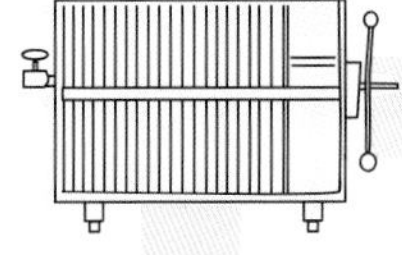

Filtration unit
If the wine contains residual sugar, filtering is essential. It removes any yeasts which might otherwise ferment in the bottled wine.

Bottling

Pressing

Sometimes whole bunches of grapes by-pass the crusher and go directly to the press. The press is the first port of call for premium quality, hand-harvested bunches destined to make elegant wines as well as red varieties that are to make white wines.

Where the fruit has been crushed into separation tanks and had its free-run juice drained away into another vessel, the skins and pips left in the bottom of the tank after maceration are pumped to the press to extract the last remnants of juice.

Varieties press differently

Fleshier, thick-skinned varieties suit slow pressing with gentle increments in pressure, for example. Winemakers programme presses accordingly – the harder they press, the more phenolic the wine.

Types of presses

- **The pneumatic 'airbag' press** with its pressurised, inflatable inner bag presses the must against the walls of its cage and sends the juice out through mesh screens. It gently extracts about 600–630 litres of free-run juice per tonne of grapes from fruit despatched directly to the press (without breaking the pips which would otherwise impart bitter flavours into the wine). Or when pressing the juice-saturated skins from the separation tanks it extracts about 100–150 litres of juice per tonne of grapes.
- **The traditional basket press** is quite common in small New Zealand wineries. It has a solid, lid-like plate that bears down upon the grapes, forcing the juice through gaps in between the vertically arranged wooden slats that comprise its circular cage (see the photographs on page 258).
- **The hard screw press** is sometimes used to press the residual 'cake' (of skins and pips) from the pneumatic press. The extracted 50–60 litres per tonne is very astringent and has limited uses. It is often distilled for brandy or grappa-type products.

The job of climbing inside tanks to shovel out the grape pulp after the juice has been drained away is a messy one. But it's unnecessary when using these New Zealand-invented tipping tanks, known affectionately as 'tommy tippers'. These tanks are tipped at the push of a button so that the crushed, slushy grape pulp pours directly into the press, which then extracts any remaining juice.

Preparing the juice for fermentation

A few winemakers take a hands-off approach now and simply press the juice directly into barrels, relying on wild yeasts present in the winery atmosphere and on the grapes' skins to initiate fermentation.

But the majority – those who want to minimise the ever-present risk of things going wrong – clarify the juice (to remove solids that risk producing 'off' smells during fermentation) and add a selected strain of cultured yeast. Which route winemakers take depends on their personal winemaking philosophy.

Most winemakers drain free-run and press juices into separate refrigerated tanks where they settle for anywhere between a few hours or up to four days. With the tanks' thermostats set at 5°C, fermentation can't start spontaneously because yeasts won't ferment at low temperatures. Any solids in the juice sink to the bottom of the tanks during this 'cold-settling' period. Afterwards the clear juice is racked (or drained) into fermentation vats.

More options

- **Clarification reagents** added before fermentation, such as bentonite clay, guard against oxidation and clarify (or remove) suspended solids. They're commonly used on juice from last pressings and also Gewürztraminer (as rendering the juice clearer helps accentuate this variety's aromatics).
- **Pasteurisation** kills bacteria, wild yeasts and the flavour-destroying enzymes released by the fungus botrytis. It also deactivates proteins so that they precipitate out of the wine during fermentation. Some say pasteurisation is contrary to the New Zealand winemaker's primary objective – preserving the wine's delicate aromas and flavours. Others argue any effect on the wine is minimal if it's done before fermentation. Studies in the United States suggest pasteurisation improves a wine's ageing potential. Winemakers rarely pasteurise premium fruit harvested in tiptop condition since it is relatively free from harmful bacteria or fungi.
- **Centrifuging** using centrifugal force to spin yeasts out of wine best suits slightly sweet wines. Removing the yeasts prevents them from consuming a wine's residual sugars.
- **Acid adjusting** the acid balance of the juice must be correct at the start of fermentation. If necessary, it can be adjusted upwards using natural grape acids or, alternatively, lowered using common chalk derivatives.

Oxygen and white winemaking

Keeping white wine juice cool prior to fermentation prevents spontaneous fermentation as well as slows oxidative browning. Winemakers who want to further prevent the juice from oxidating may blanket it in a layer of carbon dioxide gas which acts as a barrier between the juice and air in the atmosphere. Once fermentation begins, the wine then produces its own protective layer of carbon dioxide. Some winemakers, however, choose to allow the juice to oxidise, to a greater or lesser degree, depending on the style of wine they aim to make with it. Contact with oxygen causes the grapes' polyphenol compounds to become chemically unstable and thus precipitate out of the juice. The result? The finished wines are less phenolic, less fruit-driven and with age develop distinctive rounded flavours.

Fermentation

New Zealand white winemakers, ever intent on preserving fresh fruit aromas and flavours in their wines, usually put wines through a long, slow, cool fermentation in stainless steel tanks.

Typically, New Zealand white wines undergo a temperature-controlled fermentation in stainless steel tanks equipped with cooling bands around their exteriors. The cooler the temperature, the longer the fermentation takes and the fresher and fruitier the wines taste. The vast majority ferment at around 11–16°C over three to five weeks. That said, traditional barrel fermentation – warmer by far at around 16–25°C – is making a comeback in New Zealand. Wood insulates the fermenting wine, hurrying it through the sugar-into-alchohol conversion within 10 days or so. The wine picks up some subtle oak characters en route, but, fortunately, not at the expense of its fruity freshness. It's a technique which white winemakers chasing a more complex style of, say, Chardonnay, Sémillon or Sauvignon Blanc, may opt for.

A continuously trickling fountain of cold water is pumped over the exterior of these older-style fermentation tanks to control the temperature of the wine inside.

A handful of winemakers rely on the wild yeasts present in all grapes to conduct the fermentation, but the vast majority instead decide on a strain of cultured yeast for each batch and inoculate (or add it to) the juice (see opposite). When the yeasts convert 99 per cent of the sugars to alcohol and carbon dioxide, a dry (or non-sweet) wine results. But when fermentation is stopped ahead of that point, some residual sugar remains and the winemaker produces a sweeter wine. Fermentation either stops of its own accord or when the winemaker chooses. (Chilling fermenting wine and adding sulphur dioxide stops the still-active yeasts in their tracks; so does filtering or centrifuging yeasts out of wine.)

Once fermentation finishes, white wines are particularly prone to oxidation, hence the winemaker usually pumps inert gas (carbon dioxide or nitrogen) into the tank's air space (see ullage, opposite).

Winemakers taste and the laboratory analyses the wines daily throughout the winemaking process, measuring components such as the amount of sugar left to ferment and acidity (tartartic, malic and lactic acids). The developing wine's pH (alkalinity) level is all-important, since it affects the rate of all chemical reactions within the wine and thus influences its ratios of chemical components. Generally, the lower the wine's pH the better – and the greater its ability to age. Typical pHs for white wine range between 3.1 and 3.4.

More options

- **Malolactic fermentation:** an optional secondary fermentation, usually reserved for Chardonnay and some Sauvignon Blancs (see page 259).
- **Lees-contact and less-stirring:** leaving the wine to rest with its yeast sediment (or lees) after fermentation and regularly stirring that sediment gives it a creamier palate and broader mouth-feel, characteristics which suit some styles of Chardonnay. Lees-stirring may be carried out at the barrel maturation stage as well.

Yeast in winemaking

Rather than rely on wild yeasts present in the atmosphere to initiate fermentation, the majority of New Zealand winemakers innoculate grape juice with cultured yeasts – naturally occurring pure strains selected, bred and grown in a laboratory.

Yeast does much more than generate alcohol. The more than 100 strains of yeast used in winemaking also spawn a wealth of highly desirable by-products which can enrich the appeal of wines. Each strain has its own special attributes and therefore winemakers select the strains that are likely to bring the most benefit to their wines. Some strains accentuate certain varietal aromas and flavours. Some increase a wine's mouth-feel. Others can ferment at low temperatures. And a few ferment wines to a high 16 per cent alcohol, whereas others die once a wine reaches a mere 12–13 per cent alcohol (and therefore don't suit, say, ripe 24°Brix fruit with the potential to make a 14 per cent alcohol wine).

The most commonly used winemaking yeasts belong to the *Saccharomyces cerevisiae* species, a class of yeasts which gives rise to higher levels of aromatic compounds and therefore improves aromatic styles of wine. The less common *Saccharomyces bayanus* yeasts, on the other hand, impart yeasty, bready flavours into wine.

By innoculating a ferment with a purposely chosen strain of cultured yeast, the winemaker can reliably predict how the yeast will behave throughout fermentation.

Wild yeast fermentations, on the other hand, mainly depend on the naturally occurring airborne yeasts present in the winery's atmosphere to conduct the sugar-into-alcohol conversion. A few local wineries make some wild (or indigenous) yeast-fermented wines, but nowadays even the majority of European producers opt to use selected cultured yeasts rather than permit wild yeast fermentations to go ahead.

Yeasts are capricious characters. They need just the right growth-promoting, nitrogen-rich environment to multiply and initiate a ferment. Stress them and they give off a nauseating rotten-egg smell (hydrogen sulphide) and peter out before fermenting all the sugar – which spells disaster for any maker of dry wines.

Overseas research into genetic modification of winemaking yeasts aims to improve the sugar-acid balance as well as the body in some wine styles. GM developments are also being touted as having the potential to prevent hangovers on account of their special anti-microbial properties that dispense with some of the substances responsible for heavy heads. But strong consumer resistance to GM products makes it highly unlikely any prudent winemaker would use them.

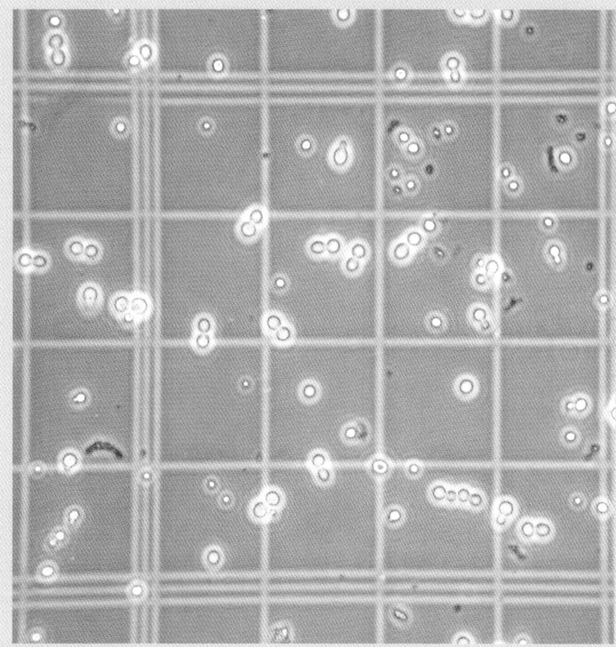

Winery laboratory technologists put samples of the winemaker's 'starter' yeasts under a microscope and count the number of yeast cells present to ensure they exist in sufficient numbers to successfully ferment a batch of juice.

Ullage

Oxygen exposure has the potential to cause many problems in wine after fermentation. Oxidation can lead to flavour loss as well as the development of acetobacter bacteria which turn wine into vinegar. To prevent oxygen from wreaking havoc on freshly made wine, winemakers have two options. Either they fill the holding tanks or barrels full to the top or they pump carbon dioxide or nitrogen gas into the tanks' head space.

Fining, blending and cold stabilisation

After fermentation the winemaker usually clarifies (or fines) white wine to remove any cloudiness, and prevent further yeast activity before blending the wines. How heavily the winemaker filters the final blend is over to the winemaker to decide.

Some simply clarify white wine by adding fine particles of bentonite clay to which any spent yeasts, proteins and other matter adhere before sinking to the bottom of tanks or barrels. Winemakers then rack the clear wine away from the sediment into a second tank or barrel. Here it settles for a few months longer, is racked once more, filtered and then bottled.

Others use a centrifuge, an altogether quicker method of removing the lees or sediment, followed by the use of fining agents (see opposite). From here, the clear wine is racked to refrigerated tanks in readiness for blending and/or cold stabilisation.

Blending

Although wine can be bottled in the batches it fermented in, more often than not the winemaker blends several batches to enhance the finished wine's complexity and balance its sensory components.

Cold stabilisation

Chilling the wine to –3°C for one to three weeks causes crystal-forming potassium bitartrate to precipitate out of the wine. Chilling the wine doesn't freeze it because alcohol lowers its freezing point to –5° to –7° C.

Tartaric acid, the most prevalent type of acid found in wine, can leave (harmless) white crystal deposits in wine. To remove tartaric acid quickly, winemakers 'seed' the chilled wine with salts of tartaric acid (potassium bitartrate). The tartaric acid in the wine clings to these salts which drop to the bottom of the tank within 12–24 hours.

Church Road winemaker Wendy Potts 'lees-stirs' a barrel of Chardonnay using a manual baton inserted through the barrel's bunghole. Each barrel is lees-stirred about once a week, a process which takes just under a minute when using a manual baton, but which can be performed inside 30 seconds with a hydraulic baton.

Filtration

It's important to filter white wines containing residual sugar in order to remove yeast particles which may ferment after the wine has been bottled.

The process commences with a coarse method of filtration to achieve clarity in the wine, using filters with stainless steel sieve-like screens coated with diatomaceous 'earth' through which the wine passes. Secondly, the wine is put through slightly less coarse cellulose pads or membrane filters which polish it or, in other words, render it brilliantly clear. Lastly, the wine passes between extremely fine membrane filters. No yeasts, bacteria or mould spores can pass through their screens, thus the wine's sterility is assured. But many winemakers prefer coarser-grained filters, nevertheless. The harder one filters, the less aromatic and fruity the wine appears, although these characters do return to the wine with time.

Maturing and finishing the wine

Freshly made white wines taste fresh and fruity and flaunt their varietal characters to the hilt.

Not all whites benefit from ageing prior to bottling, but maturing some styles in either stainless steel tanks or oak barrels does balance and integrate their characters. Those that age in oak typically do so for between six to, at the most, 18 months. A little oak can impart oaky flavours and richer textures (see page 263), but must be used with extreme caution so as not to swamp a white wine's delicate characters.

Fining wine

Virtually every wine undergoes 'fining' to clarify it (or remove any suspended matter, such as grape and yeast proteins that still remain in the wine). Without fining, many wines would taste bitter and unappealing.

Fining has been practised for centuries. The French word for fining, 'collage' (which in English means 'sticking'), goes partway to explaining how the technique works. There are two types of fining: protein fining, the adding of positively charged, proteinous fining agents to which the wine's negatively charged tannins and phenolics bind; and secondly, the adding of negatively charged bentonite clay, to which positively charged grape proteins stick.

Fining agents don't dissolve into the wine. Rather, they fall, along with the particles clinging to them, to the bottom of the tank, whereupon the winemaker filters them out of the wine. Any fining agents' residues left in wine after filtering are infinitesimal and undetectable.

Winemakers have a number of fining agents at their disposal. Egg white picks up coarser tannins in red wine but leaves the softer, more attractive tannins alone. Gelatine removes tannins, too, although it's no longer popular. Isinglass, a fish-derived protein and an alternative to gelatine, helps polish harsh tannins. Casein (from milk) is a white-wine fining agent that has decolouring and clarifying properties.

Synthetic fining agents generally haven't the same efficacy as naturally derived fining agents. Silicasol, a silica-based mineral, is used in conjunction with protein-based fining agents to speed up the bonding and settling process. It also helps strip any oxidised compounds from wine. Polyvinyl polypyrrolidone (PVPP), a nylon polymer that attracts browned and bitter compounds in the wine, improves wine colour and arms wine with a degree of resistance to further browning. It's most often used to fix problems in slightly oxidised wines.

Méthode traditionnelle and Champagne winemaking

How do winemakers put bubbles into méthode traditionnelle and Champagne? They induce a secondary fermentation inside the bottle.

The keys to making top-quality méthode traditionnelle are:

- Hand harvesting
- Light, gentle pressing
- Carefully controlled fermentations
- Skilled blending of individual and reserve base wines
- Long-term ageing on yeast lees
- Addition of liqueur d'expédition to sweeten the final wine.

Grapes destined for premium sparkling wines are usually hand-picked. Chardonnay (above), Pinot Noir and, to a lesser extent, Pinot Meunier are the three principal varieties used to make méthode traditionnelle.

Harvesting

It takes physiologically ripe grapes with comparatively high acidity to make top-quality, zesty sparkling wines. Hence, grapes are hand-picked just before their acid levels start to free-fall, when the Brix (sugar levels) are relatively low. Chardonnay destined for sparkling wine is picked at a crisp 19°Brix, whereas that bound for still wine is sweeter by far at around 23°Brix sugar level.

Vineyards dedicated to growing grapes for quality sparkling wines are mainly located in the cooler South Island, particularly in Marlborough, where the fruit retains higher, crisper acidity. Significant quantities of quality fruit are also produced in Hawke's Bay and Gisborne.

Pressing

Gently pressing whole bunches in special presses minimises contact between juice and grape matter (skins, pips and stalks) which would otherwise make the wine taste harsh and tannic.

Lightly pressing whole bunches of grapes, either in a traditional Champagne-style press or in a small basket press (see page 258) ensures few phenolic substances permeate the juice. Fruit for premium sparkling wines such as Deutz Marlborough Cuvée and Lindauer Grandeur are pressed in a dedicated Champagne press, called a Coquard press, which slowly and gently releases the juice from the grapes.

The first, light pressing releases top-quality free-run juice which has more acids and less phenolics than later pressings. Not surprisingly, free-run goes into premium-quality sparkling wines. Second pressings and any subsequent pressings – conducted under progressively higher pressure – extract greater concentrations of phenolics which can adversely affect the wine's flavours. These generally end up in lesser-quality sparklings, although small portions may be recombined with first-press wine at the blending stage to add extra complexity. All batches of juice are kept separate throughout the winemaking process. That way, the winemaker has a wide palette of base wines with which to compose the final blend.

Pre-ferment handling and clarification

The juice from each pressing is pumped into a separate vat. Grape matter settles to the bottom and the clear, clarified juice is racked into stainless steel fermentation tanks.

Chilling the juice to 0–5°C prevents spontaneous fermentation and stops bacterial growth. When making a white sparkling, winemakers quickly separate red varieties Pinot Noir and Pinot Meunier from their skins. But when making Rosé they allow the juice a little contact time with the colour-conferring skins.

This traditional Coquard Champagne press, believed to be the first of its kind introduced in the southern hemisphere, resides at Montana's Brancott Winery in Blenheim, where it presses premium Deutz Marlborough Cuvée and Lindauer Grandeur.

Méthode traditionnelle and Champagne winemaking process

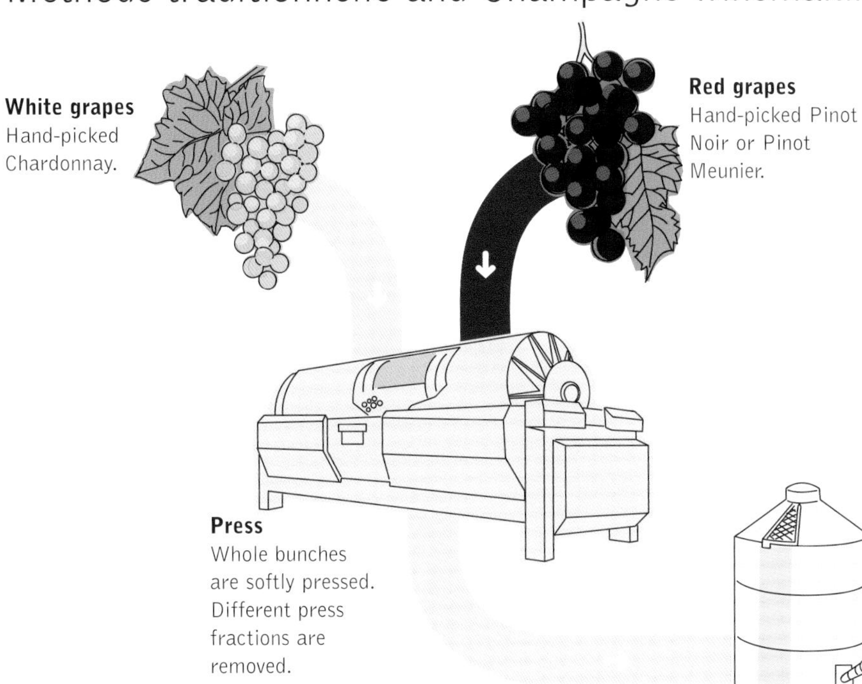

White grapes
Hand-picked Chardonnay.

Red grapes
Hand-picked Pinot Noir or Pinot Meunier.

Press
Whole bunches are softly pressed. Different press fractions are removed.

Fermentation vat
Juice is fermented in stainless steel tanks, left to age on its lees (yeast sediment).

Reserve wines
from previous vintages are kept separate.

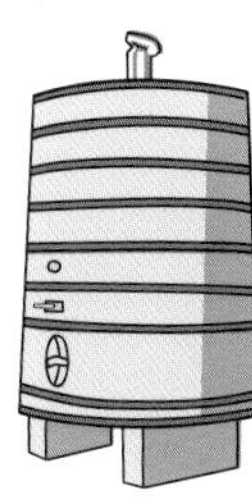

Base wines
are blended together to create the cuvée. Reserve wines may also be part of the blend.

Sugar, yeast and fining agents (tirage liqueur) are mixed in the wine. The wine is bottled and a crown seal crimped on.

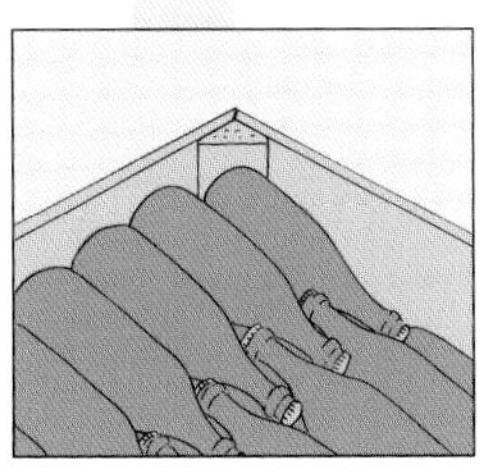

Secondary fermentation takes place in the bottle over six weeks at 12°C.

Wine is stored on lees for 18 months to three years (a period called entrillage).

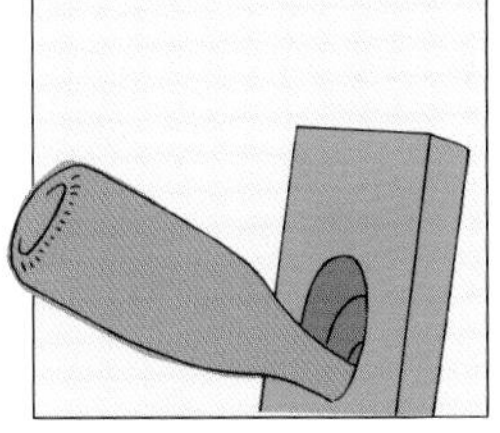

Lees (sediment) wedges in the neck of the bottle, a process called remuage or riddling.

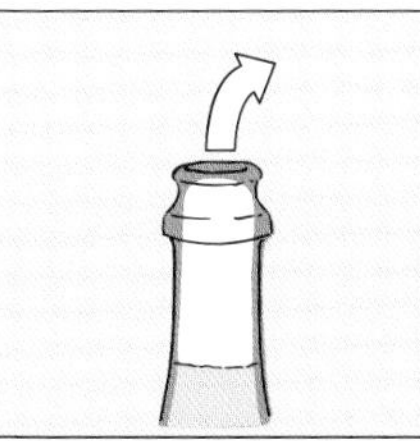

Bottle necks are frozen and the sediment is removed as a block of ice.

Liqueur d'expédition (variously containing sugar, aged brandy and old wine) is added to top up the wine.

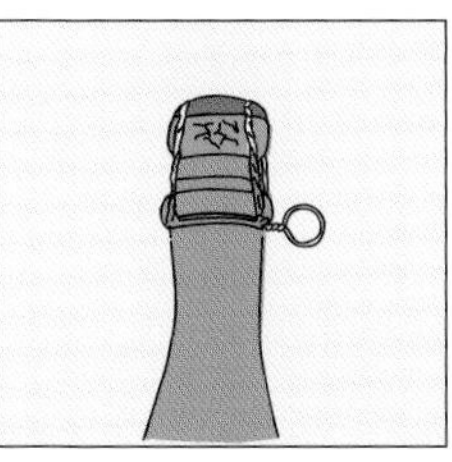

Sealed with cork and wire.

The first fermentation: fast and furious

The winemaker inoculates each individual ferment batch with a chosen strain of yeast which quickly begins converting the juice's sugars into alcohol and carbon dioxide.

It's easier to predict the behaviour of a cultured yeast fermentation (see page 271) hence the reason most New Zealand sparkling winemakers use a cultured strain.

The wine ferments for just one week in temperature-controlled, stainless steel vats typically set at 18–20°C. (Sometimes, however, fermentation is conducted at cooler temperatures of 14–15°C, to enable the wine to retain more of its primary fruit characters.) Very few Champagne houses ferment in oak. Those who choose to do so utilise old, well-used barrels which won't impart oaky characters into the wine. Some winemakers may also allow the wine to go through a malolactic fermentation (see page 259) to soften and round the wine.

Ageing on yeast lees

The three main varieties used to craft sparkling wines, Chardonnay, Pinot Noir and, to a lesser extenet, Pinot Meunier, each have the ability to age well on lees. Sparkling wine ages on its 'primary' lees (yeast sediment) for a number of months, the exact length of time being determined by the winemaker.

Fining (clarifying), cold stabilisation and filtering

Various fining agents (see page 273) can be used to clarify sparkling wine. Chilling the wine to –2°C (called cold stabilisation) precipitates any suspended solids out of the wine and prevents tartrate crystals from forming (see page 273).

Blending (or assemblage)

The most critical point in the sparkling winemaking process, the blending exercise taxes and titillates even the most masterly of palates.

Winemakers gather around scores of base wines samples, drawn from separate ferment batches. They taste, review, re-mix and reconvene many times over until, having examined every conceivable combination of wines, they fix upon the final blend that best matches their aspirations.

Each base wine must bring something special to the blend – now called cuvée in the parlance of Champagne. When blending Non-Vintage wines, winemakers incorporate base wines from previous vintages. This helps maintain consistent styles of Non-Vintage méthode traditionnelle from year to year. Reserve wines also bring additional complexity and structure to Non-Vintage blends. After blending, the wine may require another light fining.

Preparing for the secondary fermentation

Adding the tirage liqueur stimulates the secondary, bubble-inducing fermentation. Tirage liqueur contains sugar, selected yeast culture and nutrients (typically nitrogen) to encourage healthy yeast cell growth as well as 'riddling agents' that render yeast deposits slippery.

Bottling

The cuvée is bottled with a crown-seal – just like a traditional beer bottle top – and stored on its side.

Secondary fermentation: turning still wine into sparkling

The yeast and sugar in the tirage liqueur convert into alcohol and carbon dioxide bubbles. Trapped inside the bottle, these bubbles dissolve into the wine. The wine's alcohol content increases by about one per cent and pressure inside the bottle climbs to six times that of normal atmospheric pressure.

In the temperature-controlled cellar, set at a cool 12° C, bottle-fermentation takes about six weeks. The cool temperature seems to help produce smaller bubbles – and hence a finer, smoother mousse or bead.

With the Charmat method – commonly used in the production of Asti Spumante – the wine ferments for the second time in a sealed tank, not a bottle.

Storage (entrillage)

The now sparkling wine is usually stored for anywhere between 12 months and three years, during which time the yeast lees (sediment) breaks down and the wine develops new dimensions.

The top Champagne houses mature their wines in deep, underground chalk cellars. New Zealand wineries use refrigerated warehouses or cool-stores. Non-Vintage wines stay on yeast lees for at least 18 months, while vintage méthode traditionnelles typically require no less than three years on lees, often longer.

It's a very important time for the wine during which it develops harmony and complexity as well as palate structure. The texture becomes creamier, while flavours and aromas evolve. Credit, in part, goes to the yeast lees which, as they break down (or autolyse) after fermentation, interact with other fruit-derived flavourings to lend the wine savoury, biscuity, bready, yeasty characters. Furthermore, complex changes in esters, a class of naturally occuring chemicals, contribute to yet more evolutionary changes in aromas and flavours.

Riddling (or remuage)

The traditional method for removing yeast lees sees the wines cradled in wooden riddling racks, where each suspended, up-ended bottle is hand-turned by precise degrees every day for up to 14 days until gravity lodges sediment in the neck of the bottles. A more modern riddling method is to use gyropallets. These perform the same job as the riddling racks, but require nowhere near the same labour-intensive attention. Laden with bottles, gyropallets mechanically rotate every three hours. After one week, the now upside-down bottles have yeast sediment wedged in their necks.

The lees deposit can be seen in the neck of this bottle.

The neck of this up-ended bottle has been chilled in order to freeze the sediment before disgorging it.

Disgorgement

By freezing the neck of the bottle in a chilled brine bath and then removing the crown seal, the yeast lees pops straight out in a solid, icy lump, leaving the wine perfectly clear.

Dosage

Dosage means the topping up of the bottle with the liqueur d'expédition – a jealously guarded, secret recipe concocted by the winemaker.

Creating the dosage or liqueur d'expédition – a brew containing sugar, aged brandy, reserve wine and fruit acid, or a combination of any of these – is the winemaker's final opportunity to influence the taste and style of the wine. Liqueur d'expédition counters acidity and sweetens the wine. When making sweeter Demi Sec or Riche styles (see page 74) winemakers usually add a little more sugar. Lastly, they top the bottle up with freshly disgorged wine from the same batch.

Sealing

Sealed and wired, the bottle is now ready for labelling and packaging. Given an extra year or so of cellaring, the wine's flavours may integrate further and new characters develop, such as hints of nut and honey, albeit at the expense of the wine's fruit flavours.

Left: These disgorged and topped-up bottles of Deutz Marlborough Cuvée have just been sealed with their caps and wire cages. Below left: Lindauer Grandeur being labelled and packaged.

All dressed up

The Champagne makers of old first started dressing bottles with shrouds to disguise the fact that the contents were sometimes less than full after disgorging the yeast sediment. Rest assured that today all méthode traditionnelles and Champagnes contain the amount of wine stated on their bottles. Nowadays shrouds, made of foil, are merely there to look the part.

Cheap 'n' cheerful sparkling wines – such as Bernadino Spumante – are made by the 'con-gas' method, that is, injecting wine with carbon dioxide.

Sweetness levels in méthode traditionnelle and Champagne

On the label	grams of sugar per litre	on your palate
Extra Brut or Brut de Brut	0	completely dry
Brut	0–15	off-dry
Extra Dry or Extra Sec	12–20	medium-dry
Sec	17–33	medium
Demi Sec or Riche	33–50	sweet
Doux	+50	intensely sweet

The carbon dioxide in sparkling wine dries the taste, so any sugar in the wines isn't as obvious as it would be in a still wine. Serving sparking wines chilled further dims the perception of sweetness on the palate.

Sweet winemaking

It's no accident that sweet dessert wines possess thick, syrupy textures. Most are made from grapes which dehydrated on the vines – whether through the work of the fungus botrytis, prolonged exposure to the sun and the wind or icy cold weather.

Crafted from either Sémillon, Riesling, Müller-Thurgau, Muscat, Sauvignon Blanc or Muscadelle, dessert wines are extraordinarily sweet, boasting well in excess of 30 grams of residual sugar per litre. Here's how some of the most common styles are made.

Making dessert Noble Sémillon the Sauternes way

When growing grapes for sweet dessert Noble Sémillon wines, the fungus botrytis – normally the bane of the viticulturist – plays superhero.

In its good-guy guise, botrytis rolls up in autumn during late ripening (never before) to claw tiny, imperceptible holes in the grapes' skins through which moisture, or water, slowly evaporates. The increasingly parched fruit shrivels to raisin-like wrinkledness and the juice inside the grapes thickens to an exceptionally sweet, fruit juice concentrate-like consistency. Taste the grapes and you might imagine botrytis had coated them in honey.

But there are a lot of 'ifs' in this equation. Making botrytised wines is risky and expensive. Very few places boast the natural environments to produce them to quite the same quality as those made in Sauternes, south Bordeaux, France. In favoured districts, a river or lake neighbouring vineyards brings evening mists which hover over the ripening fruit until late morning, when the hot sun dries up the moist air that botrytis thrives on. It's a climate which gives botrytis enough leeway to raisin individual berries on a bunch, but also holds the fungus in check so it doesn't cause bunch rot.

In New Zealand we have at least one vineyard area ideal for growing botrytised wines – the Korokipo Estate vineyard in Taradale, Hawke's Bay, neighbouring the Ngaruroro River and near the Church Road Winery. A spring-fed stream meandering along the front of the vineyard's Sémillon-planted area generates evening and morning mists that rise to form a blanket over the vineyard before the hot Hawke's Bay sun dries the grapes out again. It takes about 10 to 14 days of these cyclical wet-and-dry conditions to shrivel the fruit to a point where the winegrower is happy with the results.

A bunch of botrytised, raisined Sémillon grapes maturing at the Korokipo Estate vineyard in Hawke's Bay.

Harvesting botrytis grapes

Those who adhere to Sauternes-style traditions pick only the botrytis-affected grapes with maximum flavour concentration once they reach 30–45°Brix (sugar

The mists which hover over the Korokipo Estate vineyard in Taradale, Hawke's Bay give rise to botrytis which dehydrates the grapes on the vines.

levels), usually in late autumn. They hand harvest the most raisin-like grapes, leaving the still-plump, non-botrytised fruit behind until the fungus dehydrates it. Then they revisit the vine maybe six or seven times, on each occasion picking only the most botrytised fruit until it is all harvested. Pickings are slim: such is the degree of dehydration required in the fruit, yields can be as low as one and a quarter tonnes per hectare.

Pressing

Inside the winery, the fruit is immediately despatched to a basket press and pressed very hard to extract as many fruit flavours as possible from the skins. It typically yields only about 450–600 litres per tonne. The highly concentrated juice is drained into tanks to settle overnight. During settling the botrytis spores – tiny black hyphae – drop to the bottom of the tank. The next day, the winemaker racks the juice to French oak barriques ready for a comparatively long four- to five-week fermentation.

Fermentation

Most yeasts struggle to ferment the thick, syrupy juice botrytised grapes produce, so the New Zealand winemaker selects a strong-fermenting cultured strain. Once the wine reaches about 14–14.5 per cent alcohol, the yeasts die off, killed by the combination of alcohol and remaining sugar. But since the sugar levels started out very high there's still plenty of sweetness left in the wine – about 80–150 grams of sugar per litre compared to just one to 10 grams per litre in the average dry wine.

Maturation

The wine is racked several times to clarify it and generally remains in barriques for 12 to 18 months. (Late-harvest or 'Noble' aromatic wines, such as Riesling, however, are not usually fermented/matured in oak.)

Filtering

Sweet wines are the most difficult to filter because botrytis-produced complex polysaccharide molecules, called glucans, form a fibrous 'mat' which can clog filter devices. Sweet wines do nevertheless require filtering since racking doesn't remove all the extremely fine, hazy particles that could cloud the wine. But the extent of filtering is discretionary.

Late-harvest wines: the last grapes to be picked

Harvested late in the autumn, when the grapes have built maximum sweet, ripe, intense fruit flavours, the extra time they spend in the sun and exposed to the wind helps dehydrate them. Occasionally botrytis aids dehydration, too – you may notice a honeyed fruit flavour in late-harvest wines, albeit less pronounced than in fully botrytised sweet wines.

Ice wines: freaks of nature

When bitterly cold frosts strike late in autumn and freeze ripe grapes still on the vines, nature presents winemakers with a rare opportunity.

Ice wines are the product of extreme, at least –7°C frosts that freeze ripe clusters on the vines, separating the grapes' frozen water content from the juice and thus concentrating the fruit's sugars, acids and flavours. Little wonder they typically hail from colder countries such as Canada, Austria or Germany.

Timing is of the essence when crafting an ice wine. As soon as the frost has the vineyard in its grip, vineyard workers race outside to harvest the fruit, either during the night or first thing in the morning when temperatures are coldest. Then they hurry the fruit into the winery for pressing. The press extracts the concentrated, syrupy juice, leaving the still-frozen ice crystals behind with the grapes' skins. Everyone has to work quickly each step of the way – if the ice starts to thaw, it waters down the juice's all-important sugars as well as dilutes the precious acid and flavour concentrations.

Pressed ice-wine juice ferments and matures in the same way as botrytised wine. Its high sugar levels at harvest allow residual sugars to sweeten the wine.

Ice wines, similar in flavour to late-harvest wines, are made in small quantities and command steep prices. New Zealand's southerly winegrowing regions only occasionally experience the exceptionally cold, early frosts responsible for true ice wines. Don't confuse the real McCoys with copycats made by freezing conventionally harvested grapes prior to pressing nor those made by freezing pressed juice and separating its water content.

Making Sherry

Winemakers fortify Sherry with spirit after fermentation finishes, not during fermentation as when making Port. All traditionally made Spanish Sherries are matured in the solera system – casks (known as butts) arranged in stacks containing progressively older wines to which a succession of younger wines are added over the years, until the finished blend boasts great complexity.

Sherry's traditional home, Jerez, is one of the hottest fine-wine regions in the world: summer daytime temperatures can exceed a sweltering 40°C. The best Sherry vineyards are located on Jerez' dazzling white soils, called albariza (literally meaning 'snow white'). Made up of 60–80 per cent chalk, they are porous and store the region's plentiful winter rain, reservoir-like, in the sub-soils and slowly release moisture to the vines during the hot, dry summers. What is more, albariza reflect the hot sun onto the grapes and help them ripen.

Fruit harvested from older vines on the best albariza soils is earmarked for premium Finos. Grapes grown on heavier clay soils tend to go into Oloroso Sherries.

Making Fino-style Sherry

After fermenting and fortifying the wines to about 15.5 per cent, traditional winemakers store the wines in five-sixths full butts or casks. Sherry bodegas (wineries) are brimful of the flor yeast that's key to the Fino style (but which won't grow on wines above 16 per cent alcohol). The yeast appears on the wine's surface and interacts with air to form a crust that looks like a thin slice of bread. The flor and oxygen convert some of the wine's alcohol into acetaldehyde, the substance that produces dry Fino-style Sherry's delicate, nutty characters. Furthermore, flor thins the wine by eating glycerol which would otherwise impart the Sherry with an illusion of sweetness.

All Sherry butts, whether they contain Fino or Oloroso wines, are stored above ground in airy cellars, quite unlike the cool, humid underground cellars of most other regions. Some of the water in the Sherry evaporates, concentrating the flavours and boosting the alcohol levels.

Sherry winemakers keep the flor alive for years by continually drawing off portions of the maturing wine and topping up the butts with younger wine, using the solera system (described on this page). Those Finos that lose their flor early on – either because the yeast has exhausted its source of nutrients or has been killed off by fortification to 16 per cent or more alcohol – become Amontillado-style Sherries and develop a browner hue due to their greater contact with air.

Making Oloroso-style Sherry

Oloroso-style Sherries are fortified to 18 per cent alcohol – conditions flor yeast cannot contend with – then matured for long periods in half-full barrels. Contact with the air oxidises the wines, making them darker and richer flavoured. Both Oloroso and Fino Sherries are naturally dry, but may be sweetened at the final blending stage (with grape juices concentrated by drying on the vine).

The solera system

Rarely is Sherry made from a single vintage. Virtually all of them are blends from several vintages, merged using the traditional fractional blending system known as the solera. Each bodega has its own solera formula, but they all work similarly. Every year a percentage of wine is drained from the oldest group of butts (known as the solera) and bottled. The part-full butts are then topped up with wine from the next oldest batch of butts (known collectively as criadera) while those butts, in turn, are topped up with wine from the next oldest criadera and so forth. Wine from the most recent harvest feeds the system. The solera keeps the flor alive in the case of Fino-style Sherries. It also helps the winemaker bottle a consistent style of wine each year. How the wine looks and tastes depends on the percentage of wine removed annually, on how long the solera has run – soleras up to 100 years old are not uncommon – and the number of criaderas involved. When conducted properly, each bottle contains at least a very small portion of wine from the solera's first vintage.

Sometimes producers note the date the solera started on the label. Don't confuse this date with a vintage – only rarely do Jerez producers make vintage-dated Sherries, called Anada or Vintage Sherry, which they mature for perhaps 30–40 years.

Making Port

Put simply, to make genuine Portuguese Port winemakers fortify wine halfway through its fermentation with highly alcoholic grape spirit or brandy, thus killing the yeasts before they've had a chance to consume all the wine's sugar.

The Douro Valley, Portugal.

Viticulture

The New World makes its Port-style wines from a handful of varieties, most commonly from Grenache, Shiraz and, to a lesser extent, Cabernet Sauvignon. But the Douro producers of Portugal use an astonishing multitude – more than 80 authorised varieties all told – and indeed may grow as many as 20 different grapes in a single vineyard. Water is scarce in the Douro Valley, so during winter vineyard labourers dig trenches to catch enough rain to help see the vines through the hot, dry summer ahead. Severe pruning takes place in November and December, so that each typically produces only about eight bunches of quality grapes the following season. Most grapes are hand harvested due to the steepness of the terrain.

Winemaking

The time-honoured way of making Port is to tip the grapes into lagares – long, low granite or concrete tanks measuring about one metre deep – fill them until two-thirds full, then invite a team of foot-treaders to trample the fruit and allow the naturally occurring yeasts on the grapes' skins (not on the feet!) to ferment the juice. Foot-treading works like a charm, breaking up the fruit without crushing the bitter-tasting pips, but since the labour shortages of the 1970s it has largely been replaced with autovinification (which works by pressure, not electrical power) and the use of stainless steel fermentation vats. Now only about five per cent of Port is made in traditional lagares.

Once the alcohol level reaches four or five per cent, the partly fermented wine is fortified using a lethal 77 per cent alcohol grape spirit or brandy which kills the still-active yeasts, stops fermentation before it converts all the sugar to alcohol and bolsters the alcohol content to around a whopping 20 per cent.

From here, the wines age in wooden casks. Winemakers taste and retaste them over the next two years before deciding their fate. Only if the Port industry's governing body, Instituto do Vinho do Porto (IVP) 'declares' a vintage exceptional are the very best wines of Portugal labelled Vintage Port. That happens about three times in a decade (although in the 1990s five vintages were 'declared').

Imported wines

New Zealanders are adventurous when it comes to experimenting with wines produced overseas. This chapter briefly outlines the styles of wines made in the key Old World and New World wine-producing countries.

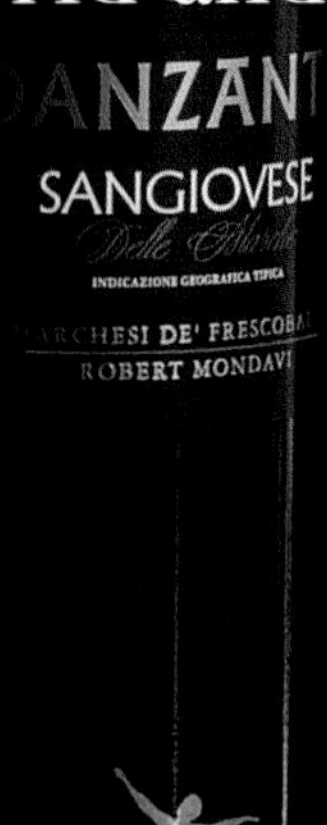

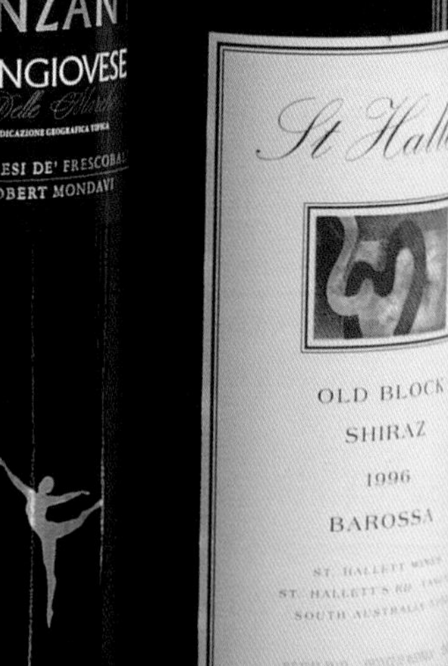

Under European wine laws, wines are generally classified under two categories: Quality Wines Produced in a Specific Region (QWPSR), such as the Appellation Contrôlée wines of France and the DOC wines of Italy; and secondly, lesser-ranked Table Wines, known as Vin de Pays in France or Indicazione Geografica Tipica (IGT) in Italy. Both the QWPSR and Table Wines classifications divide into higher- and lower-ranked classes of wines.

The New World wine regulations, by comparison, tend to be less prescriptive. Recently a number of countries, including New Zealand, signed a mutual acceptance agreement recognising this fact.

Old World wine producers

France

France produces more fine wine than any other country. To appreciate the country's many wine styles it helps to have an understanding of the diverse regions in which they grow.

Schlumberger's Kitterlé Grand Cru vineyard in Alsace.

Alsace

Alsace wines marry Germanic varieties with French winemaking techniques and are labelled by variety. Dry Riesling and Gewürztraminer dominate. Alsace itself divides into two 'départements', or winegrowing districts: the Bas-Rhin to the north and the higher altitude, more highly regarded Haut-Rhin in the south. Most wines fall under the Alsace or Alsace Grand Cru appellations, the last representing vineyards with special qualities.

Bordeaux

An extremely diverse region, especially beloved for its red-wine blends – often known as Claret – and also its sweet Sauternes.

Merlot, Cabernet Sauvignon and Cabernet Franc make the standard red blend, although some wines may include Malbec and Petit Verdot. The proportions of each vary according to where the wine comes from. Red Bordeaux from the Médoc and Graves regions (home to some of Bordeaux's most prestigious châteaux) is predominantly Cabernet Sauvignon. Red Bordeaux from the Libournais (which includes the prestigious St-Émilion and Pomerol districts) tends to contain a high proportion of Merlot. (Dry) white Bordeaux is typically a blend of Sauvignon Blanc and Sémillon; sweet Sauternes a blend of Sémillon, Sauvignon Blanc and Muscadelle.

Burgundy

Another diverse region with a huge reputation for silky, seductive red Burgundy (mostly made from Pinot Noir) and white Burgundy (mainly made from Chardonnay). It also boasts France's most notoriously complicated, hierarchical Appellation Contrôlée system, beset with traps for the unwary. A good producer's standard Bourgogne Rouge may be better than a lesser producer's Grand or Premier Cru. Study a wine atlas to learn more about growers' reputations, or ask your wine merchant for advice. Much of the Burgundy available in New Zealand is négociant (or wine dealer) wine, generally of reliable quality.

Chablis Chablis makes distinctive steely, minerally Chardonnays, classified into four levels: Chablis Grand Cru, Chablis Premier Cru, Chablis and Petit Chablis, in descending order. Look out for another of its specialities, Sauvignon de St-Bris, an inexpensive Sauvignon Blanc produced in the village of St-Bris.

The famous Corton Grand Cru on the Côte de Beaune.

Côte d'Or The heart of Burgundy, divided into the Côte de Nuits and the Côte de Beaune areas. The villages in the Côte de Nuits produce mainly red (Pinot Noir) Burgundy. The Côte de Beaune makes the finest Burgundian whites as well as reds. Every major village has its own appellation: at the top of the system sits the Grand Cru (named after a single vineyard) followed by the Premier Cru and village wine levels (the latter only mentioning the vineyard name if the wine comes from a single named vineyard). Wine mixed with other village wines from the Côte de Nuits wears the 'Villages' appellation. Wine grown anywhere within the region may carry the Bourgogne appellation. The Côte d'Or's wines can have similar-sounding names, since during the Depression many villages attached the name of their best-known vineyard to the village name to help bolster wine sales.

Côte Chalonnaise Some of Burgundy's better bargains spring from the Côte Chalonnaise (known also as the Région de Mercurey). Producer of both red Burgundy from Pinot Noir and white Burgundy from Chardonnay as well as Aligoté, a high-acid, appley-flavoured white. Mercurey is the most important village.

Mâconnais Produces generous, full-bodied wines made predominantly from Chardonnay – Pouilly-Fuissé being its most revered white. Gamay and increasingly Pinot Noir make up the balance of production. The Mâcon Supérieur appellation refers to wines with more than 11 per cent alcohol. Its other appellations are Mâcon, followed by one of the village names, and Mâcon-Villages blends (the latter for whites only).

Beaujolais Synonymous with light, affordable, berry fruit-flavoured red wines, made entirely from Gamay. Beaujolais' wines fall into four quality grades: drink-while-young Beaujolais Nouveau (also called Beaujolais Primeur); slightly weightier wines labelled simply Beaujolais; Beaujolais-Villages; and, the pick of the crop, richer, more complex Beaujolais Cru wines (which don't necessarily mention the word Beaujolais), the most famous of which are Moulin à Vent and Morgon. From the wider Burgundy region comes Bourgogne Grand Ordinaire, mostly red wine generally made from Gamay, and Bourgogne Passetoutgrains, a blend of Pinot Noir and Gamay.

Vineyards near Epernay, Champagne.

Champagne

Only sparkling wine produced in the Champagne region can bear its name. The best villages in Champagne have Grand Cru status, the next best Premier Cru, but it's the names of the big Champagne houses – Champagne Mumm for instance – people recognise first and foremost (see page 75).

Loire Valley

Whites, reds, Rosés and sparkling wine: the Loire Valley produces them all, but you won't find a wide selection available in New Zealand.

Pays Nantais and Muscadet Known for Muscadet, the best of which hail from Sèvre et Maine and may also carry the descriptor 'sur lie', meaning the wine was bottled directly off the lees in the tank.

Anjou-Saumur Famous for its many styles of Chenin Blanc and its Rosés – the better versions made with Cabernet Franc and Cabernet Sauvignon, but the majority from Grolleau, called Rosé d'Anjou in the bottle. The most notable wine of Saumur is Saumur-Champigny, a light red wine with crisp acidity and a fruity personality.

Touraine Vouvray is the region's best-known appellation. Chenin Blanc (everything from dry to sweet in style), reds based on Cabernet Franc and Cabernet Sauvignon, and sparkling wine produced in large quantities are Touraine's mainstays.

Sancerre and Pouilly The villages of Sancerre and Pouilly-sur-Loire are the spiritual home of Sauvignon Blanc.

Rhône Valley

Powerful, fuller-bodied reds are the Rhône's signature wines. Côtes du Rhône is the name of the regional appellation, but most major villages have their own appellations.

From the north come powerful reds, made from Syrah (the most famous from Hermitage), and full-bodied whites, crafted from either Viognier (the most famous being Condrieu), Marsanne or Roussanne (the latter two varieties present in white Hermitage). To the south, where the leading appellation is Châteauneuf-du-Pape, Grenache, Syrah, Mourvèdre and Carignan hold sway.

Les Bessards, Hermitage, in the Rhône, home of the world's most powerful Syrah.

Languedoc-Roussillon or The Midi

This vast, sprawling region, which stretches along the coast between Nîmes, near the Rhône delta to Perpignan, close to the Spanish border, produces some of France's best-value wines.

Vin de Pays wines grow mainly on the coastal plain; and the AC (Appellation Contrôlée) wines tend to be produced in the hills that edge the plains. Although Vin de Pays wines are generally inexpensive, value-for-money wines, a few super-premium styles command high prices.

The Vin de Pays d'Oc designation covers the entire Languedoc, but where the wine comes solely from a smaller sub-region it may bear that geographical name instead. Languedoc-Roussillon's ACs comprise blends of Syrah, Grenache, Mourvèdre, Cinsault and Carignan.

Appellations and classifications

France's strict wine laws govern every aspect of wine production: everything from which varieties may be grown where, planting densities, pruning methods, maximum yields per vine and winemaking practices.

The Quality Wine Produced in a Specific Region (QWPSR) divides into two levels:

- Appellation d'Origine Contrôlée (AC or AOC): for the highest-ranking French wines. Regional boundaries for AC wines are based on soil types, while demanding viticulture and vinification practices are laid down in law. Each region has a hierarchy of largely geographically based appellations. Most top French wines come under the AC system but, alas, not all AC wines are necessarily top quality.
- Vin délimité de qualité supérieur (VDQS): for wines classified below that of the AC system, but higher than Table Wines. VDQS rules covering maximum yields and the types of grape varieties grown may be a little less exacting.

The lesser-ranked table wine category also divides in two:

- Vin de Pays: under which areas of production, grape varieties, yields and wine standards are defined.
- Vin de Table: the most basic category of French wines and the subject of fewer regulatory laws than the other classifications.

Castello di Nipozzano in Tuscany, the site of seven centuries of winemaking by the Frescobaldi family.

Italy

Wine is everywhere in Italy. Enshrined in its customs and traditions, celebrated in its centuries-old frescos and as much a staple part of daily life as bread and olive oil.

Italy vies with France as the world's largest wine producer. Across its widely diverse terroirs there are no less than 1000 different grapes planted. As you would expect, the Italian varieties dominate, although the international mainstays – such as Chardonnay and Cabernet Sauvignon – are now gaining footholds.

Fossils show the vine flourished in Italy long before humans took any account of its virtues. The history of the cultivated vine in Italy begins with two peoples: the Etruscans who made wine in the north for centuries until conquering Romans overran their civilisation in the 4th century BC; and Greek settlers in the south who planted vines at Cumae in about 750 BC, later naming the region Oenotria, meaning Wine-Land. It was the Romans who spread knowledge of the vine and winemaking.

Classifications and regulations

Italians claim to hate rules, yet their wine legislation is incredibly complex.Its regulations conform to the EU's two-tier system: Quality Wine Produced in a Specific Region (QWPSR) and the lower-ranking table wine tier.

QWPSR

The QWPSR divides into two levels, equivalent to France's Appellation Contrôlée system:

i) Denominazione di Origine Controllata e Garantia (DOCG) Defining the geographic area, grape yields, alcohol levels, maturation times and the quality of the small number of place-named wines. Tasting panels ensure standards are upheld.

ii) Denominazione di Origine Controllata (DOC) Applies to a bigger group of place-named wines. It has similar criteria to DOCG but doesn't include a strict, panel-decided quality guarantee.

Table wines

The table wine classification system also splits into two:

i) Indicazione Geografica Tipica (IGT) Introduced in 1992 in a bid to include producers of good-to-outstanding-quality wines who choose to stay outside DOC and DOCG, such as the so-called Super Tuscans.

ii) Vino da Tavola Wine bearing no vintage or geographical marker besides Italy.

Common Italian wine words

Classico – wines grown in the central, and generally better, heartland of the named region – although that's not to say excellent wines aren't grown outside the classico zone.

Superiore – merely means has more alcohol.

Riserva – a wine that has received extended ageing in oak, and usually of higher quality.

Winegrowing regions

To make sense of Italy's winemaking regions, it helps to think of them as six 'super zones'.

The North-West

Piemonte, Liguria, Val d'Aosta Homes to some of Italy's most magnificent reds and its most delicate, aromatic whites.

Of the three most important red varieties planted here – Nebbiolo, Barbera and Dolcetto – Nebbiolo steals the limelight, most famously as Barolo. As for white wines, in the North-West they grow mainly Moscato (Muscat) which produces perfumed, sweet wines; labelled 'Moscato d'Asti' when still; and simply 'Asti' when sparkling. Cortese – a crisp, steely, limey and delicious white wine – is mostly only available from specialist wine retailers. Val d'Aosta and Liguria produce small quantities of wine rarely seen here.

The Central North-East

Veneto and Lombardia Many, for the most part good-value, Veneto wines are available in New Zealand. The most common DOC reds are easy-drinking Bardolino and Valpolicella. In the white-wine arena, the exciting DOC, Soave, leads the way. 'Vini della meditazione' are wines made from grapes raisined on straw mats, the most famous being Amarone. Lombardia produces much of its wines from the same varieties as Piemonte.

The Far North-East

Fruili-Venezie Giulia and Trentino-Alto Adige Italy's coolest corner gives rise to some of its finest whites. The coastal influence of the Adriatic Sea means the far north-east suits cool-climate-loving aromatic styles best – Pinot Grigio (Pinot Gris), Gewürztraminer, Riesling and a local variety, Tocai Friulano. As for red wines, the indigenous Refosco, Schiava and Teroldego dominate.

Central Italy

Tuscany (Toscana) and Emilia-Romagna Central Italy's reds are its best wines. Tuscany, the powerhouse of Italian winemaking, is home to six of Italy's top-ranked DOCG – that's more than in any other region. Tuscan reds are based on Sangiovese, the most well known being Chianti, from the sub-region of the same name. Quality is improving and today much of the Chianti produced is well structured and cellar worthy. Chianti itself comprises a series of sub-zones, two of the better known being Chianti Classico and Chianti Rufina.

The so-called Super Tuscans fall into the IGT classification as they tend to be made from non-traditional grape varieties.

In southern Tuscany, Sangiovese reappears as Brunello, a clone yielding the powerful, long-living Brunello di Montalcino, which vies with Barolo as Italy's greatest red. Near Brunello di Montalcino, the small town of Montepulciano produces Vino Nobile di Montepulciano from another Sangiovese clone, Prugnolo.

Traditional-style sparkling Lambrusco from Emilia-Romagna is a light red wine with good acidity – but be sure to select DOC Lambrusco sealed with a Champagne-style cork.

Umbria Umbria's most celebrated wine is a white called Orvieto, made from the Grechetto grape.

Lazio Its best-known wine is Frascati, a white blend of Malvasia and the Trebbiano di Toscana grape. Wines with a higher Malvasia content are the better styles.

Marche Marche bases its whites on the Verdicchio grape, the most famous being Verdicchio di Castelli di Jesi. The region's best red is Rosso Conero, made from the Montepulciano grape.

Abruzzi It has two DOCs, Montepulciano d'Abruzzo and Trebbiano d'Abruzzo. The former is a simple, easy-drinking red wine based upon the Montepulciano grape. White Trebbiano is rarely seen in this country, but if you find it on your travels, be aware that its quality varies.

Molise Molise for the most part produces rustic versions of Abruzzo-style. Its wines are not often seen outside the region.

Arezzo: a typical Tuscan pastoral scene.

Southern Italy

Apuglia, Basilicata, Calabria and Campania Many of this region's wines tended to be high in alcohol and a little on the rustic side. The same cannot be said for the new generation of varietal wines flowing out of Apuglia under the IGT classification, however. The most common seen here number wines made from Negroamaro (also sold as DOC Salice Salentino) as well as Primitivo (also known as Zinfandel).

Sicily and Sardinia

Sicily Like Apuglia, Sicily produces lots of wine, much of it labelled according to grape variety and now crafted under the influence of the New World. Most wines fall outside the DOC system. The best carry a 'Q' on their labels.

Sardinia Its historical links with France and Spain show in its wines, Spanish Vermentino being popular for whites and the French Grenache producing the best reds.

Germany

Germany, the world's most northerly winegrowing country, is literally the polar opposite of Central Otago, the world's most southerly winegrowing region.

Germany's best wines are sensual and elegantly structured, although it's fair to say that a great many fall into the rather unremarkable, easy-quaffing category. Virtually all Germany's wines are white, with Müller-Thurgau and Riesling dominating the planting stakes. The few red wines produced here are mostly made from the Spätburgunder, the German nom de plume for Pinot Noir – a class of wines you're unlikely to come across in New Zealand. Other varieties include Silvaner (spelt Sylvaner elsewhere), Kerner, Scheurebe, Reichensteiner and Ruländer – the last being the local name for Pinot Gris. Which variety wears the crown for best German wine? Riesling, of course.

Labelling

German wine regulations are among the most complex on the planet and, to make matters even more complicated, many of their labels are written in almost impenetrable Gothic script. Fortunately, with a little perseverance, the code is relatively easy to crack. The country's wines fall into two broad categories:

Table wines
Not necessarily from Germany unless the label states 'Deutscher Tafelwein' and rarely seen in New Zealand anyway.

Quality wines
Which themselves divide into two sub-categories:

i) Qualitätswein bestimmte Anbaugebiete (QbA)
Quality Wine from a Designated Quality Region. The most common is *Liebfraumilch*, usually a medium-sweet blend of Müller-Thurgau and Riesling. Many New Zealanders are familiar with the style, sold here under brand names such as Black Tower and Blue Nun.

ii) Qualitätswein mit Prädikat (QmP) Superior Quality Wine, rated according to the degrees of ripeness the grapes reached at harvest as follows:

Kabinett – wine made from fully ripe grapes, usually light and elegant in style with a racy acidity.

Spätlese – Spätlese means late harvest. The wines tend to be higher in alcohol than the Kabinett and have fuller bodies and flavours. Their sweetness levels may be higher, too.

Auslese – usually medium-sweet wines with remarkable intensity and flavour, produced from individually selected overripe bunches of grapes.

Beerenauslese – rich dessert wines made from individually selected overripe grapes which may be botrytised (*edelfäule* in German).

Eiswein – true Eiswein is made from grapes that freeze in severe frosts on the vine (see page 285).

Trockenbeerenauslese – intensely flavoured sweet wines made from grapes raisined by botrytis.

The Moselle vineyards give rise to some of the world's most sensual Riesling wines.

Other German wine words to look out for

Trocken (meaning dry) or *Halbtrocken* (meaning off-dry) – both styles have higher alcohol contents than normal for German wines and are becoming increasingly common in Germany, but are rarely seen in our part of the world.

VerbandDeutscher Prädikats und Qualitätsweinguter eV (VDP) – the name of a producer-group organisation to which many of Germany's best winemakers belong, and a sure-fire indicator that the wine is of high quality. Look for their definitive eagle symbol on the capsule or label.

Erste Gewäch – means 'first growth'. Since the 1999 vintage the term has been used on single-vineyard wines made by some of the country's top producers in the Rheingau Anbaugebiet region.

Sekt – a style of sparkling wine made in huge quantities in stainless steel tanks, the most well-known brand in New Zealand being Henkell Trocken.

Winegrowing regions

Germany has 13 quality wine regions (called Anbaugebiete), the most famous among them being Mosel-Saar-Ruwer, Nahe, Rheingau, Rheinhessen and Pfalz. Each Angaugebiet is split into districts comprising a collection of winegrowing villages, called Bereiche, named after the most prominent village in the area. Each Bereich encompasses a number of Grosslagen – or groups of vineyards – with each Grosslagen consisting of individual vineyards called Einzellagen. The reputation of the producer may say more about the quality of the wine than the official designation on the label, however.

Invading Romans planted the first cultivated vines in what is now Germany in about 100 BC, thus beginning the region's winemaking tradition. Throughout the Middle Ages and right up until Napoleon's invasion of the Rhinelands in 1803, various monastic orders kept the tradition alive by producing many of the area's finest wines. After that, a number of church vineyards were broken up and sold off to private individuals. The next generation of winegrowers began concentrating their efforts on quality winemaking – and the state stepped in to support them with the creation of schools of viticulture. Wars and economic depressions might have curtailed the industry's development during the first half of the 20th century, but since then the country has garnered a reputation for producing wines of exquisite finesse. A number of Germany's famous vineyards trace their origins back to the ancient monastic settlements.

Rioja in northern Spain, where Tempranillo reaches its zenith.

Spain

Spain's wine industry is riding the crest of a wave, producing a wealth of complex, yet inexpensive wines.

How has it gone from being a former rustic amateur to a world-beating wine producer? Two reasons. The majority of Spain's vineyards carry mature, high-quality, low-yielding vines. Making premium wines from their crops is as straightforward as implementing good, modern winemaking practices – which is precisely the approach progressive winemakers have taken ever since revolutionary winemaker Miguel Torres introduced the first temperature-controlled stainless steel fermentation tanks into Spain in the 1960s.

So low cropping are Spain's vines, in fact, that even though it boasts the largest vineyard area of any country, it's only the world's third largest producer.

Famous around the world for Sherry (see page 78), Spain is otherwise predominantly a red-wine country. Most of the country's wines are based on the fresh, fruity, high-quality Tempranillo grape variety and the robust, gutsy Garnacha (Grenache) grape, although increasingly these are blended with internationally recognised varieties, such as Cabernet Sauvignon and Merlot.

Cava is Spain's traditional sparkling wine. Made from Parellada, Xarello and Macabeo grapes, using the Metodo Tradicional (a replica of the Champagne method) it is produced in certain prescribed regions of the country. Cava often has attractive rubbery/burnt toast aromas. 'Cordon Negro', produced by the giant Freixenet company, is the most common example available on the New Zealand market.

In accordance with EU regulations, Spain's quality wine-producing districts are defined in law. The country is split into many Denominaciónes de Origen (DO), analagous to France's Appellation Contrôlée system, and at the higher level, Denominación de Origen e Calificada (DOCa) – so far only awarded to Rioja. Each DO or DOCa is governed by a consejo regulador, made up of growers, winemakers and local officials, the authority which awards wines that meet its criteria a seal of quality.

All Spanish wines also carry a classification based on the ageing they have received. Vino Joven is 'young' wine, sold the year after vintage, whereas Crianza is at least two years old and has spent a minimum of six months maturing in small oak barrels. Reserva, produced only during the better vintages, is at least three years old when it goes on sale and has spent no less than 12 months ageing in oak. At the top of the hierarchy are Gran Reserva wines. These are made only in exceptional vintages and to qualify for Gran Reserva status must age for at least five years, with two or three of those years spent in barrels.

> Much of Spain has a continental climate with cold winters and hot summers – searingly hot in central Spain. Exceptions are the milder Mediterranean coast and temperate, wetter Galicia in the north-west of the country. Use of irrigation systems is rare, even in the hottest, driest regions.

Portugal

Portugal has given the wine world two great gifts – the cork and the rich, sweet, high-alcohol styles of wine called Port.

Portugal supplies the world with more than half its cork and is, of course, synonymous with Port (see pages 81 and 288). But its Douro and Dão regions also produce some excellent red wines from varieties such as Touriga Nacional and Spain's Tempranillo. Internationally, it is well known for the ever-popular, ubiquitous Mateus Rosé, a lightly sparkling, off-dry wine.

New World wine producers

Australia

They don't call this vast land the 'lucky country' for nothing. From the cool Adelaide Hills, noted for Sauvignon Blanc and Pinot Noir, to the hot Barossa Valley, renowned for deeply coloured, rich Shiraz, Australia's winegrowing regions span the spectrum.

Ripening grapes is seldom problematic in Australia's warm climate; hence, as a rule the country's white wines are generous and rounded, its red wines big, bold and gutsy. And not surprisingly, Australia's most planted varieties are warmth-loving Shiraz (Syrah) and Cabernet Sauvignon.

Australian winemakers and winegrowers share with their Kiwi counterparts an innate ability to adapt and innovate. Give them a technique and they'll improve it to suit their own environments – and make better wines for their efforts. It's an approach that makes their winemaking schools, Roseworthy College and Charles Sturt University, admired throughout the world.

New South Wales

The home of some of Australia's best Sémillons, made in the dry (especially unoaked) and botrytised styles. New South Wales is well regarded for generous, warm Shiraz and rich, full-bodied Chardonnays.

Hunter Valley Chardonnay and Sémillon today dominate the Upper Hunter, Shiraz and Sémillon the Lower Hunter Valley.

Mudgee The source of the famous Mudgee mud: rich, fertile soils which grow similarly rich Chardonnay and ripe, well-rounded Sémillon. Nice, big, round Cabernet Sauvignon and Shiraz hail from this district, too.

Riverina Hot, dry, irrigated plains grow vast quantities of everyday wines and turn out some delicious sweet late-harvest and botrytised dessert Sémillons.

South Australia

Oenophiles and gastronomes delight in South Australia's wine and food traditions, born out of the influences of German immigrants to the Barossa Valley and Italian immigrants to McLaren Vale. South Australia produces more wine than any other state, thanks to the massive wineries in the Riverland area.

Adelaide and the Hills As a rule, the hot, flat plains to the north of Adelaide city do not grow the best wines. But across to the east in the Adelaide Hills, cool-climate Sauvignon Blanc as well as Pinot Noir and Chardonnay for both still and sparkling wine fare very well.

Barossa Valley and Eden Valley The Barossa Valley, famous for its German Lutheran heritage as much as its gutsy Shiraz and Cabernet Sauvignon, boasts some of Australia's and the world's oldest producing vines. Some gnarled, old gentlemanly Shiraz and Grenache specimens have seen their 100th birthday. Riesling dominates the whites, the best springing from the cooler, higher-altitude Barossa Ranges and hills of the Eden Valley rather than the Barossa Valley floor.

McLaren Vale and Langhorne Creek McLaren Vale's warm climate and moderately fertile soils produce rich, intense, full-bodied red wines, notably Cabernet Sauvignon, Shiraz, Grenache and Mataro. It's also home to many very old vines. Tropical fruit-flavoured Sauvignon Blanc and full-bodied Chardonnays epitomise the region's white wines. To the south-east of McLaren Vale, Langhorne Creek produces some excellent Cabernet Sauvignons.

Winemaking history

Australia's winemaking history shares many parallels with our own. It started confidently in the 19th century, but fell victim to phylloxera and was overshadowed by the popularity of beer and fortified wines. Then, in the 1960s, the industry's fortunes took a turn for the better. Table wines were fashionable again and a domestic boom began. By the mid-1980s, the country was in the grip of a wine glut and a government-funded vine-pull saw many old, priceless vines ripped out of the soil. Today, Australian wines are some of the world's most popular.

Clare Valley Despite its warm climate, Clare Valley makes intense Rieslings with strong lime and citrus flavours, topped off with a distinctive toastiness. Another standout style is the region's big powerful Shiraz.

Coonawarra Think Coonawarra, think Cabernet. Its continental climate yields some of Australia's top Cabernet Sauvignons from vines anchored in the region's famous terra rossa soils (shallow brick-red earth over deep limestone). Big, blackcurrant-flavoured wines with minerally flavours and a dash of mint are its trademark. Don't overlook its very good Shiraz and Merlot either.

Riverland Vast stretches of fertile, irrigated vineyards growing many different grapes, most destined for simple quaffing wines.

Padthaway A relatively cool grapegrowing region, admired for its white wines, especially ripe, bold, peachy-flavoured Chardonnays with firm acid backbones.

Tasmania Tasmania's cool climate suits Riesling, Pinot Noir and Pinot Gris as well as crisp, tangy Chardonnay for sparkling wines, the latter one of tiny Tasmania's specialities.

Victoria

Some of Victoria's districts – especially those south of the Great Dividing Range – are cool enough to be compared with Burgundy in France, while the state's central and north-eastern areas are warmer by far.

Yarra Valley and Geelong Cooler areas of Victoria, best known for smooth, yet slightly grainy, cherry fruit Pinot Noir, restrained Chardonnay and Cabernet Sauvignon. Shiraz, Sémillon and Sauvignon Blanc do well here, too.

Rutherglen Its fortes are rich, luscious liqueur Muscats and Tokay (made from Muscadelle) – underrated treasures in a world where these styles have fallen out of fashion.

Goulburn Valley and Central Victoria Marsanne rates as the Goulburn Valley's speciality. Others include Riesling, Shiraz and Cabernet Sauvignon.

McLaren Vale, where sea breezes cool the midday heat.

North-West Victoria Huge, flat, irrigated vineyards stretching from Mildura township down to Echuca grow grapes for easy-drinking fruity wines.

Mornington Peninsula Home to some of Victoria's best boutique wineries and also a few larger producers. In good years Mornington crafts excellent Pinot Noir, Cabernet Sauvignon and Chardonnay.

Western Australia

Wines from Western Australia are more European in style on account of the region's maritime climate. They generally have greater elegance and tighter structures than the upfront, fruit-driven styles of many other Australian wines.

Swan district One of the oldest – and hottest – grapegrowing regions in Australia, its most revered wine is the famous Houghton White Burgundy, a Chenin Blanc-dominant blend.

Margaret River Cooled by sea breezes from the Indian Ocean, the valley turns out a wide range of excellent wines, particularly well-balanced Chardonnay and tight, attractive Cabernet Sauvignon.

Great Southern Further south lies the Great Southern region, producing some of Western Australia's best wines, including those from Plantagenet.

United States of America

America's vibrant wine industry has impacted upon virtually every aspect of the world's wine trade in one way or another.

The New World of modern winemaking, especially, owes the US industry a huge debt of gratitude. Everything from a collection of ground-breaking advances in viticulture and winemaking techniques to the styles of wine we prefer today have been influenced by the United States to some extent.

The seminal work of Robert Mondavi of Napa Valley, California – whose experimentation with fermentation techniques, barrels and fining regimes revolutionised winemaking in the 1960s – helped set the New World on the path towards producing the fresh, fruit-forward, easy-drinking wines that are its hallmarks today. And it was the world-famous University of California, Davis, wine faculty which first promulgated 'varietalism' in the 1950s and 1960s in a bid to encourage winegrowers to plant *Vitis vinifera* varieties. By the 1970s US winemakers had adopted 'varietalism' wholeheartedly and soon so did the New World. Closer to home, it was the Davis wine faculty which in 1973 recommended Montana go ahead with Frank Yukich's plans to plant grapes in Marlborough and therefore indirectly played a part in the development of New Zealand's wine industry.

The United States is the world's fourth largest wine producer. Virtually all its wines flow out of California, but that major-league state aside, there are two other leading wine-producing regions: Washington and Oregon.

California Americans believe California is as close to a winegrowing Utopia as any place on Earth. Rain rarely falls between late spring and autumn; the nearby Pacific Ocean fans the summer heat; and a cold ocean current treading along the Californian coast forms a cooling fog that moves inland, hovering over two of its most famous viticulture regions – the (southern end of) Napa and Sonoma valleys. Cabernet Sauvignon, Merlot and Cabernet Franc (occasionally labelled Meritage, when blended) are California's star wines. Chardonnay remains the most important white variety while oak-aged Sauvignon Blanc (known as Fumé Blanc) is also popular. But the grape which California has made its own is Zinfandel, a big, spicy, high-alcohol red, which at its best makes a powerful, long-living wine.

Redwood Valley, California, operates on a huge scale.

Oregon Further up the west coast lies cool-climate Oregon, whose main grapegrowing region, the Willamette Valley, enjoys a similar climate to Burgundy and not surprisingly has made Pinot Noir its signature wine.

Washington state Most vineyards in Washington state are clustered in the dry Columbia Valley. Full-bodied reds are the region's celebrities, especially fine, fruity Merlot, Cabernet Sauvignon and Syrah.

America's wine-producing regions fall under designated Approved Viticultural Areas (AVAs). At least 85 per cent of the wine must come from the appellation specified on the bottle.

You'll find very few American wines in New Zealand – the strength of the US dollar against the Kiwi largely prices them out of our local market. Fierce competition within the US for the best wines tends to push prices above their intrinsic value – and beyond the reach of the average Kiwi wallet.

Canada

Four provinces house Canada's thriving wine industry: Ontario, British Columbia, Quebec and Nova Scotia.

In the early 1990s, their growers began placing more emphasis on producing wines from the classical *Vitis vinifera* varieties in place of the traditional, winter-hardy (North American) Labrusca species which had until then occupied most of their attentions. Now the country successfully produces a raft of classical-style wines, such as Chardonnay, Riesling and Merlot. But its wine niche is undoubtedly geniune, high-quality ice wine (see pages 77 and 285), of which Canada is the world's largest producer. This is not suprising given many of the country's ice-wine producers can almost rely on bitter frosts to freeze ripe clusters on the vines each season. Look for Canadian ice wines in specialist wine retail stores.

Argentina

Noticed an increasing number of Argentinian Malbecs and Cabernet Sauvignon blends on the shelves recently? Argentina's wine revolution is in full swing, as producers concentrate on appealing to export markets.

Visit Argentina and you will encounter plenty of wines you most likely haven't heard of – bulk varieties, such as Criolla or Cereza, packaged in wicker-encased demi-johns, tetrapaks and casks and sold as thirst-quenchers to appreciative locals, but looked upon in disdain by those with more discerning, cosmopolitan palates.

Fortunately, an increasing number of Argentinian wine producers are now focusing on the European varieties and are enjoying terrific success with Malbec. So successful are Argentinian Malbecs, in fact, that at their exalted best, they outshine those produced in the variety's original homeland, Bordeaux. Red-wine lovers appreciate their intense aromas, flavours and rich textures. Graffigna produces good examples.

Winter in the Mendoza region, Argentina.

Aside from Malbec, Argentina's main claim to fame is its reds – the Bordeaux varieties of Pinot Noir and Syrah along with the classic Italians Bonarda, Barbera and Sangiovese. It also produces some interesting Chardonnay, Sémillon, Sauvignon Blanc, Chenin Blanc and even Riesling. But when looking for something with 'Argentina' written all over it, try Torrontes, an aromatic variety of obscure, probably Spanish origins which Argentinians now claim as their own. The wine tastes like a cross between Gewürztraminer and Pinot Gris and is available on the New Zealand market.

Argentina is the world's fifth largest wine-producing country. Most of its grapes grow along the nation's western wing, between Salta in the north and Rio Negro some 2000 kilometres further south, in and around the foothills of the Andes. The finest fruit comes off the less-fertile, cooler, higher-altitude vineyards set in the mountain foothills.

Mendoza The majority of Argentinian wines flow from Mendoza – a name many New Zealanders are familiar with since Argentina's Mendoza Chardonnay is widely planted in this country.

Salta The northern province of Salta produces some of the best Torrontes in the country.

Patagonia Argentina's coolest wine-growing region, Patagonia has the potential to make very good white wines and already produces Chardonnay and Sauvignon Blanc.

Chile

Chile produces most of its wines for the export market. You'll find a number of them for sale in New Zealand.

In recent years, the standard of Chilean wine has improved markedly as a direct result of producers having invested heavily in viticultural management and new winemaking technologies. Today, the country has a reputation for soft, fruity varietal wines with relatively inexpensive price tags. Comparatively low labour costs help keep the cost of Chilean wine down, although those prices are rising as the quality of the country's wines improves.

Some Chilean producers have likened their climate to a cross between that of Bordeaux and the Napa Valley in California. Little wonder then that it is best known for warm, juicy Cabernet Sauvignons and Merlots, although Chile also enjoys success with a number of other varieties as well – fruity Chardonnays, Syrah, Pinot Noir, Gewürztraminer, Sangiovese, Zinfandel, Riesling and Viognier.

Chile is in the enviable position of being phylloxera-free, hence its vines grow on their own roots.

The Helderberg, typical of South Africa's breathtakingly beautiful vineyards.

South Africa

You won't find many South African wines on New Zealand shelves, but if you do come across a wine from an estate producer, chances are it offers good value for money.

Only since the demise of apartheid politics have wine producers turned their attentions to the classical varieties. Now they are dabbling with everything from Cabernet to Chardonnay and beginning to evaluate precisely which varieties best suit individual terroirs, rather than relying on their former scatter-gun approach to planting. Nonetheless, high-yielding grapes – the likes of Colombard and Chenin Blanc (known locally as Steen) – still hold sway, even today. The country also boasts its very own grape, Pinotage (see page 70).

Regions Most of the country's best-known wine regions lie near the Cape of Good Hope. **Stellenbosch** is the wine hub, home to some of the best labels and the focus of much capital investment. Cool, coastal **Constantia**, renowned in the 18th century for sweet wine, is now garnering a reputation for Cabernet Sauvignon, Merlot and Chardonnay. **Paarl** policed South Africa's wine industry for decades through the Koöperatieve Wijnbouwers Vereniging (KWV), a national organisation which set production limits and fixed crop prices until its regulatory role was dismantled in the early 1990s. Today, it remains an important producer. **Worcester** produces excellent fortified wines, while nearby **Robertson** makes still and sparkling wines from Chardonnay. Bottle-fermented versions are known as Méthode Cap Classique – you may find one or two in New Zealand.

South Africa's Wine of Origin system, introduced in 1973, recognises 60 appellations and guarantees consumers that the origin, grape variety and vintage stated on the bottle are accurate.

Glossary

acetaldehyde Most important aldehyde in winemaking. See aldehyde.

acetobacter Bacteria that causes the vinegary taste in wine.

acetic acid Chemical that gives wine a vinegary taste. Also called volatile acidity.

acidity All wines naturally contain acids, which should be in proper balance with fruit and other components. Sufficient acidity gives liveliness and crispness and helps white wines age.

aeration Exposing the wine to oxygen, either during winemaking or when tasting.

aftertaste The flavour impression the wine leaves after it is swallowed. This is also referred to as the finish and can be pleasant or unpleasant. Complex, fine and aged wines have a long or lingering aftertaste.

albariza Chalky, white soils of the Jerez region of Spain.

alcohol Chemical produced as a by-product of the conversion of sugar by the yeast during fermentation. Also called ethanol.

aldehyde Class of chemicals resulting from the combination of oxygen and alcohol by flor yeast that produces a nutty flavour, found mainly in dry Sherries.

ampelography The science of identifying and describing vine species.

anthocyanins Chemical compounds extracted from the skins of red-grape varieties that give wines their colour.

antioxidant 300 See vitamin C.

appellation Demarcated French wine region bound by certain rules in terms of grape variety and yields.

aroma The varietal fruit flavours present in the grape juice at harvest. See bouquet.

aromatic Term to describe wines with pronounced aromas, particularly floral and spicy aromas. Examples include Gewürztraminer and Riesling.

ascorbic acid See vitamin C.

aspiration Practice of gurgling air through wine in the taster's mouth. Also called trilling.

Asti Abbreviated term for Italian sparkling wine.

astringent Term to describe the mouth-puckering feel of tannins in wine derived from the grape skins or barrel oak. It is most pronounced in young red wines.

attack The first impression a wine gives on the palate.

austere Term to describe wine that is dry, somewhat hard, but not fruity in flavour.

back-blending Winemaking technique in which unfermented grape juice is added to wine to sweeten it.

backbone See structure.

balance Aspect of wine that relates to the harmony between its main components such as acid, sugar, tannin and alcohol.

barrique A 225-litre oak cask commonly used in New Zealand.

barrique fermented Term to describe wine that has been fermented in barriques to add an extra dimension of flavour, a softer texture and a better integration of fruit with oak flavours.

bâtonnage French for lees-stirring.

bead Term for the bubbles in sparkling wine.

Beaujolais French wine region and wine from it. Normally fruity wines made from the Gamay grape.

bentonite Clay-based fining agent used for removing protein from wine.

big Term to describe a wine that is full bodied and powerful in aroma and flavour.

bilge Rounded part of the barrel.

biodynamic Winegrowing practice based on Rudolph Steiner's holistic, environmentally friendly philosophy.

bitterness Flavour picked up on the back of the tongue. In wine this can be caused by phenolic compounds and is usually considered a fault.

blind tasting Tasting where wines are tasted without their identity being known.

body Term to express the fullness of a wine and usually proportional to the amount of extract present. Also described as viscosity or chewability.

Bordeaux French wine region and the wine from it. Normally Cabernet Sauvignon-based or Merlot-based reds.

Botrytis cinerea A mould or fungus that attacks most grape varieties. Also known as grey rot or noble rot.

bottle age The mellowing effect and taste of a wine that has spent time in a bottle.

bouquet Those smells that are derived from the winemaking process or cellaring, e.g. from yeast, oak barrels and malolactic fermentation. cf. aroma.

Brix A unit to measure the sugar content of grapes, grape juice or wine. One degree Brix of sugar is the same as one per cent sugar content.

brut Term for Champagne or méthode traditionnelle wines which taste off-dry.

bunchstem necrosis Vine disorder that causes the bunch to wilt.

Burgundy French wine region and wine from it. Normally based on Chardonnay and Pinot Noir.

buttery Term to describe the tastes associated with malolactic fermentation: rich flavours and smoothness of texture.

cap The layer of red grape skins that float on the top of a red wine ferment.

carbon dioxide The gas that is produced as a by-product of fermentation and also provides the effervescence in sparkling styles.

carbonic maceration Winemaking fermentation process whereby whole bunches ferment spontaneously. A characteristic of French Beaujolais production.

cellar To store a wine to mellow its acid or tannic structure. Also the area for storing wine.

centrifuging Technique of clarifying the wine by passing it through a centrifuge or separator, spinning out the yeast.

chalking Winemaking technique of adding calcium carbonate chalk to wine to lower acidity.

Champagne Wine region in north-eastern France famous for its sparkling wines. Also used for wines from the region.

chaptalisation The addition of cane sugar to lift juice sugar levels.

Charmat A variation of the méthode traditionnelle process whereby the secondary fermentation is carried out in a pressure tank rather than in the bottle. Commonly used in the production of Sekt and Asti Spumante.

château French winemaking estate (literally 'castle').

chewability See body.

clarification Filtering, centrifuging or fining the wine to remove yeast and particulate material.

clone A member of a group of plants propagated asexually from a single parent. Most grape varieties have different clones displaying different characteristics.

closed Term for wine that has a smell which is difficult to detect. Also shy or dumb.

coarse Term to describe wine that is harsh or rough in flavour or texture.

cold stabilisation Winemaking process by which wine is chilled to –2°C and held there for between one to three weeks to precipitate unstable tartaric acid as potassium bitartrate (cream of tartar).

collage French term for fining wine.

con-gas Winemaking process by which carbon dioxide gas is infused in still wine to create inexpensive sparkling wine.

cool ferment Winemaking process by which the temperature is kept low during the fermentation process. Used for white wines to retain more fruit flavours and aromas.

complexity Feature of a wine that has a diversity of desirable smells and tastes in harmony with each other.

concentrated Feature of a wine that has intense, full flavours.

cooper The tradesman who makes wine barrels.

copita Small, tulip-shaped glass traditionally used for drinking sherry.

Coquard press French brand of wine press.

corked A wine fault caused by cork taint, and having an unappealing mouldy smell reminiscent of a damp wardrobe.

coupe Flat, dish-like, long-stemmed Champagne glass. Now out of favour.

cover crop Inter-row plantings which influence vine vigour, soil fertility and structure, and harbour predatory insects.

Crémant French sparkling wine made outside Champagne.

criadera Term for the upper layers of barrels in a Spanish solera.

crisp Term to describe a wine with fresh acidity.

crust The sediment that often appears inside bottles of older red wine. It consists mostly of pigments, tartrate crystals and tannins.

cuve A tank for fermenting wine, traditionally made of wood.

cuvée Base wine for méthode traditionnelle before fermentation in the bottle. It means blend.

cynarin Chemical that makes wine taste bitter, found in artichokes and asparagus.

declared vintage This term relates to Champagne and Ports, where in exceptional years a vintage is declared by individual producers.

delestage Winemaking technique whereby wine is removed from its original container and then returned to it. Also rack and return.

delicate Light in fragrance, flavour and body.

dessert wine A wine that is sweet and rich and is enjoyed with desserts or strong-flavoured foods.

developed Term to describe a mature wine that displays an integration of different flavours and tastes.

diacetyl Chemical compound that imparts a buttery flavour to wine.

diatomaceous earth A fine powder made from the skeletons of tiny waterborne organisms which is used as an inert filter medium.

diurnal variation Difference between day and night temperatures.

dry Term to describe a wine that has little or no perceived sweetness. Officially less than five grams per litre of residual sugar.

dull Term to describe a wine that lacks acidity, character and freshness. Also flat.

dumb See closed.

earthy Bouquet and flavour reminiscent of certain soil types, found in young Vintage Ports and some reds.

entrillage Practice of storing sparkling wines on their lees after the secondary fermentation.

esters Chemical compounds derived from the combination of alcohol and acids. They are usually intensely aromatic.

ethanol See alcohol.

extract The measure of a wine's solids content or dry weight, incorporating sugars, minerals, glycerols, tannins, and the like. The level corresponds to the body of a wine.

extra dry Term on Champagne labels to indicate not quite dry; not as dry as brut.

fermentation The basic winemaking process in which yeast converts sugar into alcohol, carbon dioxide and heat.

filtration Winemaking process through which different types of filters are used to remove matter particles or yeast from wine.

fine-grained Term to describe tannins that are not coarse and harsh. An indication of good-quality red wine.

finesse Term to describe wines showing delicate characteristics, well-structured yet still in perfect balance.

fining Winemaking process by which a fining agent is added to a wine. This combines with a particular molecule or substance present, then settles out on the bottom of the tank, effectively removing the matter from the wine.

finish See aftertaste.

firm Term to describe red wine with obvious tannins.

flabby Term to describe wines which are out of balance owing to low acid levels.

flat See dull.

flavour A complex interaction between a number of different sensory receptor systems. The element in the taste of a substance that depends on the cooperation of the sense of smell.

flor A unique yeast which grows on the surface of Sherry and produces a characteristic nutty flavour.

floret The tiny grape flower prior to pollination.

flute Tall, thin glass, mainly used for sparkling wine.

fortified Wines to which pure alcohol spirit or brandy spirit has been added.

forward Term to describe wines that have aged more rapidly than expected.

foxy Term to describe the grapey flavours of wines made from native American grapes such as *Vitis labrusca* or hybrids.

free run The juice which runs freely by gravity from draining tanks and bag presses.

fresh Term to describe appealingly youthful, light and acidic wines.

fruit Aspects that relate to the varietal flavours of a particular grape.

fruiting zone That section of a grapevine where almost all of the grape bunches are attached.

fruity Term to describe wines where flavours and aromas of various fruits are dominant. Sometimes confused with an impression of sweetness.

full-bodied/full Term to describe gutsy, round and mouth-filling wines.

Fumé Blanc Usually Sauvignon Blanc that has been fermented and/or aged in oak barrels.

Gamay Black-grape variety used to make Beaujolais wines.

Gewürztraminer Grape variety that produces aromatic, floral wines.

glycerol A colourless substance with a smooth, warm, sweet taste which occurs naturally in very ripe grapes.

gondola A grape-bin trailer towed behind a tractor and filled by a mechanical grape harvester.

grafting Practice of joining budwood and rootstock from different varieties.

grams per litre (g/L) Often used to indicate total acidity or residual sugar in a wine.

Grand Cru Title applied to some of the best vineyards in France. Literally 'great growth'.

green Term to describe a wine with excessive acidity, generally from being picked too early. Often lacking fruit flavours.

Grenache Popular red French grape, called Garnacha in Spain.

grey rot See botrytis.

grow guards Breathable shelters placed around young, growing vines.

growing degree days (GDD) The sum of the growing season's mean daily temperatures above 10°C.

gyropallets Machines that perform the riddling of sparkling wine to move the sediment to the neck of the bottle.

hard Term to describe excessive levels of tannin dominating a wine's other characteristics.

harmonious Term to describe wine in which all elements, such as fruit, acidity and tannins, are in balance.

harsh Term to describe wine that has a rough, biting character from excessive tannin or acid.

hen and chicken berries Large and small berries occurring on the same bunch.

herbaceous Term to describe wines with aromas reminiscent of cut grass or pea shells as in Sauvignon Blanc. Similar flavours are evident in some cool-climate Cabernet Sauvignons.

Hermitage French wine appellation known for wine based on Syrah. Sometimes used as a synonym for Syrah or Shiraz.

hollow Term to describe wine with foretaste (the first impression or 'attack') and finish, but lacking flavour in the middle.

honeyed Luscious sweet characters evident in late-harvest and botrytised styles.

horizontal tasting A comparative tasting of related wines from the same vintage.

hot Term to describe wines with excessive and out-of-balance alcohol levels.

hydrogen sulphide Chemical that smells of rotten eggs. It is sometimes produced by the yeast during fermentation and is considered a wine fault.

internodes Area between nodes on vine shoots.

jammy Wine with insufficient acidity to match high sugar levels, giving a cloying finish.

jéroboam 3-litre or 4.5-litre wine bottle.

lactic acid Mild acid found in wines after malolactic fermentation. Also common in dairy products.

lagares Flat concrete tanks traditionally used to crush grapes for making Port.

late harvest Medium to sweet wine that has been made from very ripe, late-picked grapes.

lees The yeast or fining sediment that is deposited by the wine in a tank or barrel.

lees-stirring Winemaking process by which yeast lees sediment is stirred up. Also bâtonnage.

legs The streams left on the inside of a glass after a wine has been swirled. Their characteristics are proportional to the alcohol content. Also tears.

length See aftertaste.

lifted Term to describe wine flavours which are pronounced.

light-bodied/light Term to describe wines with little weight, extract or mouth-feel.

liqueur d'expédition Mixture of sugar, brandy and old wine added to sparkling wine before bottling.

lively Fresh, crisp and full of vitality.

loess Fine-grained clay and silt soils deposited by wind.

luscious Rich and smooth, applied to intensely fruity wines.

maceration Winemaking process by which colour, flavour and tannin is extracted from red-grape skins.

macroclimate Climate in the region.

magnum 1.5-litre wine bottle.

malic acid A strong, sharp acid found in grape juice. The main acid in apple juice.

malolactic fermentation Winemaking process through which bacteria change malic acid to buttery lactic acid.

marc The grape solids that remain after pressing.

mature Term to describe wine that is aged to its full potential, but with aged characteristics still in harmony with a wine's other beneficial attributes. Could also be a euphemism for wine that is past its best.

medium-bodied Term to describe wines with medium weight, extract or mouth-feel.

mellow Term to describe wine that is soft, integrated, easy drinking or older.

Mendoza Argentinian wine region where the popular Mendoza clone of Chardonnay was selected.

mercaptan Wine fault resulting from the combination of hydrogen sulphide molecules. Although it produces the same rotten egg smell as hydrogen sulphide, it cannot be removed from the wine.

mesoclimate Climate in the vineyard.

metallic Term to describe wine with a metal flavour, usually unpleasant.

méthode champenoise Disused term for méthode traditionnelle.

méthode traditionnelle Wine made by the traditional winemaking process used in the production of Champagne, incorporating a secondary fermentation in the bottle. Also méthode champenoise.

methoxypyrazines Flavour compounds responsible for the pungent, herbaceous character in Sauvignon Blanc.

microclimate Climate in and around the vine canopy.

mousse Term for the effervescence in sparkling wine.

mouth-feel The physical impact of a wine in the mouth that relates more to the sense of touch, such as astringency, weight and body.

mouth-filling Term to describe wines with a full mouth-feel.

Müller-Thurgau German grape variety that produces pleasant fruity wines.

Muscat Any of a group of grape varieties that produce sweet wines with a grapey taste.

must Crushed grapes. A mixture of grape juice, skins and pips.

musty Term to describe stale or dusty aromas in wine.

négociants Wine merchants.

nitrogen Inert gas used to protect wine from contact with oxygen.

noble rot See botrytis.

non-vintage Indicator mostly found on sparkling wine made of grapes from different vintages.

nose The smell of a wine.

NV See non-vintage.

oak The preferred type of wood used in the construction of barrels because it is easily worked, and imparts agreeable flavours into the wine.

oak aged Matured in, but not necessarily fermented in, oak barrels.

oak fermented Fermented in oak. See barrique fermented.

oaky Term to describe the aroma or flavour derived from oak barrels. Can be characterised as spicy, coconut or vanillin.

oenology The science of winemaking.

off-dry Term to describe a wine that has a perception of sweetness, but at a low level, e.g. 10 grams per litre of residual sugar.

off flavours Aroma or tastes that are indicative of a faulty wine.

oidium See powdery mildew.

olfactory mucosa Organ in the nasal cavity where many wine flavours are detected.

organoleptic In wine terms refers to wine qualities that can be sensed by sight, smell, taste and mouth-feel.

oxidation The excessive interaction of wine or juice with oxygen, which over time turns the wine brown and dulls varietal flavours.

oxidised Term to describe the unpalatable taste derived from the exposure of a wine to air through poor handling or excessive cellaring. Brown colours are usually in evidence.

pasteurisation Technique sometimes used to kill wild yeast and bacteria, as well as to denature enzymes in grape juice.

petillant Term to describe a wine that has a light sparkle. cf. spritzig.

pH Measure of acidity or alkalinity, representing the hydrogen ion concentration in the grape juice or wine.

phenolics A varied group of compounds which are mainly sourced from the grape skin and include tannins, anthocyanins and some flavour compounds.

photosynthesis Process by which plants convert water, light and carbon dioxide into sugars.

phylloxera Aphid that attacks vine roots with potentially devastating effect.

Pinotage South African red-wine variety also grown in New Zealand.

Pinot Gris Pink grape variety that makes light white wines.

Pinot Noir Cool-climate red variety grown to great effect in New Zealand.

polyphenols Class of grape substances that include anthocyanins and tannins.

polysaccharides Sugar-like molecules that soften the tannins in wine.

Port Fortified wine style from the Douro Valley in Portugal.

potassium bitartrate Cream of tartar crystals that precipitate out of wine during cold stabilisation.

powdery mildew Fungus that attacks vine leaves and bunches.

powerful Term to describe wine with very accessible, intense, rich and complex smells and flavours.

preservative 202 Potassium sorbate. Often used to maintain the sterility of cask wines.

preservative 220 See sulphur dioxide.

pressing The application of pressure to grapes or macerated skins to remove juice or wine.

pumping over Winemaking technique by which red wine is circulated over the cap of red skins during fermentation to help the extraction of colour, flavour and tannins.

puncheon A 500-litre oak barrel. Used to be popular in New Zealand but now seldom used.

pungent A wine with high levels of volatile aromas.

quaffer Easy-drinking wine, generally of lower quality.

quinta Portuguese for farm, sometimes used to identify single-vineyard Ports.

rack and return See delestage.

racking Winemaking process by which wine is transferred from one tank to another, leaving behind any sediment.

rancio A hessian sack-like flavour often found in old Ports and Sherries that has resulted from extended maturation in old oak casks.

remuage See riddling.

residual sugar The quantity of unfermented sugar present in a finished bottle of wine. This is usually detected as a degree of sweetness.

Rhône French wine region known for its powerful reds and full-bodied whites.

rich Term to describe wine with apparent sweetness, intensity and lusciousness.

riddling Inverting bottles (principally of Champagne or méthode traditionnelle) to help sediment precipitate to the neck and facilitate its removal. Also remuage.

Riesling German grape variety that makes aromatic white wines which can age well.

Riesling Sylvaner Name used for Müller-Thurgau in the past.

ripping Viticultural practice of breaking up soil using a long metal tooth.

rootstock Part of vine that bears roots, commonly grafted with budwood of the desired variety to impart resistance to phylloxera.

Rosé Pink wine made from red grapes, using limited skin contact.

rough Term to describe wine that is harsh, coarse and possibly unpleasant.

round Term to describe wine that has good body and extract.

sappy Term to describe a touch of herbaceousness or stalky character, often found in Pinot Noir and young wines.

Sauternes French winemaking region known for its botrytised dessert wine.

scented Highly aromatic smells associated with flowers or fruits.

Sekt German sparkling wine.

Sémillon French white-grape variety.

shanking See bunchstem necrosis.

sharp Term to describe wine with biting acid or tannins.

Sherry Fortified wine style from Jerez in Spain.

Shiraz See Syrah. Also Hermitage.

shy See closed.

single-vineyard wine Wine from a specified vineyard. Normally a premium wine.

skin contact The period during the winemaking process when grape skins are left in contact with the wine to impart flavour, body and colour.

smooth Agreeable, harmonious, not coarse in any way.

soft Term to describe wines with delicate flavours and gentle acidity. May relate to wines that are lacking acidity.

solera Spanish maturation system in which wine is systematically racked, creating a blend from different vintages.

spicy Term to describe wine with an aroma and flavour reminiscent of mint, cinnamon, cloves or pepper.

spirity Term to describe an obvious presence of the warm and sometimes fiery feel of alcohol.

spritzig Term to describe a hint of gassiness on the palate, adding to the freshness of a wine. The gas is residual carbon dioxide from the fermentation.

strainers Heavy posts at the end of each row of vines.

structure The composition of a wine as it relates to acid, tannin and alcohol.

submerged cap Winemaking technique that physically holds the cap submerged in fermenting wine.

sulphur dioxide Preservative added to wine. It is mentioned on the back label as preservative 220. Sulphur dioxide has antioxidant and anti-microbial properties.

sweetness The taste sensation relating proportionally to the sugar concentration in a wine.

sur lie French term for 'on the lees'. Lees being the coarse sediment, which consists mainly of dead yeast cells and small grape particles.

sustainable winegrowing Programme of growing wine grapes in ways that minimise the effects on the environment.

Syrah French black-grape variety, widely grown in Australia. Also Shiraz and Hermitage.

tannic Term to describe wine with aggressive tannins that will mellow with cellaring.

tannins Chemicals derived mainly from the skins of red grapes, but can also be sourced from grape stems, pips and oak barrels. It is responsible for the mouth-feel of red wines and can be coarse, soft, mouth-puckering or drying.

tart Term to describe wine with a hard taste of dominating tartaric acid.

tartaric acid The most important acid in grape juice and therefore wine. Can have a firm or tart taste in large amounts.

Tawny A Port style which has been aged in barrels. Also used to describe the colour of old red wine.

tears See legs.

temperature-controlled Refers to controlled temperature of the fermentation.

terroir The situation a vine finds itself in. A combination of location, climate, soil and aspect.

texture Overall structural feel of a wine, typically smooth, satiny or complex.

thin Term to describe wine that is lacking in body and flavour content.

tipper tanks Drainer and fermentation tanks that can tip the marc directly into presses.

tirage French for on lees, especially for méthode traditionnelle wines.

tirage liqueur Mixture of sugar, yeast and fining agents added to base wine before the second fermentation to create sparkling wine.

titratable acidity A measure of the acidity of a wine. Often used interchangeably with the term total acidity.

trichloroanisole The chemical responsible for cork taint. Also known as TCA.

trilling See aspiration.

topping up Winemaking practice of regularly filling barrels to avoid oxidation.

ullage The air space in the top of a bottle, tank or barrel.

upfront Term used to describe wine that has attractive, lifted flavours, particularly those fruit flavours which are typical of a grape variety.

vanillin One of the key flavours imparted to wine stored in young oak casks.

varietal Wine made from a specific grape variety. A style of wine displaying characteristics of a grape variety.

varietalism Practice of identifying wines by the grape variety from which they were made.

variety Type of grape.

vats Any wine containers, usually made of wood.

Vendange Tardive Late-harvest wine from Alsace.

veraison That point in the grapegrowing season that marks the start of ripening. Sugars start to rise, acid levels decline and red varieties change colour.

vertical tasting A comparative tasting of wines of the same variety but of different vintages, usually tasted in sequence.

vintage The time of harvest within a particular year or the year of harvest. The year that is mentioned on the label.

vintage wines Wines made from grapes harvested in a specific year as indicated on the label.

viscosity See body.

vitamin C Chemical that acts as an antioxidant and is used in small amounts in white wine.

viticulture The science of growing wine grapes.

Vitis vinifera Classical species of European vines.

volatile acidity See acetic acid.

weight Term to describe a strong, full-bodied wine.

whole-bunch pressing Winemaking technique where whole bunches of grapes are pressed from hand-picked grapes to make premium wines.

yeast Microscopic, single-celled organisms which convert grape-juice sugars into alcohol. The most common types used in winemaking are *Saccharomyces cerevisiae* and *Saccharomyces bayanus*.

yeasty Term to describe a bready or Marmite smell that is often evident in Champagne and some Chardonnay styles.

young Term to describe an immature wine.

Zweigelt Austrian red-grape variety.

Bibliography

Wine in New Zealand, by Frank Thorpy, published by Collins, 1983

A Stake in the Country: Assid Abraham Corban and his family, by Dick Scott, published by Reed Publishing (NZ) Ltd

Pioneers of New Zealand Wine, by Dick Scott and Marti Friedlander, published by Reed Publishing (NZ) Ltd, 2002

The Wines and Vineyards of New Zealand, by Michael Cooper, published by Hodder Moa Beckett, 1996

Wine Atlas of New Zealand, by Michael Cooper, published by Hodder Moa Beckett, 2002

Christie's World Encyclopaedia of Champagne sparkling wine, by Tom Stevenson, published by Absolute Press, 1998

The Oxford Companion to Wine, by Jancis Robinson, published by Oxford University Press, 1994

Taradale: The story of a village, by Janet Gordon

The Canoes of Kupe: A history of Martinborough District, by Roberta McIntyre, published by Victoria University Press, 2002

Canterbury Grapes & Wines 1840-2002, by Danny Schuster, David Jackson & Rupert Tipples, published by Shoal Bay Press, 2002

Vineyards on the edge: the story of Central Otago Wine, by David Cull, published by Longacre Press, 2001

Marlborough Wines and Vines, by Cynthia Brooks, 1992

Viticulture and Environment, by John Gladstones, published by Winetitles, 1992

Bateman Contemporary Atlas New Zealand: The Shapes of Our Nation, by Russell Kirkpatrick, published by David Bateman, 1999

Soils of the Heretaunga Plains: A guide to their management, by E. Griffiths, published by Hawke's Bay Regional Council

Water and Soil Resources of the Wairau: Volumes one and three, published by Nelson-Marlborough Regional Council

Groundwaters of New Zealand. by M.R. Rosen and P. A. White

The Production of Grapes & Wine in Cool Climates, by David Jackson and Danny Schuster, published by Daphne Brasell Associates Ltd, 1994

The Art and Science of Wine, by James Halliday and Hugh Johnson, published by Mitchell Beazley, 1992

The Australian and New Zealand Field Guide for disease, pests and disorders of Grapes, published by Winetitles

Barrel Making: An art in the service of wine, by Jacques Puisais, published by Hermé, 2000

New Zealand Winegrowers Annual Report 2002

New Zealand Winegrowers BNZ Statistical Annual 2002

Index

Bold italics refer to a major topic.

Photography credits:

All photographs in *Wine in New Zealand* are by Austin and Jane Langford, except for those attributed below:

Philip Bothwell, p 303
Brent Carville, p 91 bottom left
Malcolm Dale, p 296
Craig Potton, pp 214, 215 (except no.7)
Clive Ralph, pp 92, 121 right, 249 bottom
George Rose, pp 79 bottom right, 287 top, 289, 298, 301
Jaap van der Stoel, p 61
Zirk van den Berg, p 201.

Montana Wines also wishes to thank:

Bodegas Balbi, Argentina, p 302
Bodegas Domecq, Spain, p 286
Bosch, p 125 middle
Champagne Mumm, France, p 292 middle
Mr Khaleel Assid Corban, pp 13 top right, 185 bottom left, top right and middle
Delas Frères, France, p 293
Marchesi de' Frescobaldi, Italy, p 294
The German Wine Institute/Hartmann, p 297
Louis Latour, France, p 292 top left
Rongopai Wines, p 13 bottom left
Domaines Schlumberger, France, p 291
Tatachilla Wines, Australia, p 300
Tech Home, p 125 top left.

Uncredited photographs are from Montana's photographic archive.

All diagrams and illustrations by Harriet Bailey.

cabernet franc

cabernet sauvignon

chardonnay

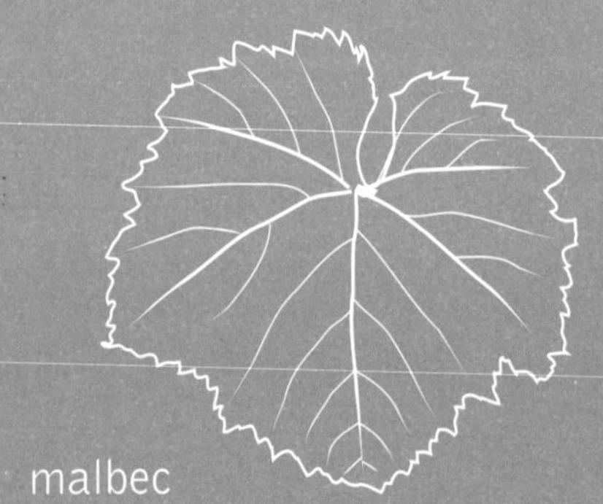
malbec

merlot

müller-thurgau

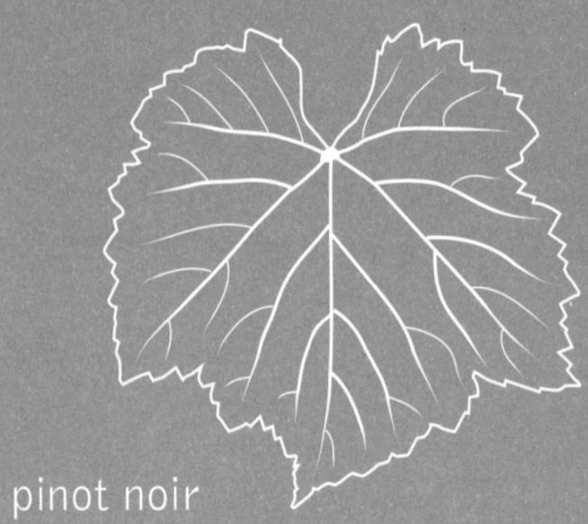
pinot noir

sauvignon blanc

sémillon